TORT LAW
AND HUMAN RIGHTS

Tort Law and Human Rights

JANE WRIGHT
University of Essex

·HART·
PUBLISHING

OXFORD – PORTLAND OREGON
2001

Hart Publishing
Oxford and Portland, Oregon

Published in North America (US and Canada) by
Hart Publishing
c/o International Specialized Book Services
5804 NE Hassalo Street
Portland, Oregon
97213-3644
USA

Distributed in Netherlands, Belgium and Luxembourg by
Intersentia, Churchillaan 108
B2900 Schoten
Antwerpen
Belgium

Hart Publishing is a specialist legal publisher based in Oxford, England. To order further copies of
this book or to request a list of other publications please write to:

Hart Publishing, Salters Boatyard, Folly Bridge, Abingdon Rd, Oxford, OX1 4LB
Telephone: +44 (0)1865 245533 Fax: +44 (0)1865 794882
email: mail@hartpub.co.uk
WEBSITE: http//:www.hartpub.co.uk

British Library Cataloguing in Publication Data
Data Available

ISBN 1-84113-035-4 (cloth)

Typeset in Sabon
by Hope Services, Abingdon, Oxon
Printed and bound in Great Britain by
Biddles Ltd, www.biddles.co.uk

Preface

My interest in the relationship between tort law and the implementation of international human rights standards, particularly the European Convention on Human Rights, was prompted by a series of cases decided in the last decade that challenged the English courts to make public authorities accountable for their actions. Perhaps the most notable was the House of Lords' decision in *X* v. *Bedfordshire County Council*, which held that no matter how gross a dereliction of duty occurred there could be no liability in the English tort of negligence where a public authority failed properly to perform its statutory obligations relating to children. This book is a development and expansion of the work that I undertook following that decision in which I began to explore the possibility for the negligence action to be the means by which the United Kingdom fulfilled its obligations under the Convention. It was *Osman* v. *UK*, in many ways a much less obvious case than *Bedfordshire*, which later proved to be cathartic for the tort of negligence. The tone of the European Court of Human Rights' decision was one of concern that human rights standards should be vindicated. Could it really be the case that, on facts such as those, there was no mechanism by which the police force could be brought to account for its actions? The dominant theme of the Court's decision in *Osman* v. *UK* and the Commission's decision in the application to Strasbourg by the Bedfordshire children (*Z* v. *UK*) was the necessity for public bodies, the instruments of the state, to be made accountable for their actions. The legal landscape has changed dramatically since the Osmans took their claim to Strasbourg: not only has the Human Rights Act (its avowed purpose to give further effect to Convention rights in English law) come into force, but English courts have demonstrated a willingness to open up liability in the wake of *Osman*. Perhaps, not surprisingly (but, unfortunately, regarding the timing of completion of this book!) a Grand Chamber of the European Court of Human Rights recently resiled from its decision in *Osman* in its judgment in *Z* v. *UK* (delivered on 10 May 2001).

This book evaluates a number of established principles of English tort law for their compliance with Convention standards. Those principles, particularly in areas such as defamation, must be rendered compatible with the Convention. The significance of *Osman* lay in its power, as English courts proved, to influence the boundaries of tort law, especially negligence; to some extent the decision in *Z* mutes the capacity of the Convention to shape tort principles. However, as this book argues, what is important is that Convention rights really are brought home, to adopt the terminology of the White Paper that introduced the Human Rights Bill. What the decision in *Z* highlights is that, even in claims against public authorities, the remedies provided by the Act will not be sufficient to achieve that purpose. As well as the public dimension, this book explores the potential impact of the Act in private litigation, as a result of the duty of the court to act compatibly with Convention rights. The English courts must develop the common law, in both public and private litigation, so that it complements the Act where necessary and individuals achieve the justice they deserve.

I have been extremely fortunate to have the opportunity to share and discuss the thoughts developed in this book with a number of colleagues in the academic community. I should like to thank members of Kent University Law School and the members of the SPTL Tort Group who attended my seminars as well as fellow speakers and participants at the panel discussion on *Z* v. *UK* which took place on 22 June 2001 at the Annual Meeting of the British Institute of International and Comparative Law. I should also like to thank all those colleagues at Essex who have been so supportive and willing to discuss the themes raised, in particular Merris Amos, Maurice Sunkin and Geoff Gilbert. Needless to say, the responsibility for errors is mine alone.

It was intended that the text would be up to date to 1 April 2001, but, in the light of the significance of *Z* v. *UK* and with the patient co-operation of Richard Hart and his staff, it has been possible, within reason, to incorporate a number of amendments at proof stage to endeavour to reflect the changed legal position. The reader's attention is therefore drawn in particular to *Note on the Text*, which discusses the decision in *Z* and its impact on *Osman*.

Finally, for ease of reference, the rights "effected" by the Human Rights Act 1998, which are set out in Schedule 1 to the Act, are appended to the text.

Essex
August, 2001

Contents

Table of Cases

Table of Legislation

EUROPEAN

NATIONAL

Austria

Note on the Text: Z v. United Kingdom in the European Court of Human Rights

Shortly after completion and submission of the manuscript for *Tort Law and Human Rights*, the European Court of Human Rights handed down judgment in *Z v. United Kingdom* ("*Z*").[1] It will be recalled that this case concerns the application to Strasbourg by the children whose action in negligence was struck out by the House of Lords in *X (Minors)* v. *Bedfordshire County Council* ("*Bedfordshire*"),[2] on the basis that no duty of care was owed to them for policy reasons. The decision of the Court in *Z* is of immense significance because it apparently marks a rejection of the application of one strand of Article 6 jurisprudence relating to the right of access to a court to English common law decisions regarding the scope of negligence: in this sense it is a retraction of the Court's decision in *Osman* v. *United Kingdom*.[3] In summary, the Court has decided that where English courts refuse to recognise a duty of care in relation to a class of actors and/or a class of harm under the third head of *Caparo Industries Plc* v. *Dickman*[4] (it would not be fair, just and reasonable to recognise a duty of care) and thereupon strike out a claim, that is not to create an immunity or an exclusionary rule that should then be evaluated for compliance with Article 6 jurisprudence regarding proportionality and legitimacy.[5] Instead, what English courts are doing in such cases is to deny that (henceforth) there is an *arguable* claim the existence of which would engage Article 6 obligations.[6] Taking the decision to its logical conclusion, the Court seems to be saying that the determination of the scope of the negligence action is purely within the prerogative of the courts and the development of these substantive rules does not engage Article 6. The decision is difficult to follow and inherently contradictory.

---

[1] Application no. 29392/95, judgment dated 10 May 2001. Judgment was also delivered in *TP and KM* v. *United Kingdom* (Application no 28945/95) (the application to Strasbourg by the plaintiffs in *M* v. *Newham LBC* (*Newham*) (appeal consolidated with *Bedfordshire*). For discussion of the decisions by the Commission see text accompanying n.62 in Chapter 4. As in the case of *Z* (*Bedfordshire*), the European Court of Human Rights found that the claims in *TP and KM* had been properly and fairly examined by the House of Lords and did not therefore disclose a violation of Article 6.

[2] [1995] 2 AC 633.

[3] [1999] 1 FLR 193.

[4] [1990] 2 AC 605.

[5] Cf text accompanying n.31 in Chapter 4.

[6] On the question of "arguability", see discussion below.

In contrast with the decision of the Court in *Osman* and the Commission in Z, which were both unanimous, the Court's decision in Z was a majority decision (12–5) and Sir Nicholas Bratza, the appointed English judge, voted against the United Kingdom government in the Commission. His place in the Court was then taken by Lady Justice Arden as an ad hoc judge. The hearing took place on 28 June 2000, but almost eleven months elapsed before judgment was pronounced. It might reasonably be surmised that agreement was difficult to reach and the appended dissents reveal a significant level of dissatisfaction with the outcome of the Article 6 complaint. What the Court seems to have done is to endeavour to retain the integrity of its supervisory jurisdiction as laid down in *Ashingdane* v. *United Kingdom*,[7] but to deny that the control tests of legitimacy and proportionality deriving from that case were applicable to Z. It is extremely difficult to grasp precisely why the House of Lords' decision in *Bedfordshire* did not amount to the creation of an exclusionary rule effecting a restriction on access to the court. That is, however, what the Court in Z decided. The decision in *Osman* v. *United Kingdom* provoked a great deal of criticism, both judicial and academic, but it seems unlikely that Z will lay the *Osman* ghost to rest, because it in turn has created its own litigation-provoking uncertainties.

In Z, the United Kingdom Government conceded that both Articles 3 (the right not to suffer inhuman and degrading treatment) and 13 (the right to an effective remedy) had been breached. The European Court of Human Rights made the highest ever awards of just satisfaction (compensation) under Article 41 for psychological and physical damage totalling £320,000, with one child receiving £132,000. The awards comprised sums in respect of pecuniary damage to include the cost of psychiatric treatment and loss of employment opportunities. Sums (£32,000) in respect of non-pecuniary damage for the pain and suffering of each of the children were included in the award.

The aim of this Note is to evaluate the decision in Z and to consider what impact it may have on the common law. It is understood that the arguments put forward by Gearty in his article '*Unravelling Osman*'[8] were put to the Court[9] and have influenced the outcome. With that in mind the analysis will also make reference to those views, where relevant. Before examining the Strasbourg Court's decision the decisions of the House of Lords and the Commission on Human Rights will be summarised very briefly in order to place the discussion in context.

---

[7] Series A no 93 (1985).

[8] (2001) 64 MLR 159.

[9] I am grateful for the comments on this point made by D Anderson QC, Counsel for the Government in Z, at a Seminar held on 19 July 2001 on the subject of "Human Rights and Tort Remedies in English Public Law" at the British Institute of International and Comparative Law.

Background to *Z* v. *United Kingdom* in the European Court of Human Rights

In *Bedfordshire*, five children attempted to mount an action in negligence against the local authority charged with responsibility for their welfare under a range of statutes. They had suffered appalling neglect by their parents over a period of almost five years at the end of which they were taken into care. The leading judgment for a unanimous House of Lords was given by Lord Browne-Wilkinson who held that the action should be struck out on the basis that a direct duty of care was not owed to the children by the local authority, because it would not be "fair, just and reasonable" to recognise a duty of care for a range of policy reasons. To summarise[10] these reasons included: the interdisciplinary nature of responsibility for child welfare, involving social workers, the police, educational bodies and doctors, which would make it unfair to single out one defendant; the task is delicate; a fear of defensive practice; fear of vexatious and costly litigation and the consequent diversion of human resources and money from the performance of the requisite service. The children then petitioned Strasbourg alleging violations of Article 3 (inhuman and degrading treatment), Article 6 (right of access to a court), Article 8 (right to respect for private life) and Article 13 (the right to an effective remedy). The subsequent discussion will focus largely on the Article 6 issue, because it is that part of the decision that constitutes a rejection of *Osman*.

The Commission had found that Articles 3[11] and 6 had been violated. The Commission considered first of all whether Article 6 was applicable to the claim. In line with its constant jurisprudence, the Commission stated that Article 6 does not guarantee any particular content of substantive law and that the obligation in Article 6 extends to obligations that can be said "at least on arguable grounds to be recognised by domestic law".[12] The Commission saw no reason to distinguish *Z* from *Osman* (the applicants must be taken to have had a right, derived from the law of negligence to seek an adjudication on the admissibility and merits of a claim that they were owed a duty of care). The Commission then proceeded to examine whether the decision of the House of Lords, since it amounted to the deprivation of access to the court (the strike out meant that no hearing took place on the merits), satisfied the requirements of legitimacy and proportionality laid down by *Ashingdane*[13] and *Lithgow* v. *United Kingdom*.[14] In other words, did the restriction pursue a legitimate aim and was there a reasonable relationship of proportionality between the means employed (the denial of a duty of care) and the aim sought to be achieved. The aim of

---

[10] For the author's critique of the House of Lords decision see J Wright, "Local Authorities, the Duty of Care and the European Convention on Human Rights", (1998) 18 OJLS 1.

[11] For discussion of the Article 3 dimension see text accompanying n.36 in Chapter 3.

[12] Citing *James* v. *UK* Series A no. 98 (1986) at para. 81 and *Ashingdane, supra* n.7 at para. 55.

[13] Supra n.7.

[14] Series A no 102 (1986).

preserving the efficiency of the public service was legitimate, but the restriction was a disproportionate interference with the Article 6 right, because there was no consideration of the seriousness of the damage or the degree of negligence or the fundamental rights of the applicants which were involved.[15]

After the Commission had delivered its Report, the United Kingdom government conceded that Article 3 had been breached, but contested the Article 6 complaint before the Court.

Z IN THE EUROPEAN COURT OF HUMAN RIGHTS

Recalling its jurisprudence that the guarantees encompassed by Article 6 extend only to disputes that can be said "at least on arguable grounds", to be recognised by domestic law,[16] the Court held that, at the outset, in the proceedings before the English courts, there was a genuine dispute about the existence of the right to sue in negligence and the applicants therefore arguably had a claim in domestic law.[17] It was agreed by the parties that, prior to *Bedfordshire*, there was no precedent that suggested that a local authority could be liable in the tort of negligence for the improper performance of child protection duties. Therefore Article 6 was engaged. In a remark heavy with significance for future claims to Strasbourg, the Court stated that:

> "The Government's submission that there was no arguable (civil) right for the purposes of Article 6 once the House of Lords had ruled that no duty of care arose has relevance rather to any claims which were lodged or pursued subsequently by other plaintiffs".[18]

Thus far, the Court's approach accorded with what it had said in *Osman*. It is at the next stage of the analysis that the Court parted company with *Osman*.

The Court recalled its decision in *Golder* v. *United Kingdom*[19] which laid down the principle that where a person does have an arguable claim there should be access to a court: without access to court "the procedural guarantees laid down in Article 6 concerning fairness, publicity and expeditiousness would be meaningless". However, at paragraph 93 of the judgment, the Court relying on established authority, recalled that the right enshrined in Article 6 is not absolute; it may be subject to limitations such as statutory limitation periods, security for costs orders and so on. The Court then went on to refer to its judgment in *Ashingdane* and stated that:

---

[15] *Z* v. *United Kingdom* (1999) 28 EHRR CD 65 at para 114.

[16] The right to a fair trial in Article 6 is expressed to apply "[in] the determination of his civil rights and obligations . . .".

[17] *Z, supra* n.1 at para. 89.

[18] *Ibid.*

[19] Series A no 18 (1975).

"Where the individual's access [to a court] is limited either by operation of law or in fact, the Court will examine whether the limitation imposed impaired the essence of the right and in particular whether it pursued a legitimate aim and there was a reasonable relationship of proportionality between the means employed and the aim sought to be achieved".[20]

Clearly, the effect of this statement is that the question of whether English law requires to be evaluated for legitimacy and proportionality will depend upon whether the applicant's access to the court has been "limited". It is on this crucial issue that Z differs from *Osman v. United Kingdom*. It will be recalled that in *Osman*, the Court of Human Rights took the view that the decision of the House of Lords in *Hill* v. *Chief Constable of West Yorkshire*[21] (no duty of care in negligence in relation to the investigation/suppression of crime) had created an exclusionary rule in favour of the police force which acted as a restriction on the right of access to a court. As described in Chapter 4, the Court (applying the *Ashingdane* and *Tinnelly*[22] line of jurisprudence) concluded that the decision of the Court of Appeal in *Osman v. Ferguson*[23] had violated Article 6, because, although the aim of the exclusionary rule (maintenance of an effective police service) could be regarded as legitimate, the principle of proportionality was not satisfied, in that there was no consideration of degrees of harm or degrees of negligence.

In Z, it was contended by the applicants that the decision of the House of Lords in *Bedfordshire* deprived the applicants of access to a court (as a result of the claim being struck out on the basis of no duty, there was no determination on the merits) because it was effectively an exclusionary rule. The Court rejected this argument, stating that the procedural guarantees laid down in *Golder* had been observed because the case had been litigated with vigour up to the House of Lords and the applicants had not been prevented in any practical manner from pursuing their claim: no procedural rules or limitation periods had been invoked. In a complete rejection of its conclusion in *Osman*, the Court stated that it was not persuaded "that the House of Lords' decision that there was no duty of care may be characterised as either an exclusionary rule or an immunity which deprived [the applicants] of access to a court".[24] In *Osman*, of course, the Court had come to the very opposite conclusion. How then could the Court justify its departure from the reasoning employed in *Osman*? Ironically, the justification lay in part in the case law that has emerged from the English courts subsequent to *Osman* and which clearly manifested the imprint of *Osman*, if not always explicitly, certainly implicitly. In Z, the Court stated that

---

[20] Supra n.1 at para. 93.
[21] [1989] AC 53.
[22] *Tinnelly* v. *United Kingdom* (1998) 27 EHRR 249.
[23] [1993] 4 All ER 344.
[24] *Supra* n.1 at para. 96.

its decision in *Osman* was based on an understanding of the law of negligence that now had to be

> "reviewed in the light of the clarifications subsequently made by the domestic courts and notably the House of Lords. The Court is satisfied that the law of negligence as developed in the domestic courts since the case of Caparo and as recently analysed in the case of *Barrett* v. *Enfield LBC* includes the fair, just and reasonable criterion as an intrinsic element of the duty of care and that the ruling of law concerning that element in this case does not disclose the operation of an immunity. In the present case, the Court is led to the conclusion that the inability of the applicants to sue the local authority flowed not from an immunity but from the applicable principles governing the substantive right of action in domestic law. There was no restriction on access to court of the kind contemplated in the Ashingdane judgment".[25]

Putting it at its crudest the court has justified a retraction of its reasoning in *Osman*, because English courts have demonstrated in cases such as *Barrett* v. *Enfield LBC*,[26] that in some instances there may in fact be liability. *Barrett* was distinguished from *Bedfordshire* by the House of Lords on the thinnest of grounds, namely, that the arguments applied in *Bedfordshire* did not apply with the same force to children where the decision had been made to take them into care and the House of Lords clearly felt the pressure of the Strasbourg decision in *Osman*. It is of course illogical to say that because one class of persons may bring proceedings in negligence against a public body there can, therefore, be no immunity in relation to another class of persons. The dissent on this point by Judge Thomassen (joined by Judges Casadevall and Kovler) makes this very point:

> "To reach its conclusion that the decision by the House of Lords was no immunity, the Court's majority observes, in para. 99, that in cases concerning the liability of local authorities in child care matters brought after the applicants' case the domestic courts have held that a duty of care may arise. But this does not change the fact that an immunity was conferred on the authorities in the applicants' case. Apparently the immunity applied in the applicants' case was found no longer appropriate in subsequent cases, the national courts taking into account, amongst other factors, the Court's approach in the *Osman* case."[27]

In the author's view, the House of Lords in *Bedfordshire* clearly applied an exclusionary rule to prevent the children pursuing their claims to trial. Public policy arguments, as perceived by the House of Lords, meant that those children could not sue. In a common law system where the judiciary is responsible for the delineation of civil responsibility no distinction should be drawn between immunities (exclusionary rules) that are laid down and circumscribed by Parliament on the one hand (*Ashingdane*) and the courts on the other. Both

---

[25] *Supra* n.1 at para. 101.
[26] [1999] 3 WLR 79.
[27] Z, *supra* n.1.

statutory and common law rules are capable of creating immunities that constitute a restriction on the right of access to the court.

It is also apparent that the Court was not entirely convinced by its own reasoning. The Court states, without explaining adequately why, that the application of the fair just and reasonable criteria in *Bedfordshire* did not disclose the operation of an immunity and there was therefore no restriction on the right of access to a court. As described above, in the constant jurisprudence of the court it has been held that where there *is* such a restriction, then such should be assessed to ensure that it pursues a legitimate aim and accords with the principle of proportionality. Having reached its decision that no exclusionary rule had been applied in *Bedfordshire*, the corollary must be that these tests were quite clearly irrelevant and should logically have been disregarded. This is not quite what the Court did, manifesting an obvious discomfiture with its own finding. For the Court stated that the House of Lords' decision in *Bedfordshire* was reached after a careful balancing of the policy reasons for and against the imposition of liability, because Lord Browne-Wilkinson weighed the principle that wrongs should be remedied, which requires very potent counter considerations to be overridden, against other public policy concerns. In this part of its judgment, the Court was attempting to establish that, although there was no exclusionary rule, the House of Lords had in any event satisfied the standards against which such a rule would be evaluated. This is a complete misrepresentation of Lord Browne-Wilkinson's speech in *Bedfordshire*. To adopt the terminology of the Court of Human Rights in *Osman* and the Commission in *Z*, Lord Browne-Wilkinson gave no consideration to the degree of harm, the degree of negligence or the fact that fundamental rights were engaged. It is indeed scarcely conceivable (even taking account of the then general hostility to negligence actions against public authorities) that had Convention arguments been put before the court,[28] the House of Lords could have reached its decision with such alacrity.

The outstanding question from the Court's decision in *Z*, which is not answered clearly by the judgment, is why did the refusal to recognise a duty of care in *Bedfordshire* not constitute a restriction on access to the court of the kind contemplated in the *Ashingdane* judgment? This question requires us to revisit that authority and to examine the arguments put forward by Gearty as to how the line of authority stemming from this seminal case should be interpreted.

Ashingdane v. *United Kingdom*

This case is discussed in Chapter 4, but in view of its significance and for the sake of convenience an expanded discussion will take place here. Ashingdane wanted to challenge the failure of the Secretary of State and health authority to

---

[28] See Wright, *supra* n.10.

provide appropriate hospital care for his mental health. He was an offender patient who had suffered from paranoid schizophrenia and had been detained in Broadmoor Hospital. Several years after his detention it was considered by experts that he no longer posed the threat of violence that he previously did and the Home Secretary gave consent for his transfer to a local psychiatric hospital. The staff at the most suitable hospital did not consider that they had the resources to care for an offender patient such as Ashingdane and refused to admit him, warning that industrial action might be taken were he to be transferred.

Ashingdane, having obtained legal aid, instituted proceedings to challenge the legality of his continued detention at Broadmoor. Various relief was sought in the form of declarations that, inter alia, the Department of Health and Social Security and the local health authority were acting ultra vires in refusing to transfer him, as well as declarations that the members and officers of the union were acting unlawfully. The matter was litigated up to the Court of Appeal where the proceedings were stayed because there was no allegation of bad faith or lack of reasonable care and it was found that the acts complained of fell within the immunity created by the Mental Health Act 1959. The Court of Appeal found that Ashingdane's civil action against the local health authority and the Department of Health and Social Security was barred by operation of law on account of section 141 of the Mental Health Act 1959 which provides that:

"(1) No person shall be liable . . . to any civil . . . proceedings to which he would have been liable apart from this section in respect of any act purporting to be done in pursuance of this Act . . . , unless the act was done in bad faith or without reasonable care.

(2) No civil . . . proceedings shall be brought against any person in any court in respect of any such act without the leave of the High Court, and the High Court shall not give leave under this section unless satisfied that there is substantial ground for the contention that the person to be proceeded against has acted in bad faith or without reasonable care."

Thereupon Ashingdane took his case to Strasbourg alleging that the United Kingdom had breached its obligations under Article 5 paragraphs (1) and (4), which are not relevant for present discussion, and Article 6(1).

The Government contended that Article 6 (1) was not applicable because the claims did not relate to a "civil right". The Court of Human Rights declared that it was not necessary to settle this issue, because assuming that Article 6(1) was applicable, the requirements of the Article had not been violated. The Court referred to the *Golder* holding that Article 6(1) secured the right of access to a court. In *Ashingdane*, the applicant did have access to the court, both the High Court and the Court of Appeal, where he was told, predictably enough, that his actions were barred by the statute. The Court stated that:

"[to] this extent, he thus had access to the remedies that existed within the domestic system. ... This of itself does not necessarily exhaust the requirements of Article 6(1).

It must still be established that the degree of access afforded under the national legislation was sufficient to secure the individual's 'right to a court', having regard to the
rule of law in a democratic society".[29]

In the passage that has come to assume enormous significance the Court
declared that the right of access to a court under Article 6 is not absolute and
may be subject to limitations. Such limitations must not:

"restrict or reduce the access left to the individual in such a way or to such an extent that
the very essence of the right is impaired . . . a limitation will not be compatible with
Article 6(1) if it does not pursue a legitimate aim and if there is not a reasonable relationship of proportionality between the means employed and the aim sought to be
achieved".[30]

As we see in Chapter 4, the Court took the view in *Ashingdane* that these tests
were satisfied. It is difficult to see why it was appropriate to apply these criteria
to the staying of proceedings in *Ashingdane*, but not to the strike-out in
Bedfordshire. It is emphasised also that the Court in Z evinces no explicit
willingness to cast doubt on the authority of *Ashingdane*; rather, the Court has
taken the view that those principles do not apply in Z. The perspective adopted
by Gearty provides illumination on this question.

In *Unravelling Osman*,[31] Gearty traces the development of Strasbourg supervision in relation to Article 6 and suggests an alternative interpretation of
Ashingdane that would have led to different outcomes in both *Tinnelly*[32] and
Osman.[33] Gearty's thesis is that the appropriate interpretation of *Ashingdane*
(but not the one adopted in *Osman* or *Tinnelly*) is that Strasbourg supervision
under Article 6 operates at two levels that are mutually exclusive. First, where a
person can show that she has an arguable civil claim in domestic law, that will
engage Article 6 and secure the procedural guarantees laid down in *Golder*.
This he describes as the "threshold" test for the engagement of Article 6
guarantees. Thus, in Z, the Court found that the threshold of arguability was
satisfied and then moved on to ensure that the procedural guarantees had been
observed. Gearty then suggests that, where a person cannot show an arguable
claim, the tests of legitimacy and proportionality should be applied as a
"fallback" test in order to ensure that Strasbourg retains a proper supervisory
jurisdiction over states. He has argued that the fact that Ashingdane's claims
were barred by operation of law should naturally have led the Court to conclude
that, therefore, Article 6 was not applicable as the threshold test of arguability
had not been satisfied. He suggests that the further evaluation of the degree of
access for compatibility with principles of legitimate aim and proportionality
should rightly be regarded as a "European fallback test" that would only apply

---

[29] *Supra* n.7 at para 57.
[30] *Ibid.*
[31] *Supra* n.8
[32] *Supra* n.22.
[33] *Supra* n.3 and see text accompanying n.46 *et seq* in Chapter 4.

when the threshold test of establishing an arguable claim in domestic law (thus engaging Article 6) had not been met. Gearty has argued that:

> "it was clear enough from the Court's reasoning [in *Ashingdane*] that this test could only apply where the threshold test had not been passed and that, once it was brought into play, it would take effect notwithstanding that the impugned deprivation or restriction of access had been clearly set out in national law, and in respect of which therefore no issue of unlawfulness could have arisen at the domestic level (and thus by definition no arguable case): indeed this was the whole point of the test".[34]

In the author's view, this interpretation is at odds with the express words of the Court in *Ashingdane*: it is not clear at all from the reasoning of the Court that this was intended to be only a fallback test. Indeed, a substantial leap of inference is required to make this assertion. The Court did not find that Ashingdane had no arguable case. It spoke instead of degrees of access and the court's fallback position applies, *whatever* the degree of access. Gearty does not suggest that there can be degrees of arguability: either an applicant is within Article 6, or they are not in which case the fallback test will apply. It is suggested that such an approach is also unduly formalistic: can it really be said that a claimant has access to a court when (as in *Bedfordshire*) all argument in favour of liability is rejected peremptorily on the grounds of judicially conceived notions of public policy that mean certain claims cannot be entertained, whatever their merits. The corollary of the Gearty interpretation is that the degree of scrutiny applied by Strasbourg differs depending upon which route an applicant takes into Article 6. Where an applicant can show an arguable claim simpliciter, Article 6 is simply a guarantee of the procedural requirements of a fair trial. If a claimant cannot show an arguable claim the stricter level of supervision which requires an evaluation of exclusionary rules and hence, possibly, a pronouncement on the legitimacy of substantive law comes into play. Adopting Gearty's perspective, though, the children in *Bedfordshire* did have an arguable case so that the threshold for entry to Article 6 was satisfied, and in view of that there was no mandate for invoking the fallback test. It is presumably this thinking that led the Court to conclude that the applicants had had access to a court with all the procedural rights enshrined in Article 6: as the Court of Human Rights observed, the case had been litigated with vigour all the way up to the House of Lords.

Thus, according to Gearty, a claimant cannot on the one hand have both an arguable case that engages Article 6 and then also seek to engage another level of supervision, the jurisprudence relating to the right of access (proportionality and legitimacy) that is properly the fallback test. This approach is unduly restrictive and out of tune generally with Strasbourg jurisprudence which eschews narrow formalism. There is also no support for this view in the caselaw, apart from Z itself. There is jurisprudence in which as Gearty puts it

---

[34] *Supra* n.8 at 169.

this second limb of *Ashingdane* is "jettisoned without explanation",[35] but this is rather more indicative of the Court of Human Rights' haphazard approach to the use of precedent rather than a concerted effort to develop doctrine. Subsequent authority, beginning with *Fayed* v. *United Kingdom*[36] picked up the *Ashingdane* level of supervision in its entirety, paving the way for *Tinnelly* and *Osman*. It should finally be emphasised that the Court of Human Rights in *Z* seemed scarcely convinced by its own reasoning, in light of the fact that it (ostensibly) satisfied itself in any event that the criteria applicable under the fallback position (legitimacy and proportionality) had been fulfilled by the House of Lords' decision in *Bedfordshire*.

The sceptic might argue, however, that the Court had its eye to the future when it observed that the control tests of legitimacy and proportionality had been satisfied. The point was made above that in *Z* the Court observed that *henceforth* claimants in the position of the Bedfordshire siblings will not have "an arguable case" in domestic law: thus, the threshold test for engaging Article 6 would not be satisfied. It might be thought then that the fallback test as it has been described by Gearty would apply in full rigour. However, by ostensibly scrutinising Lord Browne-Wilkinson's speech in *Bedfordshire* for compliance with the tests of legitimacy and proportionality, the Court has effectively closed off that argument.

Article 13—The right to an effective remedy

Before the Court, the Government accepted that, in the "particular circum-stances of the case", the range of available remedies (compensation from the Criminal Injuries Compensation Board, invocation of the complaints procedure under the Children Act 1989 and complaint to the Local Government Ombudsman) was insufficient to satisfy the demands of Article 13. In view of the seriousness of the violation of one of the most important Convention rights, the Government accepted that a legally enforceable right to compensation should be available and pointed out that such a right would exist on the coming into force of the Human Rights Act 1998.

In its observations on Article 13, the Court began by highlighting the princi-ple of subsidiarity: it is for states to enforce Convention rights in "whatever form they happen to be secured in the domestic legal order".[37] However, there is a limit to the discretion afforded to the state and the scope of the Article 13 obligation will vary depending upon the nature of any violation. The Court held that where an allegation is made that there has been a failure to protect someone from the acts of others there should be a mechanism for establishing liability and in the case of breaches of Articles 2 and 3 compensation should in

---

[35] Gearty, *supra* n.8 at 171, citing *James* v. *United Kingdom*, *supra* n.12 and *Lithgow* v. *United Kingdom*, *supra* n.14.
[36] Series A no 294 (1994).
[37] *Supra* n.1 at para. 108.

principle be available for non-pecuniary damage. However, the Court declined to make any finding as to whether on these facts only court proceedings could provide effective redress, "though judicial remedies indeed furnish strong guarantees of independence, access for the victim and enforceability in compliance with the requirements of Article 13 (see ... *Klass* v. *Germany*[38])".[39]

Nevertheless, the Court held that the applicants did not have available to them an appropriate mechanism for determination of their allegations that they had suffered inhuman and degrading treatment and nor did they have any possibility of obtaining an enforceable award of compensation. Therefore, Article 13 had been breached. In view of the fact that the only realistic means of securing damages was the tort action, this finding gives a strong signal to the English courts that on analogous facts where proceedings under the Act are unavailable the common law must fill the breach.

CONCLUSION

For the reasons described above, Z is an unsatisfactory decision and one that is out of step generally with recent Strasbourg jurisprudence.[40] In the period since *Osman*, as Chapter 4 describes and as the Court in Z observed, the starkness of the legal landscape has been relieved by a number of cases being permitted to go to trial with facts that may lead to an expansion of common law obligations. In relation to acts occurring after 2 October 2000 (section 22(4) Human Rights Act 1998), claimants will have the right to take proceedings under section 7 of the Human Rights Act, where it is considered that a public authority has acted incompatibly with Convention rights. In Z, it was conceded by the Government that the state had acted incompatibly with its positive obligation under Article 3 to protect the children from inhuman and degrading treatment. However, the decision of the House of Lords did not amount to a violation of Article 6; rather, the United Kingdom failed to ensure that the plaintiffs had an appropriate remedy in accordance with Article 13. The question remains then as to how English law will accommodate claims brought in relation to acts that occurred before 2 October 2000, of which there are many in the judicial system, and which may now legitimately be the subject of strike-out orders on the basis that the third limb of *Caparo* is not satisfied. The effect of Z is that striking out claims in negligence will not amount to a violation of Article 6. Although the Court of Human Rights relied in part on post *Osman* English cases to find that there was no immunity, in the author's view that does not alter the fact that Z effectively upheld an immunity recognised in *Bedfordshire*. It is arguable that it has been the threat of proceedings against the United Kingdom under Article 6

---

[38] Series A no 28 (1978).
[39] Z, *supra* n.1 at para. 109.
[40] See Chapter 4.

that has resulted in English courts being rather less willing to strike out claims in negligence against public bodies.[41] The question that arises is whether English courts are likely to regard Z as the green light to revert to a general pattern of hostility towards negligence actions against public authorities. A number of arguments outlined in the following brief observations suggest that this outcome may be unlikely.

Z is a case in which on the one hand a positive obligation under Article 3 arose and was breached but on the other the fact of inability to sue in negligence did not amount to a violation of Article 6. In such cases there is therefore, English precedent aside, nothing to prevent English courts from rejecting claims in negligence. However, where such claims engage Convention rights, other than Article 6, petitions will continue to be made to Strasbourg unless an effective remedy is given in this country. It is therefore appropriate that the common law should be reflective of Convention standards (as a minimum, the Convention is after all a floor of rights) and that a remedy should be available for breaches at domestic level, where a claimant cannot avail herself of the Human Rights Act. Although the Strasbourg Court declined to indicate that a judicial process was necessary to vindicate the rights concerned, the only possible remedy at that time, other than the remedies effectively discounted, was the action in negligence. In Chapter 2, the role of the court as a public authority with a concomitant obligation to act in a way which is compatible with Convention rights (section 6(1) Human Rights Act 1998) is discussed, although largely in connection with the extent to which horizontal effect of Convention rights is achieved. There is now the highest authority for the proposition that the common law should be rendered compatible with Convention rights. This observation applies whether a defendant is public or private, although as Chapter 5 reveals the scope of positive obligations that require action in the private sphere is generally limited.

Thus, it can be forcefully argued that if English courts are to act in a manner that is compatible with Convention rights they must ensure that, where appropriate (and this would arguably be the case in relation to Articles 2 and 3 of the Convention) a judicial remedy is available for the violation of Convention rights, where a claim under the Human Rights Act is not available. One option would be for courts to continue the trend we have seen in cases such as *Barrett v. Enfield LBC*[42] which signify an expansion of the circumstances in which claims may be brought in negligence in terms of both the identity of defendants and recognised harms. It seems highly unlikely that the courts will ignore the steer given to them in Z, that it was the prevailing trend to open up negligence that reassured the Court of Human Rights that immunities were not being applied to public authorities.

---

[41] See, for example, the speech of Lord Browne-Wilkinson in *Barrett* v. *Enfield LBC* [1999] 3 WLR 79 and see Chapter 4 generally.

[42] *Supra* n.26.

The analysis in Chapter 5 demonstrates that there is no necessary equivalence between the criteria used to establish whether a duty of care at common law exists and when a positive obligation to protect a person from the criminal acts of another arises under Articles 2 and 3 of the Convention. That discussion reveals that the test for establishing a duty to act in Convention law is not a reasonable forseeability and proximity test. The threshold appears to be higher: the existence of a "real and immediate risk" to the victim of which the authorities "knew or ought to have had knowledge".[43] Policy issues are taken into account by Strasbourg in determining whether a positive obligation has been breached, because such obligations should not be interpreted so that they would impose "an impossible or disproportionate burden on the authorities".[44] The criteria applied by Strasbourg (real and immediate risk of which there is/should be knowledge) seem to have more in common with the application of the public law test of *Wednesbury* unreasonableness introduced by Lord Browne-Wilkinson in *Bedfordshire* (and subsequently jettisoned by the House of Lords in *Barrett*[45]) than with a reasonable forseeability threshold. To paraphrase, according to Strasbourg, a positive duty to act arises where it is obvious that action should be taken: in *Wednesbury* language no reasonable authority could possibly have come to the conclusion that action was not required. Public authority defendants are therefore likely to argue in novel cases engaging positive obligations that the standard *Caparo* criteria (overlaid with the test of justiciability laid down in *Barrett*[46]) are unsuitable for circumscribing the parameters of responsibility where Convention rights are engaged. Positive obligations to act are recognised in English law, *inter alia*, where a defendant has made an assumption of responsibility for the well being of the claimant. An assumption of responsibility *per se* would not engage Articles 2 or 3 of the Convention. In cases such as *Z*, something in the nature of knowledge of "real and immediate risk" is required. On the facts of *Osman* this was not satisfied because there was, according to the Court of Human Rights, no decisive stage at which the police knew (ought to have known) of the risk to the Osman family.

It is anticipated that in such cases English courts will be invited to construct proximity criteria designed to accommodate the urgency conveyed by the concepts of real and immediate risk. An analogy could be drawn with the specificity of the proximity criteria that have been developed in cases concerning pure economic loss and psychiatric damage suffered by secondary victims. In these types of claim the notion of proximity is shorthand for a clutch of indicators that determine whether in principle liability may lie. Further, a *Wednesbury* type of pre-condition to establishing a duty to act might be

---

[43] *Osman v. United Kingdom, supra* n.3, *Z v. United Kingdom supra* n.1 and see text accompanying n.24 *et seq.* in Chapter 3 and Chapter 5.

[44] *Osman, supra* n.3 at para. 116 and see text accompanying n.30 *et seq.* in Chapter 5.

[45] See text accompanying n.83 in Chapter 4.

[46] See text accompanying n.85 in Chapter 4.

required. It is of course difficult to separate notions of duty and breach, but it must be must be remembered that in *Osman* v. *United Kingdom* the Court of Human Rights rejected the government argument that only gross negligence should found liability.[47] Liability would flow from a failure to take reasonable measures in the face of a real and immediate risk. It is important, therefore, in this context to separate clearly the duty to act and the measures required to discharge that duty.

An intriguing question posed by Z is whether claimants will argue that a new cause of action *against the state* for breach of the rights effected by the Human Rights Act should be recognised at common law. Such a right of action would be analogous to developments in New Zealand, heralded by *Simpson* v. *Attorney General (Baigent's Case)*.[48] In *Baigent's Case*, the police obtained a search warrant in respect of a property that they believed was inhabited by a suspected drug dealer. In fact the suspect had no connection with the property which was occupied by Mrs. Baigent. However, having discovered that fact, the police nevertheless went ahead with the search. The New Zealand Court of Appeal (by a 4-1 majority) held that a cause of action against *the state* would lie for breach of the Bill of Rights Act in making an unreasonable search contrary to section 21. Unlike the Human Rights Act, the New Zealand legislation does not contain an express remedies provision but this did not trouble the court, since effective remedies should be available for its breach and the main remedy granted prior to *Baigent's Case* (exclusion of evidence) was inappropriate in this case. The action was held to be a public law action for compensation and not an action in tort which meant that the immunity in section 6(5) of the Crown Proceedings Act 1950 did not apply. For many claimants (like the siblings in Z) any impugned conduct will have taken place before the Human Rights Act came into force, so that the Convention rights were not at the relevant time "effected" in English law. It is difficult to see therefore that such an argument could be made successfully. However, the development of the common law in accordance with section 6 subsections (1) and (3) of the Act should now take place with the *obligation* of the court to take account of Convention rights[49] rather than the opportunity to have regard to Convention rights that existed formerly.[50] This obligation of the court is not confined to claims in respect of acts taking place after 2 October 2000: the challenge for English courts is to deploy their creative thinking such that Convention rights really are brought home.

---

[47] See text accompanying n.30 in Chapter 5.

[48] [1994] 3 NZLR 667.

[49] By virtue of the court's role as a public authority under section 6(1) taken together with section 2 of the Human Rights Act which requires courts to take account of Convention jurisprudence.

[50] *Derbyshire County Council* v. *Times Newspapers Limited*, see text accompanying n.36 in Chapter 2.

1

Introduction

INTRODUCTION

IT IS FREQUENTLY remarked that the United Kingdom not only had a prime role in drafting the European Convention on Human Rights (hereafter "the Convention"), but was also the first state to ratify. In addition, the right of individual petition and the compulsory jurisdiction of the European Court of Human Rights were accepted by Harold Wilson's government in 1966.[1] Prior to this only Contracting States could take proceedings against the United Kingdom in Strasbourg. However, it took nearly fifty years for the United Kingdom to take the necessary and logical step of "giving further effect" to the Convention in domestic law through the medium of the Human Rights Act 1998, in order, in the parlance of the new Labour government, to "bring rights home". It should be mentioned that the United Kingdom is also party to the United Nations International Covenant on Civil and Political Rights. This instrument, along with the International Covenant on Economic, Social and Cultural Rights came into force in 1976, but the UK government has no plans to incorporate either into domestic law, nor are there plans to ratify the Optional Protocol to the Covenant on Civil and Political Rights. The Optional Protocol affords the right of petition to those whose rights have allegedly been violated to the quasi-judicial supervisory body, the United Nations Human Rights Committee. Unlike the European Court of Human Rights, the Human Rights Committee has no power to render judgments; rather, its powers are limited to making recommendations that the state may or may not disregard. Thus, the enforcement mechanism is much weaker than the Convention procedures.

The challenge which English lawyers must now meet is that of analysing and developing English law from a human rights based perspective, grounded in the Convention, in order that an accommodation of the standards laid down by the Convention, and fleshed out by the Strasbourg jurisprudence, may be achieved. What is required is a change in the mind-set of the English lawyer something akin to that which has followed the European Communities Act 1972, albeit the Human Rights Act 1998 has been drafted in order to preserve the constitutional

---

[1] For a revealing account of the political background to the decision to accept the Strasbourg jurisdiction see Lord Lester of Herne Hill QC "UK Acceptance of the Strasbourg Jurisdiction: What Really Went on in Whitehall in 1965", [1998] *PL* 237.

balance of ultimate power resting with Parliament.[2] However, there is a significant difference: when the United Kingdom acceded to the European Communities, the European Court of Justice was in its infancy; in contrast, Strasbourg has been developing its jurisprudence for nearly half a century. Thus, English lawyers are confronted with the task of familiarising themselves with a large body of principles, and at the same time addressing the issue of how those principles will impact on English law as a result of the Human Rights Act.

The enactment of the Human Rights Act has spawned the publication of an immense number of books and academic articles which address in general terms the interpretation of the Act and the concomitant impact of the Convention on English law. Attention has focused particularly on the issue of horizontal effect: the question of the extent of the Act's impact in litigation between non-state actors, a matter which is addressed in detail in Chapter 2.

The aim of the present work is more specific than those general texts, namely, to consider the potential impact of the Human Rights Act on tort law generally, and to identify those areas of Convention law which through the medium of the Act now speak to, and are likely to bear significance for, the development of principles of English tort law. This work is not intended to be an exhaustive and comprehensive treatment of tort principles; rather, the author's aim is to provide an analysis of the Act and against that background to identify key obligations recognised by the Strasbourg jurisprudence and then to postulate how tort law may be shaped by both those principles and the Act. The Act naturally leads us to debate the twin questions of what the Convention requires of English law, in terms of compliance with a Strasbourg standard, and how those standards are to be accommodated by English law. This work contributes to that debate.

A number of recent tort decisions have highlighted the failure of English lawyers to perceive the relevance of human rights standards generally, and the Convention in particular, in the realm of tort law.[3] English law has long committed itself to the Diceyian premise that the rule of law means "equality before the law, or the equal subjection of all classes to the ordinary law of the land administered by the ordinary Law Courts". Dicey explained that the reason for this is that the notion of having special bodies to deal with disputes involving government or its servants "is fundamentally inconsistent with our traditions and customs".[4] In principle, therefore, until the advent of the Act, a person who claimed that they had suffered harm as a result of tortious conduct by a public body would seek

---

[2] The courts do not have power to strike down legislation for incompatibility with the Convention. Instead, the court may, if satisfied that a provision of primary legislation is incompatible with a Convention right, make a declaration of that incompatibility (Human Rights Act 1998, s. 4(2)). Cf Scotland Act 1998, s. 28, which provides that a legislative provision is outside the competence of the Scottish Parliament so far as any provision is "incompatible with any of the Convention rights or with Community law".

[3] See, for example, *X (Minors)* v. *Bedfordshire County Council* [1995] 2 AC 633, discussed by the author: "Local Authorities, the Duty of Care and the European Convention on Human Rights", (1998) 18 *OJLS* 1.

[4] A V Dicey, *Introduction to the Study of the Law of the Constitution*, 5th edn (London, Macmillan and Co. Ltd, 1897) at 194.

redress by bringing proceedings in the ordinary courts through the usual actions begun by writ such as negligence, misfeasance in public office etc. However, the English courts, despite the pioneering zeal of their forbears, have proved timorous in bringing public bodies to account and have therefore failed in some instances to ensure that human rights standards have been upheld. A number of authorities illustrate the point and are discussed in detail in this work. Questions of whether: abused children can sue a local authority for negligence;[5] victims of crime who have repeatedly requested police assistance can sue the police;[6] and whether those held in custody for extended periods should have a cause of action in negligence against the Crown Prosecution Service,[7] have all been decided in a human rights law vacuum. A myriad of policy arguments have been put forward to deny the possibility of liability, but the most consistent is probably the fear that the imposition of liability would lead to a diversion of scarce public resources from the functions a public body should be fulfilling. The Human Rights Act will surely put an end to such judicial isolationism and the aim of this work is to expose those areas of tort law that are particularly susceptible to a human rights critique.

It is essential to consider also the interplay of the potential development of tort principles, in response to the domestic obligation to achieve compatibility with the Convention, with the framework of remedies established under the Act. Chapter 2 analyses the structure of the Act and considers the potential impact of the Act on tort actions, particularly the negligence action, against public bodies. The recent decision of the European Court of Human Rights ("the Court") in *Osman* v. *United Kingdom*,[8] as well as the Act, have been heralded as likely to open up common law liability and there are judicial decisions to suggest that the negligence action may be freed from the constraints that have been applied in a number of cases to deny a duty of care. Thus, following *Osman*, English courts have been reluctant to strike out claims in negligence.[9] However, this process may falter following the Court's retraction of *Osman* in its recent judgement in *Z.* v. *United Kingdom*, which is discussed in Note to the Text. It is possible also that the Act may stultify common law development if the possibility of awarding damages against a public authority under the statute is regarded as preferable to the expansion of the common law, because in that way the boundaries of negligence may be contained. This is likely to be of particular concern to the English courts in view of the fact that Strasbourg recognises and compensates a much wider range of heads of damage than would currently be recognised by the English tort of negligence. When *Osman* v. *United Kingdom* was decided by the Court the action for negligence at common law was the only effective means of seeking to make the police accountable. Now, section 8 of the Act sets out a framework for seeking a remedy under the Act.

[5] *X (Minors)* v. *Bedfordshire County* Council, *supra* n.3.
[6] *Osman* v. *Ferguson* [1993] 4 All ER 344.
[7] *Elguzouli-Daf* v. *Commissioner of Police of the Metropolis* [1995] 2 WLR 173.
[8] [1999] 1 FLR 193.
[9] See, for example, *Barrett* v. *Enfield London Borough Council* [1997] 3 All ER 171, discussed in Chapter 4.

Alternatively, the common law may expand to take account of human rights law obligations, so that courts make explicit that liability is more likely to be found where fundamental rights are at stake. The decision in *Kent* v. *Griffiths*[10] is apposite here: the ambulance service took an inordinate amount of time to respond to a call, arguably contributing to the cause of the claimant's respiratory arrest and resulting brain damage. The ambulance service was held to owe a duty of care to the claimant. In contrast, in *Capital & Counties plc* v. *Hampshire County Council*,[11] the fire service was held not to owe a duty of care in responding to a call where the plaintiff argued that the fire service was legally responsible for damage to property. In terms of traditional common law analysis, the legal issue was the same: should there be liability for an omission. In each case the orthodox view would be that since the defendants did not cause harm, rather they failed to improve matters or confer a benefit, there should be no duty of care. The decisions appear irreconcilable. While there was no discussion of the Convention in *Kent*, the standards laid down in the Convention, as interpreted by the Commission and Court of Human Rights, may provide a solution: we attach greater weight to the protection of human beings than property, a fact that is recognised by the "ranking"[12] of human rights standards and by the requirement that states take "positive" steps to protect the right to life (Article 2) and to secure respect for private life (Article 8).[13]

Quite obviously, the fact that the Convention has only recently been "brought home" does not imply that the United Kingdom has hitherto failed to protect the human rights of its citizens. The struggle to secure the rights of the aristocracy was made manifest as early as Magna Carta and the ensuing centuries witnessed the gradual subjection of the monarch to the will of the people and the piecemeal development of constitutional guarantees such as the Bill of Rights 1688 and the Habeas Corpus Act 1679. However, despite the introduction of a number of Bills in Parliament,[14] the United Kingdom resisted for many years the introduction of a domestic bill of rights and incorporation of the Convention. The English approach to the protection of human rights has been premised upon the basis that citizens are free to do that which is not prohibited: this is the Diceyan world of residual liberties where individual freedom is not determined or laid down by a constitutional document but is the outcome of the ordinary law of the land enforced by the courts. For Dicey, the danger of constitutional documents and bills of rights was that that which has been given can be taken away and very frequently is, by despotic government. The traditional English position was famously summed up by Sir Robert Megarry in *Malone* v. *Metropolitan Police Commissioner*: "England, is not a

---

[10] [2000] 2 WLR 1158.

[11] [1997] QB 1004.

[12] See introductory comments in Chapter 3.

[13] See discussion of omissions and positive obligations in Chapter 5.

[14] Sir Edward Gardner QC MP introduced a Private Member's Bill into the House of Commons in 1987 and Lord Lester of Herne Hill QC introduced two Bills on incorporation into the House of Lords in 1994 and 1996.

country where everything is forbidden except what is expressly permitted: it is a country where everything is permitted except what is expressly forbidden".[15]

There are a number of problems with this approach. First, it assumes benign public power. A laissez-faire approach to civil liberties does not in principle protect the citizen from the exercise of arbitrary power and an overweening executive, as was amply demonstrated by the facts from which the famous dictum of Megarry VC sprang. The judge was referring to the power of the police to tap private telephone conversations which, at the time, was unregulated and led to the Court finding the United Kingdom to be in violation of the Article 8 right to respect for private life. The finding of that violation was foreseen by Megarry VC, but he felt unable to restrain it because neither Parliament nor the common law had recognised a right to privacy. Secondly, many complaints of human rights violations relate to non-interference by the state, in the sense that third parties have been permitted to harm the individual, unrestrained by state action. In such cases, the complainant is arguing that the state has violated its positive obligation: for example, allegations that the right to life has been inadequately protected in the face of a known danger.[16] In *Z v. United Kingdom*,[17] the five children who were denied the possibility of bringing a negligence action against their local authority by the House of Lords,[18] have taken proceedings against the United Kingdom in Strasbourg arising from the failure of the local authority to take them into care in a timely fashion. Although human rights standards are generally conceived as being necessary to guard the individual against the actions of the state, it is well-recognised by the Strasbourg jurisprudence that the rights enshrined in the Convention may require positive action by states, including the regulation of the relationships between private parties. Finally, and overlapping with this second consideration, it is inadequate to deal with a situation where one person complains that his rights have been interfered with by the actions of another exercising a conflicting right: the classic example is the tension between the assertion of freedom of speech by one person and a complaint of infringement of privacy by another. The person whose privacy has been infringed does not want to exercise a liberty in the Diceyan sense: rather, he wants to be left alone, a situation that can only be achieved if laws are in place to restrain the intrusive acts of others. Indeed as Bradley and Ewing have observed, "unrestrained liberty, particularly of private as opposed to public power, can be the antithesis of the liberty of others".[19] An example can be

[15] [1979] 1 Ch 344 at 357. Cf *R v. Somerset County Council, ex parte Fewings* [1995] 1 All ER 513, where Laws J stated at 524 that the opposite principle applies to public bodies: "for public bodies the rule is opposite, and so of another character altogether. It is that any action to be taken must be justified by positive law. A public body has no heritage of legal rights which it enjoys for its own sake; at every turn, all of its dealings constitute the fulfilment of duties which it owes to others; indeed, it exists for no other purpose".
[16] *Kilic v. Turkey* App no 22492/93, judgment dated 28 March 2000: http://www.hudoc.echr.coe.int
[17] (1999) 28 EHRR CD 65.
[18] *X (Minors)* v. *Bedfordshire County Council, supra* n.3.
[19] A W Bradley and K D Ewing, *Constitutional and Administrative Law*, 12th edn (London, Longman, 1997).

gleaned from Strasbourg jurisprudence in the context of the Article 11 right to freedom of association. In *Plattform "Ärtzte für das Leben" v. Austria*,[20] the applicant anti-abortion group claimed that their right to freedom of association had been violated by the failure of the police to provide adequate control and protection for a demonstration. On the facts no violation was found, but the Court held that states have an obligation to protect groups exercising their Article 11 rights peaceably. Thus, it is clear that according to Strasbourg a state may be enjoined to take positive steps to enable a group to exercise its right to freedom of association, through, for example, the control of counter-demonstrators. It would be no answer to those wishing to demonstrate that the law did not prevent them from doing so, if others could effectively prevent them from exercising their rights without any fear of legal restraint. In order for the right to be upheld the state may have to take positive steps to regulate the rights of others; a system of residual liberties is not adequate to that task.

European Community law apart, the English legal mind is unaccustomed to thinking in terms of overarching general legal principles. The development of English law, dominated as it was by the forms of action, took place in a procedural atmosphere. In his first essay on the Forms of Action, Maitland described substantive English law as being "secreted in the interstices of procedure". The writ system required lawyers to understand forms, rather than to systematise and theorise the law. The result has been the development of causes of action, each with their own rules which, generally, have not been examined with a view to ensuring compliance with a standard emanating from either a domestic bill of rights or a supranational legal body. The task that English lawyers confront now is to examine those causes of action from three perspectives by asking: first, whether they in themselves are compatible with Convention standards; secondly, could those causes of action be the appropriate vehicle for the implementation of Convention standards; and, finally, what are the implications (if any) for the former of the framework of remedies established by the Human Rights Act. Thus, in relation to the first question, where the issue of duty of care in negligence is under consideration, the decision of the Court in *Osman v. United Kingdom* may bear relevance.[20a] However, it will also be relevant to consider whether a cause of action and the framework of remedies provided by the Act may now satisfy the requirements of the Court as laid down in Convention jurisprudence. This issue is discussed in Chapters 2 and 4. As to the second question, an apposite example is the issue of whether the action for breach of confidence already is, or should be, tailored appropriately to meet UK obligations in relation to privacy under Article 8 of the Convention. This question is addressed in detail in Chapter 6.

Article 1 of the Convention obliges states to "secure to everyone within the jurisdiction the rights and freedoms defined in Section 1 of [the] Convention". What the Convention does not do is prescribe for states the precise methods and

---

[20] Series A no 139 (1988).
[20a] But see now Note on the Text, pp. xxiii–xxxvii

mechanisms by which compliance should be achieved. This is a matter for the contracting Parties and Strasbourg retains a supervisory jurisdiction in this regard. It is suggested that a combination of two factors has led to the United Kingdom being one of the most persistent violators (second to Italy) of the rights and freedoms secured by the Convention. Clearly, a failure to incorporate the Convention at domestic level and the dualist nature of the United Kingdom, which has generally[21] remained wedded to the notion of parliamentary sovereignty, are major contributory factors, but the issue is not as simple as that. The fact that the United Kingdom Constitution has not been codified, that there has been no modern bill of rights, nor, more importantly, a "rights consciousness" in the United Kingdom, has exacerbated the tendency for lawyers simply to fail to perceive the potential relevance of human rights treaty obligations to the development of national law.

In many common law cases, it seems that parties to litigation have not appreciated that there is a human rights issue to be determined, nor a human rights argument to put in the balance. Cases such as *Osman* v. *Ferguson* and *X (Minors)* v. *Bedfordshire County Council* illustrate the point: in neither case was the Convention even mentioned. In his groundbreaking and impressive analysis of the impact of the Convention on English law, *Using Human Rights Law in English Courts*, Hunt on the other hand, placing emphasis on *Derbyshire* v. *Times Newspapers*[22] has argued that "the reality of what has been taking place . . . is nothing short of the emergence of a common law human rights jurisdiction". [23] While English courts over the last decade displayed an increasing tendency to refer to Strasbourg authority, that is not the same as complying with it, or using the Convention to shape English legal thought. In their work on the "Democratic Audit of the United Kingdom",[24] Klug, Starmer and Weir conducted a research project in 1993 using the LEXIS facility, the purpose of which was to study all cases from 1972 to 1993 in which either the Convention or the International Covenant on Civil and Political rights was cited. Their research revealed that the Convention was cited in only 173 cases (0.2 per cent), but the Convention impacted in only twenty-seven of these, of which eighteen concerned freedom of expression. They concluded that the Convention affected the outcome in only three cases, one of which was *Derbyshire* v. *Times Newspapers Ltd.* Klug and Starmer repeated this exercise in 1996, searching all reports of English court decisions on LEXIS for the period between 1973 and 1996. This research revealed that half the references to the Convention occurred in the period post-*Brind*,[25] but Klug and Starmer cautioned against drawing conclusions regarding the impact of the Convention on the common law. Their research revealed that:

[21] Subject to the supremacy of EC law as recognised by the *Factortame* litigation, *R* v. *Secretary of State for Transport, ex p. Factortame (No 2)* [1991] 1 AC 603.

[22] [1992] 1 QB 770.

[23] (Oxford, Hart Publishing, 1997) at 205.

[24] F Klug, K Starmer and S Weir, *The Three Pillars of Liberty* (London, Routledge, 1996) at 106.

[25] *Brind* v. *Secretary of State for the Home Department* [1991] 1 All ER 735.

"In numerical terms, only 59 of the 316 in which [the Convention] has been cited in domestic judgments have involved the development of the common law as a body of law. Only 18 of these post-date *Derbyshire*. As for actually influencing the outcome of the case, only two could be said to have fallen into that category. Moreover, both concerned freedom of expression – the Convention right that the judiciary has been most willing to accept is already recognised in the common law".[26]

The point that Klug and Starmer are making is that the Convention may have been referred to, but references in themselves say nothing about the quality of human rights protection achieved as a result. The courts have tended, for example, to assert the compatibility of Article 10 of the Convention (freedom of expression) with the English common law, usually as "a prelude to ignoring the [Convention], or, at best playing lipservice to it".[27] Examples of this approach can be found in many authorities. In *Attorney-General* v. *Guardian Newspapers*, Lord Goff stated, without examining any of the relevant jurisprudence, that the English law of breach of confidence is consistent with Article 10 and went on to say: "[t]his is scarcely surprising, since we may pride ourselves on the fact that freedom of speech has existed in this country as long, if not longer than, it has existed in any other country in the world".[28]

The apparent inattention of English lawyers to the Convention in tort claims may have been due to the fact that many cases brought against public authorities have concerned what may be categorised as omissions and such cases have perished in the face of the monolithic duty of care device. As Lord Goff observed in *Smith* v. *Littlewoods Organisation Ltd*, "the common law does not impose liability for what are called pure omissions".[29] The public law/civil libertarian aspect of these cases has perhaps been obscured by the technical requirements of the negligence action and a subliminal tendency to dismiss the relevance of the Convention in cases outside proceedings for judicial review. It is startling, though, that the leading cases in negligence over the last decade have largely been cases brought against public bodies which have exercised considerable power over the lives of individual plaintiffs. It is all the more remarkable, therefore, that English common lawyers have been so silent regarding the Convention in actions outside judicial review. Prior to the introduction of the Human Rights Bill, the author argued[30] that the Convention should be taken into account by the court under the third head of *Caparo* v. *Dickman*,[31] in order to assess whether it would be "fair, just and reasonable" to recognise a duty of care. It is difficult to understand, for example, why no argument of a Convention character was put in *X (Minors)* v. *Bedfordshire County Council*.[32]

---

[26] F Klug and K Starmer, "Incorporation Through the Back Door?", [1997] *PL* 223.
[27] *Ibid.* at 227.
[28] [1990] 1 AC 109 at 283.
[29] [1987] 2 AC 241 at 247.
[30] *Supra* n.3.
[31] [1990] 2 AC 605.
[32] *Supra* n.3.

Human rights arguments are capable of pervading large swathes of law quite apart from the obviously "public law" type of cases concerning applications for refugee status or public housing.

Early indications are that, quite apart from the technical requirements of the Human Rights Act 1998, the *Osman* decision of the Court has put an end to such inhibition. In *Osman*, which is discussed in detail in Chapter 4, the Strasbourg Court found that the United Kingdom had violated the Article 6 right to a fair trial as a result of the Court of Appeal's decision in *Osman* v. *Ferguson*.[33] The Court of Appeal had held that the police did not owe a duty of care to the victims of crime when carrying out investigation. Although subject to criticism and effectively overruled by *Z* v. *United Kingdom*, *Osman* has had a significant impact on the tort of negligence. Equally, the point should be made that the Convention has a great deal more to offer the claimant than the Article 6 right of access to a court, important though that right undoubtedly is. The question which should be asked in any case is: first, do the facts suggest either that the state has interfered with an individual's rights or that a third party should have been restrained by the state from interfering with an individual's rights and, secondly, if so does the relevant legal rule/mechanism, or an amalgam of such rules and mechanisms, secure to that person the substance of the right accorded by the Convention?

The response of the Judicial Studies Board to the Human Rights Act was to put in place a training programme in both the Act and the Convention for all full- and part-time members of the judiciary. The 1998–99 Annual Report of the Board acknowledged that "only a few judges can claim expertise in this field". To the untrained eye such an admission might be surprising in view of the fact that the Convention has constituted a treaty obligation embracing a range of (broadly) civil and political rights for nearly half a century. However, it is a fact that in some fields, largely those outside administrative law, the relevance of the Convention has only lately been perceived and usually as a result of the United Kingdom having been found to be in violation of the Convention.[34] It should not be supposed, however, that English law was unaffected by the Convention prior to the Human Rights Act. While there is room for disagreement over the extent to which Convention jurisprudence and thinking permeated the English legal psyche, the Convention was not without effect as the following discussion demonstrates.

BACKGROUND: THE CONVENTION AND THE DEVELOPMENT OF ENGLISH LAW
PRIOR TO THE HUMAN RIGHTS ACT 1998

When the United Kingdom signed the Convention it entered into treaty obligations with the other Contracting States, whereby each state agreed to secure to

---

[33] *Supra* n.6.

[34] See, for example, *Barrett* v. *Enfield London Borough Council*, *supra* n.9, decided following the decision of the Strasbourg Court in *Osman* v. *United Kingdom*, *supra* n.8, and distinguishing *X (Minors)* v. *Bedfordshire County Council*, *supra* n.3.

all those within its jurisdiction the rights and freedoms set out. Those obligations take effect as part of international law. The status of treaty obligations within domestic law is a matter for each Contracting State: some states are dualist, some monist. The difference between the two lies in the conceptualisation of the relationship between international and national law. As Dame Rosalyn Higgins has observed:

> "For the monist, international law is part of the law of the land alongside labour law, employment law, contract law, and so forth. Dualists contend that there are two essentially different legal systems, existing side by side within different spheres of action—the international plane and the domestic plane".[35]

Thus, for the monist, international law is a subset of national law. The United Kingdom is a dualist state which means that international treaty obligations bind the state and do not create rights and obligations enforceable in domestic law unless and until they are transformed into national law by statute. It is for this reason that a right under the Convention has not constituted a right which is directly enforceable in English law.[36]

The failure of the United Kingdom to embrace fully the precepts of the Convention (and, indeed, other international human rights treaties) as a matter of English law has been caused in part by the dualist nature of the state. However, monism is not a guarantor of state compliance. A survey by Frederik Sundberg of the effect of the status of the Convention in domestic systems reveals that incorporation is no necessary guarantee of compliance with the Convention standards:

> "Whatever the level of incorporation it is at least clear that the domestic courts cannot remedy the kind of violation found for example in the *Kruslin* and *Huvig* cases against France:[37] here it was the lack of precision of the existing jurisprudence regulating telephone tapping which was at the basis of the violation found of Article 8 . . . Only a legislative change could introduce the necessary precision within a reasonable period of time and this notwithstanding the fact that the Convention is in principle incorporated at a 'supra-legal' level meaning that national statutes can be reviewed as the basis of the Convention".[38]

The Human Rights Act 1998 does not incorporate the Convention into English law: it is an Act designed to give "further effect" to the Convention and it remains to be seen whether rights will be brought home sufficiently that the number of applications to Strasbourg decreases. The White Paper made clear that the aim of the Act is to provide an effective alternative to the cost and delay in taking proceedings in Strasbourg. There is, however, the merest hint of legal

---

[35] R Higgins, *Problems and Process: International Law and How We Use It* (Oxford, Clarendon Press, 1994) at 205.

[36] *Malone, supra* n.15; *Kaye* v. *Robertson* [1991] FSR 62.

[37] Series A nos 176-A and B (1990).

[38] Frederik Sundberg, "Status of the Convention in Member States", in L Betten (ed), *The Human Rights Act 1998—What it Means* (The Hague, Martinus Nijhoff, 1997) 87 at 91.

nationalism when it is observed that the corollary of bringing rights home is that the Strasbourg Court will be enabled to become familiar with the laws and customs of England and thus English legal tradition will "influence" the development of case law by the Court.[39]

Although the Convention did not enjoy statutory force until the advent of the Human Rights Act, its influence on the development of the common law has not been without significance. The extent to which the values enshrined in the Convention have permeated the common law is a matter for debate,[40] but the following principles of English law reflected a judicial willingness in some areas to ensure conformity with the Convention standards.

(1) It was well settled that international treaty obligations might be used to resolve an ambiguity in legislation. In *Salomon* v. *Commissioners of Customs and Excise*, the Court of Appeal was required to construe a statute based on an international convention which was not included in a schedule nor otherwise referred to in it. Diplock LJ held that:

> "There is a prima facie presumption that Parliament does not intend to act in breach of international law, including therein specific treaty obligations; and if one of the meanings which can reasonably be ascribed to the legislation is consonant with the treaty obligations and another or others are not, the meaning which is consonant is to be preferred".[41]

Applying the presumption in *Waddington* v. *Miah*,[42] the House of Lords interpreted an ambiguous provision in the Immigration Act 1971 by reference to Article 7 of the Convention in order to avoid the introduction of retrospective penalties. The inherent limitation in this canon of construction was that it was triggered by an ambiguity in legislation and the conferment of apparently unlimited discretion on the executive would not amount to an ambiguity. Thus, in *Brind* v. *Home Secretary*,[43] the House of Lords refused to interfere with the broadcasting ban, prohibiting the television and radio media from broadcasting interviews with members of proscribed terrorist organisations as well as Sinn Fein. In future, the Human Rights Act will subject such executive action to evaluation for compatibility with Article 10 of the Convention.

(2) In *Derbyshire County Council* v. *Times Newspapers Ltd*,[44] the Court of Appeal was called upon for the first time to decide whether a local authority, which is a body corporate, can sue for libel. All members of the Court of Appeal agreed that where the common law was uncertain (as in this case)[45] or ambiguous then the court should have regard to the Convention in order to decide the

---

[39] *Rights Brought Home: The Human Rights Bill* (Cm 3782) at para. 1.18.
[40] Cf Hunt, *supra* n.23 and Klug, Starmer, and Weir, *supra* n.24.
[41] [1967] 2 QB 116 at 143.
[42] [1974] 1 WLR 683.
[43] [1991] 1 AC 696.
[44] [1992] QB 770.
[45] There were two conflicting decisions on the point: *Manchester Corp* v. *Williams* [1891] 1 QB 94 and *Bognor Regis UDC* v. *Campion* [1972] 2 QB 169.

case. Balcombe LJ and Butler-Sloss LJ observed also, on the authority of *R v. Chief Metropolitan Stipendiary Magistrate, ex parte Choudhury*,[46] that the court would have regard, where appropriate, to the Convention even where the common law is certain. For Ralph Gibson LJ, uncertainty was required for Convention considerations to be permitted.

As we have seen, despite these dicta, as well as a number of other authorities referred to by Balcombe LJ which supported recourse to the Convention, there was little attention paid to human rights law obligations in English tort cases prior to *Osman v. United Kingdom*.

(3) In the field of judicial review, the courts demonstrated a willingness to develop a "common law human rights jurisdiction",[47] according to which the degree of scrutiny to which a decision was subject would vary according to the status of the subject matter: if fundamental rights were at stake the scrutiny would be stricter. In *R v. Secretary of State for the Home Department, ex parte Bugdaycay*,[48] the applicant had been refused asylum and the Home Secretary had directed that he should be returned to Kenya. There was no attempt to verify the applicant's claim that he would be sent from Kenya to Uganda with risk to his life. Lord Bridge stated that:

> "The most fundamental of all human rights is the individual's right to life and when an administrative decision under challenge is said to be one which may put the applicant's life at risk, the basis of the decision must surely call for the most anxious scrutiny".

Although, as we have seen, the applicant's claim failed in *Brind*, nevertheless Lord Bridge confirmed that the human rights context would be an important factor in judicial review, stating that any restriction on fundamental human rights "requires to be justified and nothing less than an important competing interest will be sufficient to justify it".[49]

(4) Finally, the different status accorded to the Convention prior to the Human Rights Act, in the field of EC, law should be mentioned. This discussion remains relevant, the Human Rights Act notwithstanding, because of the difference in status between European Community law on the one hand and Convention law on the other.

The jurisprudence of the ECJ has recognised that fundamental rights form part of the general principles of EC law, which constrain the acts of both Community institutions and also Member States. There is now a body of case law in which "the Convention has been employed by the ECJ as an aid to the construction of Community provisions or as a yardstick for determining the validity of Community acts".[50] In addition Article 6(2) of the Treaty of

---

[46] [1991] 1 QB 429.

[47] Borrowing Hunt's terminology, see *supra* n.23, at Chapter 5.

[48] [1987] AC 514.

[49] *Supra* n.43 at 723.

[50] N Grief, "The Domestic Impact of the European Convention on Human Rights as Mediated Through Community Law", [1991] *PL* 555.

European Union has been made justiciable by the Treaty of Amsterdam. Article 6(2) provides that:

"the Union shall respect fundamental rights as guaranteed by the [Convention] . . . and as they result from the constitutional traditions common to the Member States as general principles of Community law".

The difficult question to answer is under what circumstances are the "general principles" binding on Member States. In *Ellinki Radiophonia Tileorassi AE* v. *Pliroforissis*,[51] it was held by the ECJ that it could examine national measures for compatibility with the general principles where such measures "fall within the scope of Community law". Precisely what this means beyond the fact that the general principles apply to measures taken to implement or derogate from Community law is not clear. Grosz, Beatson and Duffy have observed that "[A]ccording to the present state of the case law it would appear to be necessary for the national measure to be adopted under powers conferred or duties imposed by Community law".[52]

The effect of EC jurisprudence is, therefore, that, the court may disapply primary legislation where it contravenes EC law,[53] which includes the Convention principles. Demetriou cites *P.* v. *S and Cornwall County Council*,[54] as an example of the English courts having greater power to protect Convention rights through the medium of EC law. Following a ruling by the ECJ that discrimination on the ground of transsexuality is prohibited by the Equal Treatment Directive (76/207 EEC), because, *inter alia*, the Convention so requires, the industrial tribunal disapplied the Sex Discrimination Act 1975 and decided the case on the basis of the Directive. Under the Human Rights Act, the courts do not have power to disapply primary legislation, so there will be cases where the claimant has enhanced protection of Convention rights through the medium of EC law.

CONCLUSION

The absence of a bill of rights in the United Kingdom led inevitably to a somewhat "piecemeal" protection of rights through the application of various fields of law; but, as Lord Bingham has observed it is the law of tort "which has borne the heat and burden of the battle".[55] At bottom, the rules of tort law reflect policy decisions by the judiciary about the interests that are protected and the type of conduct that is sanctioned. Lord Cooke's speech in *Hunter* v. *Canary Wharf Ltd*[56]

---

[51] Case C-260/89 [1991] ECR I-2925. For a helpful discussion of these issues, see M Demetriou, "Using Human Rights Through European Community Law", [1999] *EHRLR* 484 at 488 *et seq.*

[52] S Grosz, J Beatson and P Duffy, *Human Rights The 1998 Act and the European Convention* (London, Sweet & Maxwell, 2000) at 13 citing Case C-2/92 *R* v. *Maff, ex parte Bostock* [1994] I ECR 955.

[53] *Factortame, supra* n.21.

[54] Case C-13/94 [1996] ECR I-2143; Demetriou, *supra* n.51 at 492.

[55] Lord Bingham of Cornhill, "Tort and Human Rights", in P Cane and J Stapleton (eds), *The Law of Obligations, Essays in Celebration of John Fleming* (Oxford, Clarendon Press, 1998) 1 at 2.

[56] [1997] 2 All ER 426 at 462.

was refreshing for its honesty in acknowledging that the determination of who has standing to sue in private nuisance cannot be a matter of legal analysis alone, but a policy choice. All that legal analysis can do is expose the alternatives. The "policy" that should inform the development of tort law, and indeed all law, in the United Kingdom is that legal rules must be rendered compatible with the Convention rights.

2

The Human Rights Act 1998

INTRODUCTION

THE HUMAN RIGHTS Act 1998 has been described as "an unprecedented transfer of political power from the executive and legislature to the judiciary, and a fundamental restructuring of our political constitution".[1] However, unlike the Scotland Act 1998, the Human Rights Act does not give the courts power to strike down primary legislation on the grounds of incompatibility with the European Convention on Human Rights ("the Convention"). Instead, the power of the court is limited to issuing a declaration of incompatibility following which remedial action may be taken by a Minister under section 9 of the Act. Thus, while there has been a transfer of power, the constitutional balance between the courts and Westminster is maintained with sovereignty remaining with Parliament. It seems that rivers of ink have been spilled in order to examine the likely impact of the Human Rights Act on English law and much of the language employed by commentators has been that of "incorporation". Indeed, the government White Paper spoke of "[t]he case for incorporation".[2] But, the Human Rights Act does not incorporate the Convention into English law: rather as, Ewing has observed, certain of the Convention rights acquire "a defined status in English law".[3] The Convention rights have no autonomous existence in English law: they have been given "further effect", to the extent that the legislation so prescribes.

The basic scheme of the Act is set out in section 6(1), which makes it "unlawful for a public authority to act in a way which is incompatible with a Convention right". However, section 6(3) defines "public authority" to include in sub-paragraph (a) "a court or tribunal". Thus, one of the key questions arising is the extent of the court's duty to develop the common law so that it is compatible with Convention rights. In particular, will the courts consider that they are permitted or mandated to recognise new causes of action when it is considered that this is necessary to give effect to Convention rights? Clearly, the degree to which the recognised and established parameters of tort law are extended, hinges upon the view the courts take of their role under section 6. It seems likely,

---

[1] K D Ewing, "The Human Rights Act and Parliamentary Democracy", (1999) 62 *MLR* 79. See also G Marshall, "Patriating Rights—With Reservations" in J Beatson, C Forsyth and I Hare (eds), *Constitutional Reform in the United Kingdom: Practice and Principles* (Oxford, Hart Publishing, 1998) at 75.

[2] *Rights Brought Home: The Human Rights Bill* (Cm 3782, 1997) at para. 1.4.

[3] Ewing, *supra* n.1 at 84.

in the light of jurisprudence emerging since the Act came into effect on 2 October 2000, that the initial response of the courts to this question will be conservative.

The Act creates a framework of remedies in section 8, the main thrust of which is that a claim for damages will lie against a public authority (other than a court), which has acted incompatibly with Convention rights. Thus, where a public authority acts negligently and that negligent behaviour also amounts to a violation of a Convention right,[4] a claim will lie against the public authority under section 7 of the Act, as well as in any recognised tort action. The potential impact of the section 8 remedy is discussed in the final section below.

This chapter will examine the effect of the relevant Convention rights in English law as a result of the Act under five broad headings: (i) the Convention rights covered by the Act; (ii) the role of the courts in relation to legislation; (iii) the issue of "horizontal effect": what effect will the Act have on actions between private parties; (iv) remedies under the Act; and (v) the implications for tort law of the scheme of remedies established by the Act.

THE CONVENTION RIGHTS

The Human Rights Act 1998 was enacted in order to give further effect to certain Convention rights and freedoms and they are listed in section 1 as follows:

"(a) Articles 2 to 12 and 14 of the Convention,
 (b) Articles 1 to 3 of the First Protocol, and
 (c) Articles 1 and 2 of the Sixth Protocol
 as read with Articles 16 to 18 of the Convention".

The Articles are set out in Schedule 1 to the Act. Detailed discussion of Strasbourg jurisprudence and related tort law issues takes place in the subsequent chapter and attention will focus here on the Articles that have been excluded and the status of Convention jurisprudence under the Act.

Two important Articles have been excluded from the Act: Article 1, according to which states agree "to secure to everyone within the jurisdiction the rights and freedoms set out", and Article 13 which provides that everyone whose rights and freedoms are set out shall have "an effective remedy before a national authority". Article 1 embodies the interstate obligation by which each Contracting Party (state) agrees to give effect to the Convention rights and freedoms and as such is not appropriate for inclusion in the Act. It has been observed by a number of commentators[5] that Article 1 has constituted the

---

[4] Chapter 3 provides an analysis of key obligations under the Convention.
[5] G Phillipson, "The Human Rights Act, 'Horizontal Effect' and the Common Law: a Bang or a Whimper?", (1999) 62 *MLR* 824 at 836; R Buxton, "The Human Rights Act and Private Law", (2000) 116 *LQR* 48 at 52 *et seq.* and S Grosz, J Beatson and P Duffy, *Human Rights: The 1998 Act and the European Convention* (London, Sweet & Maxwell, 2000) at 4.

vehicle through which the positive obligations[6] generated by the Convention have been developed by the European Court of Human Rights, through a reading of Article 1 in conjunction with the relevant substantive provisions. Thus, in *A v. United Kingdom*,[7] the Court found the United Kingdom in violation of the Article 3 right to be free from inhuman and degrading treatment as a consequence of failing in its positive obligation derived from Article 1, read together with Article 3, to protect a child from brutal beatings by his stepfather. However, an examination of the authorities, reveals that Article 1 did not feature in the early jurisprudence in which positive obligations were found. The Article 8 right to respect for private and family life was the key right here and the Commission and the Court inferred the positive obligation from "the right to respect", without the need to rely on Article 1.[8] In any event, the United Kingdom has entered into the obligation at Treaty level and all the Strasbourg jurisprudence, regardless of the substantive Article number in issue, is to be taken into account under section 2 of the Act.

The omission of Article 13 is likely to be more problematic, particularly in the light of recent jurisprudence which has highlighted the role that Article 13 has to play in ensuring the effective enjoyment of the substantive rights laid down. In his trenchant criticism of the Human Rights Bill, Marshall suggested that the White Paper needed a subtitle to the effect: "Rights Brought Home: All Bar One; and That the Most Important".[9] A number of explanations for the omission of Article 13 were given, including a statement by the Home Secretary in Committee:

> "We took the view that the best way of applying Article 13 in the context of incorporating the Convention was to spell out in specific clauses how those remedies should be made available. Therefore, we take from Article 13 that 'everyone whose rights and freedoms . . . are violated shall have an effective remedy' and then set out in the Bill what those effective remedies should be and how they can be accessed".[10]

In resisting attempts during the Lords' Committee stage to have Article 13 included in the scheduled rights, the Lord Chancellor declared that:

---

[6] The notion of positive obligations in this context refers to the recognition by Strasbourg of state obligations to act in the private sphere to regulate the relationships of non-state actors. Strasbourg has also recognised positive obligations on public bodies to act to secure rights through the institution of operational measures in certain circumstances: *Kilic* v. *Turkey* App no 224/92, judgment dated 28 March 2000 (operational measures by the police required to protect the applicant's right to life under Article 2), see text accompanying n.34 in Chapter 5.

[7] (1998) 27 EHRR 611.

[8] In *Marckx* v. *Belgium* Series A no 31 (1979), *Airey* v. *Ireland* Series A no 32 (1979) and *X and Y* v. *The Netherlands* Series A no 91 (1985) which are pivotal for the recognition of positive obligations, Article 1 is not even mentioned; cf, *Young, James and Webster* v. *United Kingdom* (Series A no 44 (1981)) where the closed shop arrangements of the United Kingdom were found to be in violation of the Article 11 right to freedom of association, notwithstanding that the employer in question was private. The Court invoked the Article 1 obligation to "secure the" right laid down in Article 11 to freedom of association (which includes the negative freedom not to associate).

[9] *Supra* n.1 at 77.

[10] HC Deb vol 312 col 986 20 May 1998, quoted by G Phillipson, *supra* n.5 at 837.

> "If Article 13 were included, the courts would be bound to ask themselves what was intended beyond the existing scheme of remedies set out in the Bill. It might lead them to fashion remedies other than Clause 8 remedies".[11]

Thus, essentially the government's justification for exclusion is that section 8 of the Act provides the domestic analogy for Article 13. The problem with that view is that the concept of "effective remedies" under Article 13 is not, to adopt a mathematical analogy, delineated by a "closed set" while section 8 of the Act is clearly intended to be. Section 8 of the Act has been described as being "framed in the widest possible terms",[12] but the court's powers are limited to granting remedies "within its powers as it considers just and appropriate"(section 8(1)) and awards of damages are circumscribed by "the principles applied by the European Court of Human Rights" (section 8(4)). Recent jurisprudence demonstrates the very important substantive role that Article 13 has to play: it may be an auxiliary right in the sense that an evaluation for compliance is only triggered when an applicant can demonstrate an arguable claim that a Convention right has been violated,[13] but it is an autonomous right.[14] The effect of Article 13 is to require the provision of a domestic remedy allowing the competent national authority both to deal with the substance of the relevant Convention complaint and to grant appropriate relief. In *Aksoy* v. *Turkey* (concerning, *inter alia*, allegations of torture by state agents), the Court held that:

> "The scope of the obligation under Article 13 varies depending on the nature of the applicant's complaint under the Convention . . . where an individual has an arguable claim that he has been tortured by agents of the State, the notion of an 'effective remedy' entails, in addition to the payment of compensation where appropriate, a thorough and effective investigation capable of leading to the identification and punishment of those responsible and including effective access for the complainant to the investigatory procedure".[15]

The Court found that there had been a violation of Article 13 since there had been no investigation, despite the evidence of torture. It should be noted that the Court has also held that the obligation of the state to protect life under Article 2 requires that there should be some form of effective official investigation where individuals have been killed as a result of the use of force,[16] but the Court has held that the requirements of Article 13 are broader than the obligation to investigate imposed by Article 2.[17]

---

[11] HL Deb vol 583 col 521, quoted by Marshall, *supra* n.1.

[12] Grosz, Beatson and Duffy, *supra* n.5 at 138.

[13] *Silver* v. *United Kingdom* Series A no 61 (1983).

[14] See D J Harris, M O'Boyle and C Warbrick, *Law of the European Convention on Human Rights* (London, Butterworths, 1995) at 461.

[15] (1996) 23 EHRR 553 at paras 95–100. *Cf Osman* v. *United Kingdom* [1999] 1 FLR 193, where the Court found a violation of Article 6 and recalled that the requirements of Article 13 are less strict than and are absorbed by Article 6.

[16] *McCann and others* v. *United Kingdom* Series A no 324 (1995); *Kaya* v. *Turkey* (1999) 28 EHRR 1 and *Kilic* v. *Turkey* App no 22492/93, judgment dated 28 March 2000.

[17] *Kilic* v. *Turkey*, *ibid.* at para. 93.

A recent decision taken by the Court illustrates the potential shortcomings of failing to give effect to Article 13. In *Keenan* v. *United Kingdom*,[18] the applicant petitioned Strasbourg after her mentally ill son committed suicide in prison, having been put in solitary confinement in a segregation block following an adjudication that he had assaulted two prison officers. The applicant alleged that Articles 2 (right to life), 3 (inhuman and degrading treatment) and 13 had been violated. The Article 13 complaint was based on the fact that under (pre-Act) English law, there was no mechanism by which the applicant could apply for compensation for non-pecuniary damage in the nature of grief or distress suffered by her or her son. There was no evidence that her son had suffered additional psychiatric harm prior to his death and as a non-dependent parent of an adult child she was unable to claim under the Fatal Accidents Act 1976. The Court held that Articles 3 and 13 had been violated. The Article 13 violation consisted in the fact that there were no means by which the applicant could seek compensation and there was no remedy by which responsibility for the death of Mark Keenan could be established.

Sir Stephen Sedley entered a concurring judgment in which he pointed out that what Mrs Keenan really needed was an effective inquiry into her son's death: an inquest to determine responsibility is required. However, Rule 42 of the Coroners' Rules 1984, made in the exercise of delegated legislation, forbids the framing of a verdict in such a way as to appear to determine civil liability or a named person's criminal responsibility. Sir Stephen Sedley pointed out that, because Article 13 has not been included in the Schedule to the Human Rights Act, there is no mandate for English courts to interpret section 11 of the Coroners' Act 1988 (requiring a finding as to how a deceased person died) to achieve compatibility with Article 13.

It is difficult to see how applicants in the position of, for example, Stephen Lawrence's family could achieve the remedy they required, namely an effective investigation into their son's death, through invoking section 8 of the Act, which is couched in terms of remedial orders within the recognised powers of the court and damages. As the Lord Chancellor acknowledged, it is not intended that the Act should enable the courts to fashion remedies other than those prescribed by section 8, so there will clearly be cases where redress at domestic level for violation of Convention rights is not afforded. A family who consider that the police are failing properly to investigate a suspicious death would have no effective remedy under the Act, because the court's power does not extend to ordering such an investigation. Compensation may be sought under section 8, but this would not satisfy the Article 13 (and probably Article 2) right to have the matter properly investigated.

There would clearly have been conceptual problems in bringing Article 13 home in view of the interpretative obligation imposed on the courts by section 3 of the Act and discussed in the next section. Where the court is forced to make

---

[18] App no 27229/95, judgment dated 3 April 2001.

a declaration that primary legislation is incompatible with a Convention right, the litigant will have no remedy in relation to that incompatibility, because section 3(2)(b) provides that the validity of such legislation is not affected by such incompatibility and section 6(1) does not apply to an act if as the result of a legislative provision the authority could not have acted differently (section 6(2)). Thus, the offending legislation cannot effectively be impugned by a claimant in proceedings under the Act, leaving the victim of a violation without a remedy.

However, Strasbourg jurisprudence under Article 13 will impact indirectly on English law by being taken into account by the courts under section 2 of the Act, which is discussed below. During parliamentary debates, in response to a question put by Lord Lester as to whether the courts could have regard to Article 13 jurisprudence, the Lord Chancellor replied that they could do so "when considering the very ample provisions of Clause 8 (1)". He went on to say: "One always has in mind *Pepper* v. *Hart* when one is asked questions of that kind".[19]

THE EFFECT OF THE ACT ON LEGISLATION

Section 3(1) of the Act provides that:

"So far as it is possible to do so, primary legislation and subordinate legislation must be read and given effect in a way which is compatible with the Convention rights".

Where a court determines that a provision in primary legislation is incompatible with a Convention right, its powers are limited to making a declaration of that incompatibility (section 4(2)). The same principle applies in the case of subordinate legislation where the court is satisfied that the relevant primary legislation prevents the removal of the incompatibility (section 4(4)).

It is apparent that the Act imposes a very strong interpretative obligation upon the courts. The White Paper acknowledged that the drafting goes far beyond the rule hitherto applied that the courts could resort to the Convention in order to resolve ambiguity in legislation. Henceforth, the courts would be required to interpret "legislation so as to uphold the Convention rights unless the legislation itself is so clearly incompatible that it is impossible to do so".[20] The section applies to all legislation, whether enacted before or after the Act, and makes no distinction between public and private bodies.

Kentridge has described the provisions on incompatibility as "a subtle compromise between the concepts of parliamentary sovereignty and fundamental rights" and has suggested that such declarations will be rare. He gives two reasons: first, there is no incentive for the litigant to seek such a declaration and, secondly, Parliament, the executive and the courts will all strive to avoid the necessity for such declarations.[21] The wording of section 3, " so far as it is

---

[19] Quoted by F Klug, "The Human Rights Act 1998, *Pepper* v. *Hart* and All That", [1999] *PL* 246.
[20] *Rights Brought Home: The Human Rights Bill, supra* n.2 at para. 2.7.
[21] S Kentridge, "The Incorporation of the European Convention on Human Rights" in Beatson, Forsyth and Hare, *supra* n.1 at 69.

possible", is reminiscent of the standard applied by the ECJ to the interpretation of directives in *Marleasing*,[22] and cases like *Webb* v. *EMO Air Cargo (UK) Ltd*,[23] where the House of Lords went to great lengths to accommodate the ruling from the ECJ, suggest that English courts will be reluctant to make declarations of incompatibility. It is true that the Act contains no equivalent of sections 2(1) and 2(4) of the European Communities Act 1972, but section 3 gives statutory force to the obligation to search for compatibility, possibly at the expense of truth.[24]

WHO IS BOUND BY THE HUMAN RIGHTS ACT: VERTICAL/HORIZONTAL EFFECT?

Undoubtedly, the most important question for the common lawyer is: who is bound by the Human Rights Act? Is the Act intended to create rights and duties as between the individual and the state, or does it go wider than this and have a role to play in the relationships between individual citizens *inter se*? In other words, is the Act intended to operate in the sphere of private law as well as public law? This issue is commonly ascribed the epithet "vertical/horizontal" effect to convey the reach of bills of rights in visual and spatial terms and a range of responses can be seen in a number of jurisdictions, from the aggressive "state action" doctrine of the USA to Ireland, "which appears to be unique in recognising a cause of action against private parties for breach of constitutionally protected rights".[25] Ireland is an example of a jurisdiction embracing "direct" horizontal effect; other states are illustrations of "indirect" horizontal effect, where the values embodied in the constitutionally guaranteed rights, while not directly applicable, inform the development of the rules of private law. Germany is an example of indirect effect: the constitutional rights set out in the Basic Law of 1949 are treated as values that permeate the entire legal system, finding their way into the ordering of private relations through the interpretation of the "general clauses" in the Civil Code.[26] This section will discuss the position that appears to be occupied by the Act on the horizontality spectrum.

---

[22] Case C-106/89 *Marleasing SA* v. *La Commercial Internacionale de Alimentacion SA* [1990] ECR I-4135: "in applying national law, whether the provisions in question were adopted before or after the directive, the national court called upon to interpret it is required to do so, as far as possible, in the light of the wording and purpose of the directive in order to achieve the result pursued by the latter".

[23] [1993] 1 WLR 49.

[24] See M Beloff, "What Does it all Mean", in L Betten (ed), *The Human Rights Act 1998: What it Means* (The Hague, Martinus Nijhoff, 1999) 11 at 28, quoting Lord Cooke of Thorndon: Hansard HL Deb vol 52 col 1272.

[25] M Hunt, "The Effect on the Law of Obligations" in B S Markesinis, *The Impact of the Human Rights Bill on English Law* (Oxford, Clarendon Press, 1998) at 428–9: "there exists in Ireland *a sui generis* 'constitutional tort', a breach of a constitutional right. In marked contrast to the American requirement of 'state action', the Irish constitutional jurisprudence allows individuals to sue other private parties by directly invoking their constitutional rights as the source of their claim".

[26] B S Markesinis, *The German Law of Torts* (Oxford, Clarendon Press 1994) at 365 *et seq.*

As we have seen, as regards the interpretative obligation of the courts in relation to legislation, no distinction is drawn between public and private law: section 3 applies to all primary and subordinate legislation. Therefore, all legislation affecting the law of obligations must, "so far as it is possible to do so", be read and given effect in a way which is compatible with Convention rights. Therefore, to this extent at least the Act has horizontal effect. But, what about the development of common law principles as between non-state actors? The Act makes no explicit mention of the common law. However, section 6, which sets out the framework of the Act, provides in subsection 1 that: "It is unlawful for a public authority to act in a way which is incompatible with a Convention right". A non-exhaustive definition of "public authority" is provided by subsection 3:

> "In this section 'public authority' includes—
>   (a) a court or tribunal, and
>   (b) any person certain of whose functions are functions of a public nature,
> but does not include either House of Parliament or a person exercising functions in connection with proceedings in Parliament".

It seems clear that the scheme of the Act precludes direct horizontal effect, in the sense that a claimant may found a cause of action purely on a Convention right, as would be the case in Ireland, since only "public authorities", as defined, are required to act in a way which is compatible with Convention rights. Wade, alone amongst commentators on the Act, has expressed the view that it will make no difference whether a defendant is a public authority or a private person, since the courts will be required to enforce the Convention rights having regard to section 2 in any case.[27] If direct horizontal effect along the lines of the Irish model were intended, the drafting of the Act and the careful differentiation between "public" and other bodies would be otiose. However, contrary to the view expressed by Kentridge, who has denied that the Act will apply at all between individual litigants,[28] it is clear both from the Act itself and from judicial interpretation both before and since the Act came into force, that some horizontal effect has been achieved. While the views put forward by academic commentators regarding the horizontal effect of the Act have seemed widely diverging, it is submitted that frequently apparent disagreements really amount to differences in emphasis, rather than differences in substance. A number of commentaries on the Act have examined the experience of interpretation of bills by higher courts in other (common law, anglophone) jurisdictions as a source of inspiration to determine the reach of the Act. While not in agreement with the conclusions on horizontal effect put forward by Buxton,[29] the author would agree that the impact of

---

[27] Sir William Wade, "The United Kingdom's Bill of Rights" in Beatson, Forsyth and Hare, *supra* n.1 at 63.

[28] Save to the extent that the courts are "acting in their own sphere" so that they "must give effect to such fundamental rights as the right to a fair trial; and to more particular rights such as a right to an interpreter": S Kentridge, "The Incorporation of the European Convention on Human Rights", in Beatson, Forsyth and Hare, *supra* n.1 at 69 *et seq*.

[29] R Buxton, "The Human Rights Act and Private Law" (2000) 116 *LQR* 48.

the Act should be assessed by reference to textual interpretation and that comparative references, whilst of academic interest, do not necessarily assist. It is particularly important to bear in mind that Commonwealth and other jurisdictions which have recently adopted bills of rights,[30] have not done so in order to give further effect to a supranational obligation analogous to the United Kingdom's obligations under the Convention. Where states have modelled their bills on the International Covenant on Civil and Political Rights and presumably to give domestic effect to those obligations in international law,[31] the analogy with the Human Rights Act is inapposite in view of the fact that supervision of the ICCPR is of a quasi-judicial nature by the Human Rights Committee which has no power to render judgments. The express purpose of the Act is to bring rights home and to save the victims of violations the cost (on average £30,000) and the delay in achieving justice through having to follow the long road to Strasbourg.[32]

The fact that the courts are bound by section 6(3) to act in a manner that is compatible with Convention rights suggests that the Act will be of indirect horizontal effect, so that in the development of the common law (in the broadest sense, including the doctrines of equity) the courts will be obliged to accommodate Convention principles, regardless of the identity of the defendant. The substantive development of English principles in private litigation will then be shaped by the extent to which Strasbourg has required obligations to be implemented in the private sphere. Not only is section 6(3) crucial here, but also section 2 of the Act, which, as we have seen, requires the court to "take account" of Convention jurisprudence in "determining a question which has arisen in connection with a Convention right". Support for this view is demonstrated by the recent House of Lords' decision in *Reynolds* v. *Times Newspapers Ltd.*[33] In *Reynolds*, the defendant newspaper sought to argue, unsuccessfully, that English law should recognise a new *genus* of information attracting the defence of qualified privilege, namely political information. On the question of the status of the Convention as a result of the Act, Lord Nicholls (with Lord Cooke and Lord Hobhouse concurring) stated that:

"The common law is to be developed and applied in a manner consistent with Article 10 of the [Convention], and the court must take into account relevant decisions of the European Court of Human Rights (sections 6 and 2). To be justified, any curtailment of freedom of expression must be convincingly established by a compelling countervailing consideration, and the means employed must be proportionate to the end sought to be achieved".[34]

---

[30] For example, the Canadian Charter of Rights and Freedoms (1982), the Hong Kong Bill of Rights Ordinance, Ordinance No 59 of 1991, the South African Interim Constitution of 1993, each of which is considered by Hunt, *supra* n.25.

[31] For example, Hong Kong, see Hunt, *ibid.* at n.7.

[32] See *Rights Brought Home: The Human Rights Bill*, *supra* n.2 at para 1.14 which may be taken into account by the courts when construing the Act: *Duke* v. *GEC Reliance Ltd* [1988] 2 WLR 359 and see F Bennion, *Statutory Interpretation* (London, Butterworths, 1992).

[33] [1999] 3 WLR 1010.

[34] *Ibid.* at 1023.

Lord Steyn spoke of the new legal landscape and the fact that:

"[it was] common ground that in considering the issues before the House and the development of English law, the House can and should act on the reality that the Human Rights Act 1998 will soon be in force".[35]

According to Lord Cooke regard should be paid to international human rights law, generally, in the development of the common law, with particular importance attaching to the Convention:

"bearing in mind that by section 6(1) of the Human Rights Act 1998 it is unlawful for a public authority to act in a way which is incompatible with a Convention right. By section 6(3)(a) 'public authority' includes a court or tribunal. By section 2(1)(a) decisions of the European Court of Human Rights must be taken into account".

These remarks are clear authority to support the view that the inclusion of courts and tribunals in the definition of public authority renders the Convention rights of indirect horizontal effect. The important consequence of the Act is that there is now an interpretative *obligation* on the courts in relation to the Convention, rather than the permissive approach described by Balcombe LJ in *Derbyshire County Council* v. *Times Newspapers Ltd*, that the Convention "may be used when the common law . . . is uncertain".[36] The fact that the Act has indirect horizontal effect is also implied by section 12, which governs the issuing of remedies in relation to freedom of expression and requires the court to have particular regard to the right to freedom of expression and to any privacy code. This section applies whether the parties before the court are public or private and this right is more usually invoked in private litigation between powerful sections of the media and individual litigants.

It would, though, perhaps be unwise to draw any conclusions from a case like *Reynolds* regarding the extent to which the Convention will shape the development of the common law in future, since the decision-making of the common law courts prior to the introduction of the Human Rights Bill reveals a consistent pattern of regard to the Convention in matters concerning freedom of expression. In their survey of pre-Act English jurisprudence, Klug and Starmer have demonstrated how potentially misleading it is to attempt to draw lessons regarding the permeation of English law by the Convention from cases concerning freedom of expression.[37] Similarly, the author has previously criticised the failure of English courts and litigators to have regard to the Convention in cases outside the field of freedom of expression which clearly raised Convention issues. An examination of recent authorities reveals an inconsistent pattern of regard to the Convention. A number of recent tort decisions at the highest level demonstrate an increased awareness of both the potential relevance of Convention principles and the obligation upon the court to act compatibly with

---

[35] [1999] 3 WLR at 1030.
[36] [1992] 1 QB 770.
[37] F Klug and K Starmer, "Incorporation Through the Back Door?", [1997] *PL* 223.

section 6 of the Act, but the reasoning still tends to be isolationist and in some cases the Convention has simply been ignored.

Although decided before the Act came into force (July 2000), the Convention had some impact in *Arthur J. S. Hall and Co.* v. *Simons*,[38] where the House of Lords departed from the principle laid down in *Rondel* v. *Worsley*,[39] and struck down the advocate's immunity from suit in both civil and criminal (by a four to three majority) cases, but not all members of the House showed equal regard to the Convention. It will be recalled that in *Reynolds*, it was, as Lord Steyn put it, "common ground" that the House should act on the reality that the Act would soon be in force and extensive consideration was given to leading Convention authorities. Lord Hoffmann (with whom Lords Browne-Wilkinson and Hutton agreed) observed that he had said nothing "about whether the immunity, if preserved, would be contrary to Article 6 [the right of access to a court for the determination of civil rights] of the Convention. The question does not arise".[40] He was correct in the sense that Article 6 is engaged where an individual's right of access to a court is curtailed with the effect that any restriction on that right of access must be justified by reference to Convention standards. Since the House of Lords decided that both civil and criminal suit immunity should be struck down, the right of access to the court has in fact been expanded. However, a legitimate objection to the reasoning employed by the House of Lords can be raised regarding the arguments to which greatest weight was attached. A wealth of comparative material was placed before the court, but by far the greatest emphasis was placed on the common law authorities, with Canada providing an example of a jurisdiction which had refused to follow the *Rondel* v. *Worsley* decision, but without adverse consequences.[41] Lord Steyn, with whom Lords Browne-Wilkinson and Millett agreed, considered that (despite the fact of differences in the roles of judge and advocate in the common law and civil law worlds) "the fact that the absence of an immunity has apparently caused no practical difficulties in other countries in the European Union is of some significance: Markesinis, Auby, Coester-Waltjen and Deakin *Tortious Liability of Statutory Bodies: a Comparative and Economic Analysis of Five English Cases* (1990) p 80". However, he went on to say that the "Canadian empirically tested experience" was the most relevant.[42] It is only to be expected that English courts should look to a shared common law heritage in the search for guidance in shaping the common law, but the rather grudging nod towards Europe is out of tune with our membership of the Council of Europe, which should naturally lead to a search for shared European values as the lodestar for the development of human rights standards.[43] On the other hand, the minority members who

---

[38] [2000] 3 All ER 673.

[39] [1969] AC 191.

[40] *Supra* n.38 at 707.

[41] *Demarco* v. *Ungaro* (1979) 95 DLR (3d) 385.

[42] *Supra* n.38 at 683.

[43] See the Strasbourg jurisprudence, which speaks of the search for a shared European consensus, for example, *Handyside* v. *United Kingdom* Series A no 24 (1976) and *Sheffield and Horsham* v. *United Kingdom* (1998) 27 EHRR 163: see text accompanying n.3 in Chapter 3.

dissented on the removal of immunity in criminal law cases recognised that the effect of the immunity was to restrict the right of access to a court and satisfied themselves that the restriction was not a violation of Article 6.[44] It will be appreciated that the court here was shaping the development of the common law as it will apply in private litigation and whatever the outcome, the decision is authority for the proposition that the court must ensure that it is acting compatibly with Convention rights when developing common law principles.

The Convention did not feature at all in another recent decision of the House of Lords in *Gregory* v. *Portsmouth City Council*.[45] This decision was handed down shortly after *Reynolds* (January 2000), but this time there was no acknowledgement of the impending effect of the Act. In view of the fact that four members of the House in *Gregory* also sat in *Arthur J. S. Hall & Co.* it is regrettable that the Convention was presumably considered an irrelevance by both bar and bench. In *Gregory*, the House of Lords was asked to determine whether the tort of malicious prosecution is capable of extending to the malicious institution of domestic disciplinary proceedings by a local authority against a councillor. Lord Steyn, giving the leading speech for a unanimous House, made extensive reference to principles applied throughout the common law world, but completely neglected the European dimension, and concluded that the tort does not extend to the institution of disciplinary proceedings. This was an opportunity missed to "take account" of a number of decisions rendered by the Strasbourg Court in relation to the Article 6 right of access to a court. The Article 6 guarantee to a fair and public hearing by an independent and impartial tribunal applies to the determination of "civil rights and obligations". Gregory, who had been elected as councillor to Portsmouth City Council, complained that he had suffered loss of reputation and distress as a result of the malicious institution of disciplinary proceedings against him, which were discontinued after he had ceased to be a councillor. He sought damages for financial loss as well as injury to his reputation and feelings. A number of Convention decisions are relevant here. The Court has held that decisions taken by professional disciplinary bodies should fulfil the requirements of Article 6 which means that such bodies, or those to which appeal from such decisions lies, should have full appellate jurisdiction on the law and facts of the case.[46] In a previous application for judicial review the Divisional Court had quashed the decision in the disciplinary proceedings.[47] However, the Court has in any event held on a number of occasions that the English (pre-Act) form of judicial review did not satisfy the requirements of Article 13, namely, that there should be an effective remedy for

---

[44] Any restriction on the right of access to a court must pursue a legitimate aim and be proportionate to achieving that legitimate aim: see discussion of *Fayed* v. *United Kingdom et al* in Chapter 4.

[45] [2000] 1 All ER 560.

[46] See *Le Compte, Van Leuven and De Meyere* v. *Belgium* Series A no 51 (1998) discussed by D J Harris, M O'Boyle and C Warbrick, *Law of the European Convention on Human Rights* (London, Butterworths, 1995) at 192 *et seq*.

[47] *R* v. *Portsmouth City Council, ex parte Gregory* [1990] 2 Admin L R 681.

a violation of a Convention right at domestic level.[48] Arguing by analogy from Convention jurisprudence, the tort of malicious prosecution should be opened up to cover the institution of disciplinary proceedings since these are quasi-criminal in nature and may cause financial loss, damage to health and damage to reputation (in Mr Gregory's case, he was struck off the list of official candidates and he incurred expense standing as an independent) in a situation where no action for defamation would lie.

In terms of general awareness of the potential impact of the Convention on English law, it is striking that the Article 6 issue in *Osman* v. *United Kingdom*,[49] for example, has provoked an enormous amount of comment, but the potential reach of other Convention articles has been overlooked. On the facts in *Osman*, no violation of the Article 2 right to life was found, but the Court's examination of this issue requires tort lawyers to reorient their thinking from the Article 6 considerations of duty of care/immunity to consideration of other substantive articles of the Convention and to consider how "negligent" behaviour of public authorities may also constitute substantive violations of those other articles. Whether a duty of care is found in relation to a particular set of facts is a matter for the common law, as informed by Convention jurisprudence. The rejection of *Osman* in *Z.* v. *United Kingdom* seems likely to increase the prominence of argument focusing on Convention rights, other than Article 6, as well as the English court's obligation under section 6 of the Act.[49a]

CAN THE COURTS RECOGNISE "NEW" CAUSES OF ACTION TO GIVE EFFECT TO CONVENTION RIGHTS?

Reynolds then is an example of the court's readiness to comply with the Act and to take account of Convention jurisprudence in developing the common law in private litigation, but what precisely is the *extent* of the obligation? In particular, does the Act mean that there should now be equivalence between the common law and Convention rights, so that the courts are required to recognise new causes of action, for example, a right to privacy? Or is it still the case that a Convention right is not, or cannot, be a right under the common law?[50] Klug has produced a guide to key ministerial statements made during the passage of the Bill through Parliament which would be admissible in proceedings following *Pepper* v. *Hart*.[51] A number of statements made by the Lord Chancellor go to the extent of "horizontal effect" of the Act. Lord Wakeham, Chairman of the Press Complaints Commission, a body criticised on account of its weak powers

---

[48] *W* v. *United Kingdom* Series A no 121 (1987); *Chahal* v. *United Kingdom* 23 EHRR 423 (1997). Cf *D* v. *United Kingdom* (1997) 24 EHRR 423.

[49] [1999] 1 FLR 193.

[49a] See Note on the Text at pp. xxiii.

[50] *Malone* v. *Metropolitan Police Commissioner* [1979] Ch 344.

[51] [1993] AC 593. See F Klug, "The Human Rights Act 1998, *Pepper* v. *Hart* and All That", [1999] PL 246.

in relation to privacy protection, sought to move an amendment which would have had the effect of removing the courts from the definition of public authority when the parties before the court did not include a public authority,[52] and thereby restricting the possibility for the courts to develop privacy protection. The Lord Chancellor rejected the amendment and declared:

> "We also believe that it is right as a matter of principle for the courts to have the duty of acting compatibly with the Convention not only in cases involving other public authorities but also in developing the common law in deciding cases between individuals . . . the courts will be able to adapt and develop the common law by relying on existing domestic principles in the laws of trespass, nuisance, copyright, confidence and the like, to fashion a common law right to privacy".

However, he went on to say that the development of the common law should not extend to the courts acting as legislators: "In my view, the courts may not act as legislators and grant new remedies for infringement of Convention rights unless the common law itself enables them to develop new rights or remedies".[53]

The effect of these statements seems to be that the courts should develop the common law, within the constraints of existing legal principles. Early indications on this question are mixed. The area of law that provoked the fiercest debate on the horizontality question is privacy and it is not surprising that within a few weeks of the Act coming into force the courts were confronted with two high-profile matters regarding the extent to which, and the appropriate vehicle by which, English law should fulfil its obligations in relation to the Article 8 right to respect for private life. The topic of privacy is fully discussed in Chapter 7, but two recent decisions are relevant for the present discussion. In *Douglas, Zeta-Jones and Northern & Shell plc* v. *Hello! Ltd*,[54] the applicants sought an order to restrain the defendants from publishing photographs of their wedding after they had sold the exclusive rights to publish to Northern & Shell plc, the proprietor of *OK!* magazine, the defendant's arch-rival in the field of celebrity gossip magazines. In *Venables and Thompson v. News Group Newspapers Limited Associated Newspapers Limited and MGM Limited*,[55] the applicants sought a continuation of the injunction that would prevent disclosure of their identity and whereabouts following the age of majority and release from secure accommodation.

It was accepted by the Court of Appeal in *Douglas* that the effect of the Human Rights Act is that judges should develop the law to give appropriate recognition to the Article 8(1) right to respect for private life and the court concluded that it was arguable that the claimants would be able to demonstrate at trial that English

---

[52] The Home Secretary had previously expressed the view that the press would not be a public authority within section 6(3) of the Act: "It will ultimately be a matter for the courts, but our considered view is that the Press Complaints Commission undertakes public functions but the press does not": HC Deb vol 314 cols 406, 414 quoted by Klug, *ibid*.

[53] HL Deb vol 583 cols 783–785, quoted by Klug, *ibid*.

[54] Court of Appeal judgment dated 21 December 2000, http://www.courtservice.gov.uk/

[55] QBD judgment dated 8 January 2001, http://www.courtservice.gov.uk/

law now recognises a right to privacy. Brooke LJ stated that it was not for the Court of Appeal in the instant decision to predict how this would happen: whether through "extension of the existing frontiers of the law of confidence, or by recognising the existence of new relationships which give rise to enforceable legal rights as has happened . . . since the decision of the House of Lords in *Donoghue v. Stevenson* [1932] AC 562". Sedley LJ took the view that this inter-locutory application was not the place to resolve the contentious question of the court's obligation under section 6, but he acknowledged that some "attitude" had to be taken to the claimants' submission that the court was obliged to give some effect to Article 8. However, having concluded that the claimants had an arguable case to claim a right of privacy, Sedley LJ observed that even if English law is not currently configured adequately to respect the Convention:

"if the step from confidentiality to privacy is not simply a modern restatement of the scope of a known protection but a legal innovation – then I would accept his submis-sion (for which there is widespread support among commentators on the Act: see in particular M. Hunt, 'The "Horizontal Effect" of the Human Rights Act', [1998] PL 423) that this is precisely the kind of incremental change for which the Act is designed".[56]

Keene LJ was more cautious, stating that the section 6 obligation on the courts arguably includes their decision-making in:

"interpreting and developing the common law, even where no public authority is a party to the litigation. Whether this extends to creating a new cause of action between private persons and bodies is more controversial, since to do so would appear to cir-cumvent the restrictions on proceedings contained in section 7(1) of the Act and on remedies in section 8(1)".[57]

In this case there was no need to determine the issue, because reliance was placed on the action for breach of confidence, an established cause of action. The scheme of remedies (where the defendant is a public authority other than a court) laid down in the Act is discussed below, but suffice at this point to observe that Keene LJ's view is open to criticism, because the Act expressly preserves the right to bring other proceedings,[58] apart from proceedings under the Act, and where the defendant is not a public body, proceedings will be brought otherwise than under the Act. As Brooke LJ remarked in his judgment, the development of new common law remedies has long been the preserve of the courts. It was surely not Parliament's intention to fetter the power of the courts in their devel-opment of the common law. Perhaps, ultimately, the debate about whether courts are merely able to *develop* or *adapt* the common law, rather than to *recognise* a new cause of action is an exercise in semantics. To take the apposite example of Brooke LJ, when the House of Lords decided *Donoghue*, it created

---

[56] *Supra* n.54 at para. 129.
[57] *Supra* n.54 at para. 166.
[58] 1998 Act, s. 11.

the possibility for an expansion of liability to new situations, but as far as Lord Atkin was concerned he was distilling a general principle from existing authority, the effect of which was that new categories of liability opened up.

In *Thompson and Venables*, Butler-Sloss LJ had no doubt that the obligation of the court is to act compatibly with Convention rights "in adjudicating upon existing common law causes of action and does not encompass the creation of a freestanding cause of action based directly upon the Articles of the Convention".[59] Apart from Wade, no commentator has argued that Convention articles should be pleaded directly in litigation along the lines of the Irish model; it seems likely that the common law will be shaped by reference to the Convention rights so that Convention rights are, when appropriate, mediated into English law though the adaptation of common law rules. However, the potential for English law to accommodate the Convention principles hinges upon the attitude of the judiciary—the common law may be more or less elastic, adaptable and capable of being configured appropriately to Convention rights depending upon whether the court will take an expansive view of its role.

The point is that there may arise cases where English law, prior to the Act would stubbornly deny any remedy on account of well-established English legal principle, while Strasbourg jurisprudence on the same facts would suggest that no domestic remedy gives rise to a violation of the Convention.[60] The Lord Chancellor's statement is arguably at odds with the avowed purpose of the Act as expressed in the White Paper, that:

> "Our aim is a straightforward one. It is to make more directly accessible the rights which the British people already enjoy under the Convention. In other words to bring those rights home".[61]

The question of horizontal effect must be linked to the Strasbourg jurisprudence which demonstrates that the United Kingdom may have a positive obligation to act in order to ensure that private parties do not behave in such a way that they interfere with the rights of others.[62] Clearly, at the Strasbourg level, the responsibility to procure compliance with such positive obligations is that of the state and a failure to act will result in a violation of the Convention by the state. But, at domestic level, it will fall to the courts to interpret and develop the law to secure any positive obligation that arises under the Convention. The Preamble to the Act states that it has been enacted in order "to give further effect to rights and freedoms guaranteed under the European Convention on Human

---

[59] *Supra* n.55 at para. D4.D

[60] See *Kaye* v. *Robertson* [1991] FSR 62 and *Spencer* v. *United Kingdom* (1998) 25 EHRR CD 105, discussed in Chapter 7. See also *X (Minors)* v. *Bedfordshire County Council* [1995] 2 AC 633, discussed in Chapter 4 and in Note on the Text.

[61] *Rights Brought Home: The Human Rights Bill, supra* n.2 at para. 1.19.

[62] See text accompanying nn.17–19 in Chapter 1 and see *X and Y* v. *The Netherlands* Series A no 91 (1985); *Plattform "Arzte Fur Das Leben"* v. *Austria* (1991) 13 EHRR 204; *Spencer* v. *United Kingdom* (1998) 25 EHRR 105 and *Lopez Ostra* v. *Spain*, text accompanying n.56 in Chapter 5 and Chapter 8.

Rights". The obligations on the state, the corollary of the rights laid down, can only be understood by examining the jurisprudence. A purposive approach requires us to bear in mind all the time that the aim of the Act is that victims should receive in their own courts the justice they would expect at Strasbourg. Therefore, as Hunt has observed, the effect of the Act is that courts are required "to ensure that all law which they apply accords with the Convention, and to that extent the law which governs private relations will have been 'constitutionalised' by the passage of the Human Rights Act".[63]

As Hunt has observed, the inclusion of courts and tribunals in the definition of public authorities which are bound to act compatibly with Convention rights is of crucial significance for the horizontality issue. He referred to the decision of the South African Constitutional Court in *Du Plessis* v. *De Klerk*[64] where Kentridge AJ considered the "absence of reference to the 'judiciary' in cl 7(1) of the Interim South African Constitution to be of great significance as an indicator that court judgments were not to be equated with state action and that the doctrine of horizontal effect was therefore not to be imported into South African law".[65] In contrast with both the Canadian Charter and the Interim South African Constitution, the courts are expressly included within the interpretative obligation of the Act. Further, "the whole scheme of the Human Rights Act is premised on the proposition that the only domestic law which is not to be subjected to Convention rights is legislation which cannot possibly be given a meaning compatible with Convention rights".[66]

Phillipson has argued that "looked at in the round",[67] the Act does not impose an unequivocal duty on the court to act compatibly with Convention rights. But, that is exactly what section 6 says. However, it is true to say that in many cases those rights are loose-textured and not susceptible of precise delineation: therefore, the effect of the court's obligation in relation to the common law may be difficult to determine, particularly in the field of positive obligations under the Convention. But this comment goes to the nature of Strasbourg jurisprudence, rather than the court's obligation under section 6. Section 2 of the Act provides that the courts are to have regard to the Convention jurisprudence in determining a question which has arisen in connection with a Convention right. The content of Convention rights can only be understood by examination of the Strasbourg jurisprudence and to the extent that it is clear from that jurisprudence that certain rights and obligations exist between non-state actors,[68] English courts must give effect to those rights unless they are to act incompatibly with Convention rights and therefore unlawfully in breach of section 6. Phillipson observed that:

[63] M Hunt, "The 'Horizontal Effect' of the Human Rights Act", [1998] *PL* 422 at 424.
[64] 1996 (3) S.A.850.
[65] M Hunt, *supra* n.63 at 439.
[66] M Hunt, *supra* n.63 at 439.
[67] Phillipson, *supra* n.5.
[68] Derived from the state's positive obligation to act to regulate such relationships, discussed *infra*, text accompanying n.5, ch. 5 *infra et seq.*

"if the courts are simply bound to make law compatible with the Convention, then
their duty rules out allowing any non-Convention considerations to override the
Convention right; and if non-Convention considerations can never override
Convention rights what would be the point in considering what they should be
allowed to do. Courts, under the Hunt model, would thus simply have to disregard the
rules of the relevant current tort and the values underpinning it and change automatically all its pre-existing rules into compliance with whatever the relevant
Convention article demanded".[69]

A number of points need to be made here. First, the intention of the Act is to
bring rights home, to stop applicants having to take the long, expensive road to
Strasbourg. The application of a teleological approach to interpretation of the
Act is therefore necessary and appropriate.[70] Secondly, Convention jurisprudence is premised on the basis that it is for the state to determine how to meet
the demands of the Convention, so that the area of law to be shaped to meet
Convention demands is a matter for the state. Finally, and most importantly,
why seek to protect and entrench legal rules that violate human rights standards
simply because they are established common law rules. The only appropriate
response to La Forest J's concern in the *Dolphin Delivery* case,[71] that a degree
of horizontal effect will mean that settled areas of private law would have to be
re-opened is, why not? It is noteworthy that Phillipson concludes that the degree
of horizontality achieved by the Act is at the weaker level: " the courts will be
obliged to have regard to the values represented by the rights in their development and application of the common law". [72] This view echoes the conclusion
that the Canadian Supreme Court came to in *Dolphin Delivery* regarding the
degree of horizontal effect achieved by the Canadian Charter. The Supreme
Court held that the effect of section 32(1) of the Charter is that it applies to
action by Parliament, government (the executive) and the legislatures in each
Canadian province. However, the judiciary should apply and develop the principles of the common law "in a manner consistent with the fundamental values
enshrined in the Constitution". Direct comparison between the Canadian
Charter and the Act, however, is inappropriate for the simple reason that the
Charter makes no express mention of any role for the courts in the application
of Charter rights, so it is suggested that the "values" argument has been influenced by inappropriate comparison. It is worth repeating also that the Canadian
Charter is not giving effect to a supranational obligation of the same character
as the Convention.

However, full horizontality in the sense that a citizen may assert directly
against another private party the rights laid down in the Convention as ground-
ing a cause of action is clearly precluded by the Act. Only public authorities are

[69] Phillipson, *supra* n.5 at 839.
[70] See discussion, *infra*.
[71] *Retail Wholesale and Department Store Union Local 580 et al* v. *Dolphin Delivery Ltd* (1985)
DLR (4th) 174 at 262–3.
[72] *Supra* n.5 at 843.

bound by the section 6(1) obligation and the *Pepper* v. *Hart* statements made during the legislative process support the conclusion of Hunt that the Act will apply to all law, but does not mandate the recognition of new causes of action so that the judiciary would be acting as legislators. However, as Hunt has observed, in analysing the reasoning of the Canadian Supreme Court in *Dolphin Delivery*, the distinction between "'extending' or 'modifying' the common law in order to make it compatible with Charter values, which is permissible, and making 'far-reaching changes' to the common law, which is not" may be "paper-thin".[73] Wade has expressed the view that the Act requires the courts to recognise and enforce Convention rights "in all proceedings, whether the defendant is a public authority or a private person".[74] There is probably little material difference between the Hunt and Wade position, rather a difference in emphasis: for Wade the Act itself mandates full horizontal applicability of Convention rights; the Hunt approach is more nuanced in that a combination of textual interpretation and Convention jurisprudence is the source of a "significant degree" of horizontal applicability.[75] The latter approach is to be preferred, but it is probably a difference in route rather than result.

The author argued prior to the introduction of the Human Rights Bill, and in the light of the decision in *X (Minors)* v. *Bedfordshire County Council*,[76] that Convention obligations are a factor that should weigh in the balance in shaping tort obligations, for example as a criterion to be evaluated under the third head of *Caparo* v. *Dickman*.[77] The Human Rights Act 1998 has now imposed that interpretative obligation upon the courts, but whether English lawyers generally, and the judiciary in particular, will embrace that challenge is open to doubt in the light of recent cases. Unsurprisingly, in the light of *Osman* v. *United Kingdom*, Article 6 of the Convention has found its way into judicial reasoning, but other Articles which might bear on the substantive development of the common law continue to be overlooked.[78]

REMEDIES UNDER THE ACT

The Human Rights Act 1998 has been drafted in such a way that the same set of facts could give rise to two different routes by which compensation may be sought. It is essential to understand the relationship between sections 6, 7 and 8 as they may apply in a tort situation. The Act has been drafted so that a claim

---

[73] Hunt, *supra* n.25 at 170.

[74] Sir William Wade, "The United Kingdom's Bill of Rights" in Beatson, Forsyth and Hare, *supra* n.1 at 63.

[75] Hunt, *supra* n.63 at 442.

[76] *Supra* n.60.

[77] J Wright, "Local Authorities, the Duty of Care and the European Convention on Human Rights", (1996) 18 *OJLS* 1.

[78] See for example *Kent* v. *Griffiths* [2000] 2 WLR 1158, text accompanying n.97 in Chapter 5 and *Hussain* v. *Lancaster City Council* [1999] 4 All ER 125, text accompanying n.73 in Chapter 5.

for damages *under the Act* will lie against a public authority, *other than a court*, which has acted incompatibly with Convention rights. The previous section has argued strongly that the Act renders Convention rights of indirect horizontal effect by virtue of section 6(3), but it is clear that very different consequences flow from the court acting unlawfully under the Act, as compared with other public authorities.[79] Where it is alleged that a court has acted unlawfully, section 9 of the Act limits the proceedings that may be taken to: (a) exercising a right of appeal; (b) an application for judicial review; or (c) such other forum as may be prescribed by rules. It should be noted that section 11 preserves other rights and other claims which exist independently of the Act. It seems likely, therefore, that in many cases against public authority defendants a claim under the Act will be made in addition to the assertion of other causes of action. Thus, in cases such as *Osman* v. *Ferguson* (action in negligence against the police for failing properly to investigate/suppress crime) or *X* v. *Bedfordshire County Council* (action in negligence by abused children against the responsible local authority for failing to take the children into care in a timely fashion), the claimants would probably frame their action against the public body defendant as a claim under the Act, as well as breach of a common law duty of care in negligence. However, it should be noted that the limitation period under the Act is one year from the date on which the act complained of took place, or such longer period as the court or tribunal considers equitable having regard to all the circumstances.[80]

The court's powers under section 8

Section 8(1) confers apparently wide powers upon the court to grant remedies for a breach of section 6(1) and provides that:

> "In relation to any act (or proposed act) of a public authority which the court finds is (or would be) unlawful, it may grant such relief or remedy, or make such order, within its powers as it considers just and appropriate".

Thus, the remedy is at the discretion of the court and there is no entitlement as such to damages under the Act. However, the ensuing provisions of section 8 make it clear that awards of damages are within the purview of section 8(1),

---

[79] This distinction is not always identified by commentators on the Act: see, for example, R English, "Remedies" in R English and P Havers (eds), *An Introduction to Human Rights and Common Law* (Oxford, Hart Publishing, 2000). In her contribution, English argues that "damages will be payable under Section 8, even if no existing tort has been developed. An obvious example is privacy. The absence of any available action in tort will not inhibit the courts from making an award under Section 8 based on the remedies provided by the Strasbourg Court for breaches of Article 8". However, infringements of privacy as usually witnessed are committed by the press and other media, non-public authorities under the Act and therefore an award of damages will not lie against such media bodies under the Act. Instead, the claimant will frame a claim by reference to the court's obligation under section 6(3), discussed *infra*.

[80] See s. 7(6). Cf Limitation Act 1980, ss 2, 11 and 14A.

such awards to be governed by the following subsections. The intention would seem to be that the court should endeavour to fit the remedy to the breach.[81]

However, the power to grant an award of damages is not unlimited: according to section 8(2) "damages may be awarded only by a court which has power to award damages, or to award the payment of compensation in civil proceedings". The most important question, and one to which Lord Lester sought an answer, was not answered in parliamentary debates and is: does section 8(2) create a new cause of action, a "public law tort", for which compensation will lie? What exactly is meant by the qualification that a court should have "power to award damages"? It is a fundamental tenet of English law that an action for damages against a public body will only lie if the claimant can show that he has a recognised cause of action. The fact that a person suffers harm as a result of the wrongful act of a public body does not in itself entitle the victim to compensation. Section 31(4) of the Supreme Court Act 1981 provides that on an application for judicial review, the court may award damages if these have been sought by the applicant and the court is satisfied that damages could have been obtained by an action brought for the purpose: "the 1981 Act did not alter the substantive rules of liability in damages and the fact that an individual suffered financial loss because of a decision that is quashed as invalid gives rise to no liability".[82] It would seem that on an ordinary reading, section 8(2) narrows the remedies available under section 8. The mere fact that the court declares an act unlawful (in accordance with section 6) is not sufficient for an award of damages to be made: section 8(2) provides that "*But* (italics added) damages may be awarded only by a court which has power to award damages, or to order the payment of compensation, in civil proceedings". So, unlawfulness of action is a prerequisite for damages awards, but no guarantee that damages will be awarded. Thus, "despite the 'wide amplitude' of section 8 . . . the Government's desire to furnish protection by way of remedies was apparently tempered by a wish not to place an undue burden on the public purse . . .".[83] Some commentators have suggested that Floodgates arguments, so familiar to tort lawyers, may have prompted section 8(3)(b) which requires the court, in deciding whether to award damages, to take account of "the consequences of any decision (of that or any other court) in respect of that act".[83a]

During the Committee Stage in the House of Lords the Lord Chancellor explained that section 8(2) means that a criminal court will not be able to award damages for a Convention breach. In *Re Waldron*, it was held that judicial review proceedings are not "civil proceedings" for the purpose of section 139 of the Mental Health Act 1983.[84] Is the subsection intended to encapsulate the

---

[81] See generally M Amos, "Damages for Breach of the Human Rights Act 1998", [1999] *EHRLR* 178.

[82] A W Bradley and K D Ewing, *Constitutional and Administrative Law* (London, Longman, 1997) citing *Dunlop* v. *Woollahra Council* [1982] AC 158.

[83] Grosz, Beatson and Duffy, *supra* n.5 at para. 6–16.

[83a] For example, Amos *supra* n.81.

[84] [1986] QB 824, discussed in Grosz, Beatson and Duffy, *ibid*.

purport of section 31(4)(b) of the Supreme Court Act 1981, which would then mean that the victim has to frame a claim for damages under the recognised heads of tort? The response of Lord Irvine to the perspicacious comments of Lord Lester was noncommittal. Lord Lester postulated:

> "what happens in, for example, judicial review proceedings, where what is at stake is a public law tort (a government tort) giving rise to direct loss, as distinct from the normal private law tort. That distinction does not normally arise under our legal system . . . except . . . where there is misfeasance in public office . . . it seems to me that one needs to be clear whether, by means of a *Pepper* v. *Hart* statement, or under the wording of Clause 8, the Bill permits the remedy of compensation for what I call public law wrongdoing as distinct from normal private law tort in the context in which the Convention would require it".

Lord Irvine observed that, clearly, a criminal court would not have the power to award damages, even if it has power to award compensation unless it also has power to award damages in civil proceedings. Claims for damages should be pursued through the civil courts. Lord Lester persisted, what would happen in the case of a judicial review application where the Convention would require payment of compensation? Will the judicial review court be able to award damages? Lord Irvine responded by referring to section 8(3) and saying that he felt " a moderate degree of confidence that the noble Lord could argue both sides of the question depending upon the client who instructed him".[85] With regard to concurrent claims in tort and under the Act, for a new "public law tort",[86] the Law Commission in its Report, *Damages Under the Human Rights Act 1998*,[87] seems to have assumed for the purposes of its discussion that a claim would lie under the Act, provided that proceedings are instigated in the appropriate forum: in other words, there is no need to demonstrate that the claim would satisfy established criteria to found a cause of action in tort. However, the Commission did state that the purpose of the Report is to examine the "consequences" of liability, rather than to "detail the circumstances in which liability may arise". The point is that a number of claims in the tort of negligence have in recent years been rejected by English courts where a violation of the Convention has subsequently been found in Strasbourg and even admitted by the UK government.[88] Such cases would certainly found a claim under the Act, although a duty of care may yet be denied.

The point has been made earlier that the Act should be interpreted teleologically. The purpose of the Act is to bring English law into harmony with another body of jurisprudence and a purposive approach is therefore appropriate. There is much judicial support to purposive interpretation generally. In the words of Lord Steyn:

[85]   HL Deb vol 583 col 855 24 November 1997.
[86]   Adopting the terminology of Lord Lester of Herne Hill and D Pannick (eds), *Human Rights Law and Practice* (London, Butterworths, 1999).
[87]   Law Com No 266.
[88]   See, for example, *Z* v. *United Kingdom* (1999) 28 EHRR CD 65.

"During the last thirty years there has been a shift away from literalist to purposive methods of construction. Where there is no obvious meaning of a statutory provision the modern emphasis is on a contextual approach designed to identify the purpose of the statute and to give effect to it. The new *Ramsay* [1982] AC 300 principle . . . was not based on a linguistic analysis of the meaning of particular words in a statute. It was founded on a broad purposive interpretation, giving effect to the intention of Parliament".[89]

If a teleological approach to interpretation is applied, it makes sense for any act of a public authority which is unlawful by virtue of section 6 and with respect to which an award of just satisfaction would be made by the Strasbourg Court, to be remedied by an award of damages where such is "necessary to afford just satisfaction" (section 8(3)). The express purpose of the Act as described in the Preamble, to "give further effect to rights and freedoms guaranteed under the Convention", would not be fulfilled, if English courts deny damages to claimants because they cannot bring themselves within a cause of action under section 31(4) of the Supreme Court Act 1981. The appropriate question should be: has the relevant body acted incompatibly with Convention rights and, if so, is an award of damages an appropriate remedy in the light of section 8 of the Act. Where a remedy in damages is denied in such a situation, a claimant will still have to go to Strasbourg; reverting to the White Paper, the government there stated:

"We therefore believe that the time has come to enable people to enforce their Convention rights against the State in the British courts, rather than having to incur the delays and expense which are involved in taking a case to the European . . . Court in Strasbourg and which may altogether deter some people from pursuing their rights".[90]

Even if a more restrictive view is taken, ie a claimant must be able to show that the court would have power to award damages in a recognised cause of action, it can be argued that the effect of section 6(1) is to create a statutory duty according to which public bodies must act in a way which is compatible with the Convention. Failure to do so is a breach of statutory duty and according to ordinary principles a claim for damages will lie where such a cause of action can be shown. There is a circularity of reasoning here, but in view of the ambiguous wording of section 8(2) and the avowed purpose of the Act, if a cause of action other than the Act itself is required, breach of statutory duty might be one peg on which to hang the argument. Section 3 of the Act is also relevant here. As we have seen this section requires the court to read and give effect to primary and subordinate legislation, "so far as it is possible to do so . . . in a way which is compatible with Convention rights". This must lead to section 31(4) of the Supreme Court Act being interpreted to include claims under the Act for damages. An analogy can be drawn between the effects of EC law on English law,

---

[89] *IRC* v. *McGuckian* [1997] 1 WLR 991 at 999–1000 quoted by Beloff, *supra* n.24 at 18.
[90] *Rights Brought Home: The Human Rights Bill, supra* n.2 at para. 1.18.

particularly, the implementation of the *Francovich*[91] and *Brasserie du Pêcheur*[92] decisions by the English courts. The effect of these decisions is that English courts are required to award damages where the three conditions[93] laid down are fulfilled. After initial uncertainty it would seem that the vehicle by which victims of breaches of Community law may seek reparation from the state is the action for breach of statutory duty. In *R* v. *Secretary of State for Transport, ex parte Factortame*, the Divisional Court held that:

> "In English law there has been some debate as to the correct nature of the liability for a breach of Community law. In our judgment it is best understood as a breach of statutory duty".[94]

Thus, the power of English courts to award damages has been expanded beyond the situations extant at the time the Supreme Court Act 1981 was enacted, and would encompass at least those situations where EC law is in issue. Since Convention principles inform the development of EC law, in some instances damages as a remedy are recognised as a result of the cross-fertilisation of EC law and Convention principles and would, therefore, be situations where the court "has power to award damages" within the meaning of section 8(2). A number of writers have described the "spillover" effect[95] of EC doctrines into areas not falling within the sphere of EC competence, with the result that remedies have expanded. In conclusion, should there be doubt as to the meaning of section 8(2), there are abundant arguments to justify the court in taking an expansive view of their powers under section 8(2).

The other alternative is for litigants to argue that the duty on the court under section 6(1) requires the development of the common law to expand remedies so that damages are available for a harm of the type which has been recognised as deserving of just satisfaction by the Strasbourg Court. In this way the category of claims which fall within section 31(4) of the Supreme Court Act will be expanded. It is as much the refusal of tort law to recognise certain types of damage as well as the restricted remedies available for judicial review which have been so problematic for plaintiffs. For the reasons described below, this argument may be the least appealing to English courts, given the traditional consequentialist arguments used by the courts for denying the existence of a duty of care on the part of

---

[91]   Joined Cases C-6 and 9/90 [1991] ECR I-5357.

[92]   Joined Cases C-43 and 48/93 *Brasserie du Pêcheur* v. *Germany* and *R* v. *Secretary of State for Transport, ex parte Factortame Ltd* [1996] ECR I-1029.

[93]   First, a rule of law intended to confer rights on individuals must have been breached: secondly, the breach must be sufficiently serious; and, finally, a direct causal link between the breach and the damage must be demonstrated.

[94]   [1998] 1 All ER 736 and see generally M Hoskins, "Rebirth of the Innominate Tort", and P Craig, "The Domestic Liability of Public Authorities in Damages: Lessons from the European Community", in J Beatson and T Tridimas (eds), *New Directions in European Public Law* (Oxford, Hart Publishing, 1998).

[95]   See discussion of *M* v. *Home Office* [1994] 1 AC 377 by M Hunt, *Using Human Rights Law in English Courts* (Oxford, Hart Publishing, 1997) at 296 and J Bell, "Mechanisms for Cross-fertilisation of Administrative Law in Europe" in Beatson and Tridimas (eds), *supra* n.94.

public bodies: diversion of resources, interference with statutory discretion and separation of powers arguments, the fear of defensive practices, to name a few of the arguments readily deployed.

It has been suggested that the effect of section 6(3) is that the court is now obliged, rather than merely permitted as previously the case,[96] to develop the principles of the common law in a manner compatible with the Convention rights set out in Schedule 1 to the Act. Public authorities are obliged by virtue of section 6(1) to act in a way that is compatible with the Convention rights. Where a public authority (other than a court) acts unlawfully, for example, a local government department, section 7(1)(a) provides that proceedings may be brought against the authority under the Act and damages may be claimed under section 8. On appropriate facts, it is also very likely that a claimant will bring a common law claim and seek to argue that the relevant area of substantive area should be developed in order to accommodate the court's obligation under section 6(3). This may also be necessary, as we have seen, in order to show that the court is acting "within its powers" in order to award damages under section 8.

Where an action is brought against a private individual no claim for damages is permissible under the Act. Rather, effect will be given to Convention rights through the development of the common law by the court in its role as a public authority. As we have seen the scope for judicial creativity will depend upon the court's view of the extent to which the Act achieves horizontal effect of the Convention rights.

Damages under the Act

According to section 8(4) of the Act:

"In determining—
   (a) whether to award damages, or
   (b) the amount of an award,
the court must take into account the principles applied by the European Court of Human Rights in relation to the award of compensation under Article 41 of the Convention".

Thus, Convention principles are a guide under the Act, but as with Convention jurisprudence generally under section 2, these principles do not bind English courts. It is difficult, however, to extract "principles" relating to the award of damages, or "just satisfaction" to use Convention terminology. Awards of damages are permitted by Article 41,[97] which provides that:

"If the court finds that there has been a violation of the Convention or the protocols thereto, and if the internal law of the High Contracting Party concerned allows only partial reparation to be made, the Court shall, if necessary, afford just satisfaction to the injured party".

[96] *Derbyshire* v. *Times Newspapers Ltd, supra* n.36.
[97] Formerly Article 50, Article 41 substituted by Protocol no 11.

"Just satisfaction" may include pecuniary and non-pecuniary damage and costs and expenses and these are awarded on what the Court has described as "an equitable basis", which appears to be something akin to a mantra waved by the Court, in that it expresses the conclusion of the Court, but does not explain the basis of an award. Extraction of principle from the jurisprudence is hampered by the fact that the Court will not always distinguish between the separate heads of pecuniary and non-pecuniary damage and does not consider that it is bound to do so. Indeed, Article 41 (previously Article 50) makes no distinction between pecuniary and non-pecuniary damage as the Court pointed out in *Allenet de Ribemont* v. *France* (interpretation),[98] where a global sum of 2,000,000 FRF had been awarded. In its interpretation the Court stated that:

> "It follows that, in relation to the sum awarded, the Court considered that it did not have to identify the proportions corresponding to pecuniary and non-pecuniary damage respectively. The Court is not bound to do so when awarding 'just satisfaction' under Article 50. . . . In point of fact it is often difficult to, if not impossible to make any such distinction, as is illustrated in several previous judgments where the Court granted an aggregate sum (see . . . *Billi* v. *Italy* . . . *Lopez Ostra* v. *Spain* . . .)."

In so far as it is possible to elicit guidance from the jurisprudence the following points have emerged:

(1) Whether a claim is for pecuniary[99] or non-pecuniary damage[100] the applicant must demonstrate a causal link between the conduct found to cause a violation and the loss or damage suffered by the applicant.

(2) If the nature of the breach allows of *restitutio in integrum*, it is for the respondent state to effect it. To the extent that national law does not allow, or allows only partial, reparation, the Court is empowered by Article 41 to award such satisfaction as appears to it to be appropriate.[101]

(3) It follows from (1) that where the damage complained of is partly attributable to the conduct of the applicant, the Court in its award of just satisfaction will take this into account.[102] Thus, a principle akin to contributory negligence is applied by the Court.

(4) The Court has held on a number of occasions that where the violation consists of a failure to accord to the victim due process, for example access to a court under Article 6(1), it will not speculate as to the outcome of the proceedings in issue had the violation not occurred.[103] Effectively, this argument

---

[98] 7 August 1996 Reports 1996-III.

[99] For example *Miloslavsky* v. *United Kingdom* Series A no 316-B (1995).

[100] For example *Goodwin* v. *United Kingdom* Reports 1996-II, *McMichael* v. *United Kingdom* Series A no 307-B (1995).

[101] *Papamichalopoulos* v. *Greece* Series A no 330-B (1995).

[102] See *A* v. *Denmark* Reports 1996-I, where the Court considered that the excessive length of legal proceedings caused non-pecuniary damage, but the applicants themselves "significantly contributed" to the length of those proceedings and this affected the amount of the awards.

[103] *Hauschildt* v. *Denmark* Series A no 154 (1989), *Saidi* v. *France* Series A no. 261-C (1993).

is another aspect of the causation requirement. In such cases the Court has asserted that the finding of a violation in itself constitutes sufficient reparation.

(5) Although a number of cases have denied compensation for the reasons set out in (4), there are signs that the Court is resiling to some extent from this position, at least to the point of awarding damages for "lost opportunity". In *Osman* v. *United Kingdom*, the applicants sought pecuniary and non-pecuniary loss calculated by reference to the level of compensation they would have received had their claim in negligence against the police force been permitted to proceed and been successful. Clearly, that would be to speculate on the outcome of those domestic proceedings and the Court refused to do this. However, each of the applicants was awarded a sum because they were "denied the opportunity to obtain a ruling on the merits of their claim for damages against the police".[104] Similarly, in *Tinnelly & Sons and McElduff* v. *United Kingdom*,[105] the applicants did not have an opportunity for their claims of unlawful discrimination to be heard owing to a violation of Article 6 by the United Kingdom. While the Court could not speculate on the outcome of such proceedings, modest awards were made because of the denial of the opportunity to have those claims heard.

(6) "Pecuniary" damage includes loss of earnings.[106]

(7) The range of categories of harm included under the umbrella of "non-pecuniary" damage is very wide when compared with the types of claim which may be brought in tort in English law. Thus, the following are included: "trauma, anxiety and feeling of injustice";[107] "feeling of helplessness and frustration";[108] "inconvenience . . . substantial anxiety and distress";[109] "distress and anxiety" (through witnessing a continuing violation and the deterioration in another's health);[110] "harassment . . . humiliation . . . stress".[111]

(8) The conduct of the victim of a violation will be relevant to the award of damages and in this sense it is true to say that the Court makes moral judgements about the applicant before it.[112] Thus, in *McCann, Farrell and Savage* v. *United Kingdom*,[113] no award of compensation was made having regard to the fact that the three terrorist suspects were intending to plant a bomb in Gibraltar.

---

[104] *Supra* n.15 at para. 164.
[105] (1998) 27 EHRR 249, see text accompanying n.31 in Chapter 4.
[106] *Young, James and Webster* v. *United Kingdom, supra* n.8.
[107] *McMichael* v. *United Kingdom* Series A no 307-B (1995).
[108] *Papamichalopoulos* v. *Greece, supra* n.101.
[109] *Olsson* v. *Sweden* Series A no 130 (1988).
[110] *Lopez Ostra* v. *Spain* Series A no 303-C (1994).
[111] *Supra* n.8.
[112] A R Mowbray, "The European Court of Human Rights' Approach to Just Satisfaction", [1997] *PL* 647.
[113] (1995) 21 EHRR 97.

(9) While the Court has not awarded aggravated or punitive damages, it also appears to make moral judgements about the conduct of states. Thus, in *Aksoy* v. *Turkey*,[114] where the defendant state was found to have violated Article 3 (torture), Article 5(3) (liberty and security) and Article 13 (effective remedy), the Court, "in view of the extremely serious violations suffered by Mr. Aksoy and the anxiety and distress these undoubtedly caused to his father",[115] awarded the full amounts of compensation sought as regards pecuniary and non-pecuniary damage and also the full amount of costs and expenses.

What are the implications of the section 8 remedies for tort law?

In Chapter 1, it was observed that, prior to the Human Rights Act 1998, it was a principle of English law that the ordinary law of the land applied to everyone, and that there was no separate system of public law through which compensation could be sought from a public authority. If an individual wished to allege that a public body had caused damage through negligence, it was necessary for a claimant to establish a cause of action at common law. Where a person considered that their human rights had been violated, it was necessary to seek redress by way of judicial review and if compensation was sought, an action by writ was required. The effect of the Act is that in relation to the violation of a Convention right set out in Schedule 1, a claim for compensation may be brought against a public body under the Act. As we have seen damages are not awarded as of right, they are at the discretion of the court. The question arises as to how proceedings under the Act may indirectly shape tort principles.

It is important to establish how the Convention may shape English law through the application of sections 6(1) and 6(3). It is helpful, perhaps, to use the facts of *X (Minors)* v. *Bedfordshire County Council*[116] by way of illustration: it will be recalled that the five children, who suffered serious neglect by their parents, brought proceedings in negligence against the local authority for failing to take the children into care at an appropriate time. Despite warnings from neighbours and schools and requests from the parents to take the children into care, social services had maintained a policy of supporting the family. Eventually, after a period of almost five years the children were removed into the care of the local authority and were found to have suffered physical and psychological injury. The House of Lords upheld the lower courts' decision to strike out the claim in negligence and the children petitioned Strasbourg. In the Strasbourg application, *Z* v. *United Kingdom*,[117] the European Commission on Human

---

[114] Reports 1996-VI.

[115] Mr Aksoy was severely tortured in custody and murdered following threats that he should withdraw his application to Strasbourg (although there was no allegation that Article 2 (the right to life) had been violated). His father took over the application following his death.

[116] *Supra* n.60.

[117] (1999) 28 EHRR CD 65.

Rights has found that the United Kingdom violated its positive obligation under Article 3 to prevent the children from suffering inhuman and degrading treatment and punishment and the Article 6 right of access to a court. The UK government has since conceded that Article 3 was violated and at the time of writing the complaint under Article 6 is pending before a full Chamber of the Strasbourg Court.[117a]

A case such as *Bedfordshire* could now proceed by way of two causes of action: first, a complaint under the Act would lie against the local authority in respect of its unlawfulness under section 6(1) for failing to act compatibly with Article 3 (the right not to suffer inhuman and degrading treatment) (and Article 8)[118] and, secondly, proceedings in negligence at common law may also be brought. The Act expressly preserves the right to bring proceedings apart from sections 7 to 9 of the Act. Section 7 of the Act gives a claimant two options where she claims that a public authority "has acted (or proposes to act) in a way which is made unlawful by section 6(1)", namely, to:

"(a) bring proceedings against the authority under this Act in the appropriate court or tribunal, or
 (b) rely on the Convention right or rights concerned in any legal proceedings".

The question then arises as to whether English courts are likely to develop the tort of negligence (where the common law has not previously recognised such a claim) to accommodate claims that also amount to incompatibility with Convention rights, or whether these claims will be confined to proceedings under section 6(1) of the Act. The Article 6 right of access to a court and the implications for English law of *Osman* v. *United Kingdom*[119] are discussed in detail in Chapter 4, but the Article 6 right of access to a court is relevant to this discussion, because when *Osman* (and indeed, *Z*) was decided by Strasbourg there was no adversarial procedure in English law, in the absence of a negligence action, through which the public body could be brought to account for its actions and required to pay compensation.

In *Osman*, the Strasbourg court held that the applicants were "entitled to have the police account for their actions and omissions in adversarial proceedings".[120] The possibility of such adversarial proceedings is now afforded by the Human Rights Act, so that, in terms of satisfying Convention standards, there is arguably no need to expand the tort of negligence beyond its current configuration. If English courts do take the opportunity to confine claimants to proceedings under the Act, the more expansive heads of damage (grief, distress, interference with family relationships)[121] recognised by Strasbourg can

---

[117a] See Note on the Text
[118] See discussion of Article 8 in Chapter 3, text accompanying n.69 *infra*. The European Commission on Human Rights in *Z* found no separate issue arising under Article 8 having regard to its finding under Article 3.
[119] [1999] 1 FLR 193.
[120] *Ibid*. at para. 153.
[121] See text accompanying nn.107–111 *supra*.

be confined within the action against public authorities under section 7. Claims brought to Strasbourg have largely resulted in modest awards and the Act requires English courts to have regard to the principles applied by the Court in determining both whether to award damages and the amount of an award (section 8(4)). In her thorough analysis of the principles applied by the Court to the award of "just satisfaction", Reid has commented that:

> "The Court has not proved unduly generous in its approach to awarding compensation under any of the heads. The emphasis is not on providing a mechanism for enriching successful applicants but rather on its role in making public and binding findings of applicable human rights standards".[122]

A constant refrain of English negligence law is that recognition of a duty of care will open the floodgates of litigation and in the case of public bodies that resources should not be diverted from the public purse and the proper performance of public functions to defending litigation and paying compensation. By confining legal action for damages against public bodies to proceedings under the Act two things follow: awards are likely to be modest and the template for liability in negligence remains within current bounds so that a body of precedent recognising expanded forms of liability is not developed and therefore there is no expansion of recognised heads of damage in the action in litigation between private parties. When *Osman* v. *United Kingdom* was decided there was no realistic alternative for the plaintiffs other than pursuing a negligence action; the legal landscape is completely different now. Unsurprisingly, in *Osman*, the Court having taken account of the fact that the right to life was engaged and that the "catalogue of acts and omissions amounted to grave negligence",[123] determined that the complaints should be heard on the merits. In future, public authority defendants can argue that such a hearing can now take place as a result of the Human Rights Act and, therefore, the action for negligence at common law is otiose.

Article 13 of the Convention is also relevant to this discussion. As we have seen, Article 13 requires Contracting States to provide an effective remedy at domestic level for those who suffer a violation of their rights. Article 13 has not been given effect by the Act, the government argument being that the enactment of this legislation provides an effective remedy. In future, the United Kingdom government when it is defending actions in Strasbourg will in many cases be able to rely on the Act as a reason to deny any violation of Article 13 and as a means of ensuring compliance with Article 6. There will in future be no rule that effectively gives public bodies immunity in negligence in relation to violations of Convention rights, albeit that the vehicle through which public authority action/inaction is evaluated is the statutory action under the Act.

---

[122] K Reid, *A Practitioner's Guide to the European Convention on Human Rights* (London, Sweet & Maxwell, 1998) at 398.

[123] *Supra* n.119 at paras 151–2.

There is a significant difference, though, between the Act and a negligence action and that lies in the application of different limitation periods. According to section 7(5) of the Act, proceedings under the Act must be brought within one year of the date on which the act complained of took place or such longer period as the court or tribunal considers equitable having regard to all the circumstances. In cases where victims of what are arguably unlawful acts find themselves outside this period that they will have no alternative to proceeding by other means. The Strasbourg Court has held that states enjoy a margin of appreciation in deciding how the right of access to a court is circumscribed, so that in the first instance the law of limitation is a matter within the state's discretion.[124] Since the limitation period under the Act constitutes a restriction on the right of access to a court, it must satisfy the criteria established under Article 6, by pursuing a legitimate aim and being proportionate to the aim sought to be achieved.[125]

CONCLUSION

The author's initial reaction to the announcement of the Human Rights Bill was that, in the light of the court's obligation under section 6, tort principles would be expanded so that in deserving cases new heads of damage, such as grief and distress, would be recoverable. This would apply in the case of both public and private defendants. However, actions relating to the violation of Convention rights by public authorities, whether arising out of negligence or otherwise, may be confined to taking proceedings under the Act.[125a] This would impede the development of a body of common law precedent that could also be invoked in private litigation.

It has been demonstrated that the extent to which the courts apply the Convention in private litigation depends upon the attitude of the courts to their role under section 6(3) of the Act and the scope of "positive obligations" recognised by Strasbourg. The issue of positive obligations to control the conduct of non-state actors is discussed in detail in Chapter 5, but it should be noted that the general approach of Strasbourg is to allow a considerable margin of appreciation to states in their assessment of both the need for such action and the means by which positive obligations are fulfilled. Thus, the impact of the Act in private litigation may well be more muted than parliamentary debates might otherwise have led us to anticipate.

Whether a claimant alleges that a public authority has acted incompatibly with a Convention right and in breach of section 6 of the Act, or that the court should develop the common law so that it is compatible with Convention rights,

[124] *Stubbings* v. *United Kingdom* (1997) 23 EHRR 213.
[125] See discussion of Article 6, in Chapter 4.
[125a] The reader's attention is drawn to Note on the Text for an analysis of the impact of the Court's decision in *Z* v. *United Kingdom*.

it is essential to understand the nature of the state's obligations. Section 2 of the Act requires the English courts to take account of Strasbourg jurisprudence in determining questions that arise in connection with Convention rights. Therefore, the following chapter identifies the key principles that emerge from the Convention jurisprudence and the rules of tort law for which they may be most relevant.

3

The European Convention on Human Rights: Its Application and Interpretation

T HE AIM OF this chapter is to convey in broad terms how the Strasbourg organs have interpreted and given substance to the rights included within section 1 of the Human Rights Act 1998 (with the exception of Article 3 of Protocol 1 which relates to the right to free elections and Articles 1 and 2 of the Sixth Protocol, which relate to the death penalty). In order to determine the potential impact of the Act, whether in actions against public authorities under the Human Rights Act or in the development of the common law, it is essential to achieve an understanding of the jurisprudence that will be taken into account by the court by virtue of section 2 of the Act. The interpretative techniques employed by Strasbourg are described: the reasoning employed by Strasbourg is frequently opaque and it will become apparent that it is difficult to predict outcomes, particularly when a complaint involves the exercise of conflicting rights. This discussion seeks to identify the nature of the interests protected by each of the articles, as well as the extent of the state's obligation to protect those interests. Against this background, features of Convention jurisprudence that are particularly germane to English tort principles are identified and the questions they raise for English tort lawyers are highlighted.

The Convention, together with its Protocols, sets out the rights that states are obliged, by virtue of Article 1 to "secure to everyone" within the jurisdiction. The United Nations Vienna Declaration on Human Rights called upon states to treat human rights "globally in a fair and equal manner, on the same footing, and with the same emphasis". However, a reading of the major human rights instruments reveals that human rights standards do not all require the same degree of protection at all times, and this comment applies with equal force to the Convention and its jurisprudence. It is possible, therefore, to conceive of the Convention rights as a hierarchy of rights. For example, states are permitted, "in time of war or other public emergency threatening the life of the nation", to take measures derogating from certain of their obligations under the Convention (Article 15), provided that certain conditions are satisfied. However, states cannot derogate from Article 2 (the right to life), except in respect of deaths resulting from lawful acts of war, nor Article 3 (the right not to be tortured or suffer inhuman and degrading treatment or punishment), Article 4(1) (prohibition on slavery or servitude) and Article 7 (no punishment without law). These rights therefore represent the irreducible core rights that must be protected under any circumstances. War, civil insurrection and other public emergency will not operate to reduce the obligation of the state.[1]

At the lower end of the "hierarchy" are the "personal freedom articles" set out in Articles 8 to 11: Article 8 (the right to respect for private and family life, home and correspondence), Article 9 (freedom of thought, conscience and religion), Article 10 (freedom of expression) and Article 11 (freedom of association). These rights may be the subject of derogation under Article 15 and they may also be subject to limitations and restrictions imposed by the state. The common structure of these Articles is that paragraph 1 sets out the right and paragraph 2 describes how and why the right may be limited. Although initially conceived in relation to Article 15 (derogations), it is in relation to these permitted limitations that Strasbourg has developed its extensive "margin of appreciation" doctrine described below. For the moment, suffice to say that this doctrine operates to create a sphere of deference on the part of Strasbourg to the Contracting States. It is a mechanism that has operated so that, in the first analysis, it is left to the state to determine whether the need to restrict or limit a right arises. This does not mean that Strasbourg does not retain supervisory jurisdiction, rather that in certain circumstances the initial assessment of the exigencies of a situation fall to be determined by the state. How great the margin is, will depend upon the interest at stake and the aim of the restriction: where national security and morals are sought to be protected a wide margin is accorded, while restricting freedom of expression in order to maintain the "authority and impartiality of the judiciary" calls for a narrower margin. The narrower margin is dictated because it is possible to achieve "an objective understanding of the content of the interest sought to be protected".[2] It is observable that a greater margin is allowed to the state when there is little common ground between states.

The story of the Convention is that of a search for shared European values, a search for consensus. Markesinis has been in the vanguard of those commentators who have advocated that English lawyers should utilise the comparative method in order to shape the common law, so that it reflects appropriately the values of our age.[3] His sustained argument for change in the field of privacy is just one example of his work in this field. The Human Rights Act indirectly mandates that approach, as Strasbourg principles have emerged from a dialogue between states that reflects shared beliefs. When English lawyers seek to flesh

---

[1] Subject to the operation of a margin of appreciation under Article 15, discussed *infra*.

[2] D J Harris, M O'Boyle and C Warbrick, *Law of the European Convention on Human Rights* (London, Butterworths, 1995) citing *Sunday Times* v. *United Kingdom* Series A no 30 (1979) at 297.

[3] See, for example, B S Markesinis, "Comparative Law—A Subject in Search of an Audience", (1990) 53 MLR 1 and B S Markesinis, J-B Auby, D Coester-Waltjen and S F Deakin, *Tortious Liability of Statutory Bodies* (Oxford, Hart Publishing, 1999).

out the bare bones of the Convention text, the domestic rules of the Contracting States may be relevant to establish whether there is consensus on an issue such that a European standard can be discerned. For example, few privacy[4] claims have found their way to Strasbourg, but this is probably a reflection of the fact that Contracting States, apart from the United Kingdom, have protected privacy as a matter of domestic law.

According to Article 1 of the Convention,[5] each state agrees "to secure to everyone within [its] jurisdiction the rights and freedoms defined in Section I" of the Convention. The Convention does not specify *how* the rights and freedoms are to be protected: the obligation on the state is to secure the substance of the right and Article 13 provides that everyone whose rights and freedoms are violated shall have an effective remedy before a national authority. Thus, the right and the remedy must be secured at national level in order to comply with Convention standards; the means by which this is achieved is a domestic issue. For example, in *Guerra* v. *Italy*,[6] the applicants complained that the local authority had failed to take appropriate steps to reduce the risk of pollution from a factory. They sought an order from the European Court of Human Rights which would have required the state to decontaminate an industrial site and to conduct inquiries to identify serious effects on residents who it was believed had been exposed to carcinogenic substances. The Court observed that it had no power under the Convention to accede to this request and stated that:

"it is for the State to choose the means to be used in its domestic legal system in order to comply with the provisions of the Convention or to redress the situation that has given rise to the violation of the Convention".[7]

Article 1 requires states to secure the rights to "everyone" within the jurisdiction. There is no requirement that a person should have citizenship rights or the nationality of a state in order to have the benefit of these rights,[8] and the Court has previously held that the responsibility of the state may be engaged where a person would be exposed to a real risk of an event which would constitute a violation of the Convention upon being returned to a state non-member of the

---

[4] Used in the narrow sense, to refer to cases concerning the dissemination of true private facts, usually by the mass media.

[5] Article 1 is not included in Schedule 1 to the Human Rights Act since it encapsulates the obligation of the states, *inter se*, under the Convention. Its significance is wider than this, though, in view of the Strasbourg jurisprudence on positive obligations, *infra*. For example, in *A* v. *United Kingdom* (1998) EHRLR 82, the Court found the United Kingdom in violation of the Article 3 right not to suffer inhuman and degrading treatment where a boy was beaten by his stepfather. Article 3 taken together with the Article 1 obligation to "secure" the right gave rise to a positive obligation on the United Kingdom to protect the child from such treatment.

[6] (1998) 26 EHRR 357.

[7] *Ibid.* at para. 74.

[8] Although Article 16 does provide that "[n]othing in Articles 10, 11 and 14 shall be regarded as preventing the High Contracting Parties from imposing restrictions on the political activity of aliens".

Council of Europe. In *D* v. *United Kingdom*,[9] the Court held that deportation of an illegal immigrant who was suffering from AIDS to St. Kitts would constitute a violation of the Article 3 prohibition on inhuman or degrading treatment, because the standards of medical care were so poor compared with what the applicant would receive in the United Kingdom.

GENERAL PRINCIPLES OF INTERPRETATION

The Convention is a treaty and is therefore to be interpreted according to the rules of international law on the interpretation of treaties. The basic rule is contained in Article 31 of the Vienna Convention on the Law of Treaties 1969 which provides that a treaty is to be interpreted in good faith in accordance with the ordinary meaning to be given to the terms of the treaty in their context and in the light of its object and purpose. Context comprises in addition to the text, including its preamble and annexes, any agreements relating to the treaty made between all parties in connection with the treaty. The Strasbourg authorities have adopted a teleological approach to interpretation, with the emphasis on purposive construction in the light of the "object and purpose" of the Convention. Brownlie has described the telelogical approach as one in which the court "determines what the objects and purposes are and then resolves any ambiguity of meaning by importing the 'substance' necessary to give effect to the purposes of the treaty".[10] The Preambular words to the Convention have played a significant role in the discovery of its "object and purpose" and have led the Court to flesh out the obligations of the state by giving an expansive reading to the text. Harris, O'Boyle and Warbrick cite as an example, the decision of the Court in *Golder* v. *United Kingdom*,[11] where it was held that the corollary of belief in the rule of law (see Preamble) was that the guarantee of fair trial in Article 6 included the right of access to a court.

Article 32 of the Vienna Convention provides that "recourse may be had to supplementary means of interpretation, including the preparatory work of the treaty" in order to confirm its meaning resulting from the application of Article 31 or where the application of Article 31 "leaves the meaning ambiguous or obscure or . . . leads to a result which is manifestly absurd or unreasonable". It is extremely rare[12] for Strasbourg to consider the *travaux preparatoires*, or preparatory work, since the Court has observed that the Convention is a "living

---

[9] (1997) 24 EHRR 423. See also *Soering* v. *United Kingdom* Series A no 161, where the Court held that extradition of the applicant to the USA would expose him to "a real risk of treatment going beyond the threshold set by Article 3" (in this case 'the death row phenomenon') and the decision to extradite, if implemented, would give rise to a breach of Article 3.

[10] I Brownlie, *Principles of Public International Law*, 4th edn (Oxford, Clarendon Press, 1995).

[11] Series A no 18 (1975).

[12] But not unknown: see *Johnston* v. *Ireland*, Series A no 112 (1986), where, upon review of the *travaux preparatoires*, both the Commission and the Court found that the omission of divorce from Article 12 was deliberate.

instrument" which must be "interpreted in the light of present-day conditions".[13] This approach has been applied in a number of areas where the Court
has considered that domestic legal rules are out of step with wider European
thinking. So, for example, laws which treated illegitimate children less
favourably than the legitimate were found to be in violation of the Convention[14]
as was the former criminal law in Northern Ireland which completely crimin-
alised homosexual sex.[15] In *Sheffield and Horsham* v. *United Kingdom*,[16] the
applicants challenged the refusal of the United Kingdom to allow amendment of
a birth certificate following gender reassignment surgery in order to reflect the
post-operative identity. They alleged a violation of the Article 8 right to respect
for private life. The Court found that there was still medical uncertainty in this
field and that there was no uniformity of approach among states. However, the
United Kingdom was advised that the matter should be kept under review in the
light of advances in science and changing social attitudes. Use of the *travaux
preparatoires* might also be positively misleading as to present day interpretation. For example, the Article 8 right to respect for private life permits
interference with the right where this is in accordance with the law and is necessary in the interests of, *inter alia*, "the economic well-being of the country".
The *travaux* reveal that these words were included at the request of the United
Kingdom which was then concerned with the enforcement of exchange control
regulations, a very specific concern and one which is now defunct given that the
relevant legislation was repealed many years ago. Although introduced to deal
with a very specific concern, in *Powell and Rayner* v. *United Kingdom*,[17] this
ground of interference was upheld by the Commission where applicants complained that the noise from Heathrow Airport interfered with private life. The
Commission declared the complaint manifestly ill-founded because the interference was necessary for the economic well-being of the country.

THE PROTECTED RIGHTS

This following discussion will do two things: first, set out in brief a description
of the rights secured by the Convention and given further effect by the Human
Rights Act 1998; and, secondly, highlight those areas of tort law to which those
rights may be particularly relevant, with a view to eliciting aspects of English
law that may arguably amount to a failure to "secure" the rights set out.

---

[13] *Tyrer* v. *United Kingdom* Series A no 26 (1978). In *Van der Mussele* v. *Belgium* Series A no 70
(1984), the Court stated at para. 32 that the Convention is to be read "in the light of the notions currently prevailing in democratic states".

[14] *Marckx* v. *Belgium* Series A no 131 (1979).

[15] *Dudgeon* v. *United Kingdom* Series A no 45 (1981).

[16] (1997) EHRR 443.

[17] Series A no 172 (1990).

Article 2: the right to life

This right, the most fundamental of all rights, is not an absolute right; however, derogation from Article 2 is prohibited by Article 15, except in respect of deaths resulting from lawful acts of war. The Court has elaborated upon the nature of the Article 2 obligation in a number of recent cases, from which it is clear that the state is enjoined not only to refrain from the intentional and unlawful taking of life, but also has a positive obligation to take appropriate steps to safeguard the lives of others. In *LCB* v. *United Kingdom*,[18] the applicant had developed leukaemia at the age of four. Her father had been present at Christmas Island during the nuclear tests of 1957 and 1958. She alleged that the United Kingdom was in breach of Articles 2 and 3 (inhuman and degrading treatment) for failing to warn her of her father's exposure to radiation which she claimed would have led to a close monitoring of her health and earlier diagnosis and treatment. The Court adverted to the positive obligation of the state to take appropriate steps to safeguard lives within the jurisdiction, but found no violation on the facts. The Court found that the expert evidence did not establish a causal link between parental exposure to radiation and childhood cancer and it could not therefore reasonably be held that the United Kingdom should have taken action in the late 1960s on the basis of an unsubstantiated link.[19] In *LCB*, there was conflicting expert evidence as to whether monitoring of the applicant's health *in utero* and beyond would have led to earlier diagnosis and treatment so that the severity of the disease was diminished. Thus, "but for" causation was not demonstrated since it could not be established that earlier diagnosis of her condition would have made any difference to the progress of the disease. However, the Court observed that:

> "It is perhaps arguable that, had there been reason to believe that she was in danger of contracting a life-threatening disease owing to her father's presence on Christmas Island, the State authorities would have been under a duty to have made this known to her parents whether or not they considered that the information would assist the applicant".[20]

The implication is that there could be a violation of Article 2, even though any failure on the part of the state would have made no difference to the progress of the disease. This raises the question of whether the House of Lords' decision in *Bolitho* v. *City & Hackney Health Authority*[21] would withstand scrutiny for compatibility with the Convention. It will be recalled that in *Bolitho*, the failure of a doctor to attend a two-year-old patient with respiratory difficulties (the child suffered a cardiac arrest and brain damage) was conceded by the defendants to be

---

[18] (1998) 27 EHRR 212.
[19] An analogy can be drawn with the objective standard applied to establish breach of duty in negligence: *Roe* v. *Ministry of Health* [1954] 2 QB 66.
[20] *Supra* n.18 at para. 40.
[21] [1998] AC 232.

a breach of duty. The parents brought proceedings in negligence, but the problem issue was causation: the defendants argued that even if the doctor had attended she would not have intubated the child and that, applying the *Bolam* standard,[22] non-intubation would have been a reasonable response and the injury could not, therefore, have been avoided. Evidence was given by two groups of expert witnesses, one group would have intubated, the other would not. The House of Lords, applying *Bolam*, considered that both views withstood logical analysis. *Bolitho* is an extremely difficult case to reconcile with human rights standards. The doctor was clearly negligent, the right to life was at stake, but because factual causation could not be established there was no legal mechanism by which the plaintiff could vindicate the right to life. In view of the fact that the doctor had not attended and did not have the opportunity to make a professional clinical judgement regarding the presenting symptoms, the judgment in *Bolitho* amounts to giving the professional a very large benefit of the doubt. The dictum of the Court in *LCB* is difficult to reconcile with the House of Lords' approach and suggests that in future, even if factual causation must be shown to establish negligence, human rights standards could be vindicated through the Act.[23]

The obligation under Article 2 requires the state to put in place appropriate criminal law sanctions to deter the commission of offences and to put in place the law enforcement machinery in order properly to enforce fully the criminal law. In addition, the Court has stated that there may be circumstances where the state is obliged to take *operational* measures to protect an individual whose life is at risk from the criminal act of another. In *Osman* v. *United Kingdom*,[24] the Court of Human Rights held that state responsibility in this respect under Article 2 was not engaged because it was not established that the police knew or ought to have known at the time of the existence of a real and immediate risk to the life of Mr Osman.[25] Where information is available to the police (or, indeed, other public authorities charged with responsibility to protect individuals from harm posed by third parties) to enable such a conclusion to be drawn, the authorities must (subject to resource considerations) act. This requirement was satisfied in *Kilic* v. *Turkey*,[26] where the Strasbourg Court found that the absence of any operational measures of protection for a murdered journalist who had been subjected to threats while working for a Kurdish newspaper was a violation of Article 2. As in the case of the Osman family, Kilic, aware of grave personal danger to himself, had pleaded for help from the authorities, but no assistance was given. The Court stated that:

---

[22] *Bolam* v. *Freiern Hospital Management Committee* [1957] 2 All ER 118.

[23] See also *Guerra* v. *Italy*, *infra* n.82.

[24] [1999] 1 FLR 193.

[25] A reading of the Court of Appeal decision in *Osman* v. *Ferguson* [1993] 4 All ER 344 throws doubt on this conclusion: the malefactor had said to a police officer that he was going to "do a sort of Hungerford". This point and its implications for the tort of negligence are fully explored in Chapter 4.

[26] App no 22492/93, judgment dated 28 March 2000.

"A wide range of preventive measures were available which would have assisted in minimising the risk to Kemal Kilic's life and which would not have involved an impractical diversion of resources. On the contrary, however, the authorities denied that there was any risk. There is no evidence that they took any steps in response to Kemal Kilic's request for protection either by applying reasonable measures of protection or by investigating the extent of the alleged risk to [newspaper employees] . . . in the circumstances of [the] case the authorities failed to take reasonable measures available to them to prevent a real and immediate risk to the life of Kemal Kilic".[27]

The implications that flow from this case for the development of tort law are more fully explored in Chapter 5. However, the line of cases beginning with *LCB*, through *Osman* to *Kilic* has a significance beyond tort law. It is trite to observe that there is no neat dividing line between civil and political rights (of which the Convention is broadly composed) on the one hand, and economic, social and cultural rights on the other: their substantive content may overlap and what is more both sets of rights carry financial obligations for states. The difference between the two lies in their justiciability: economic social and cultural rights generally occupy a weaker normative area, with recourse to judicial supervision by way of court proceedings confined to the civil and political dimension. This does not mean to say that such rights, or elements of them, cannot be justiciable, but it remains the fact that many states and courts are reluctant to see areas of justiciability expand: governments fear a demand that resources cannot possibly meet and courts are wary of overstepping the bounds of their role as the third branch of government.[28] However, it is possible to see that this line of cases with its introduction of an *operational* obligation incumbent on the state may lead to the recognition of positive obligations under Article 2 beyond the context of danger to the individual from criminal activity to, for example, claims that certain forms of medical treatment should not be denied to a very ill individual. In *Osman*, the Court addressed the issue of resources in the context of policing and stated that:

"Bearing in mind the difficulties involved in policing modern societies, the unpredictability of human conduct and the operational choices which must be made in terms of priorities and resources, such an obligation must be interpreted in a way which does not impose an impossible or disproportionate burden on the authorities. Accordingly, not every claimed risk to life can entail for the authorities a Convention requirement to take operational measures to prevent that risk from materialising".

These words echo a theme which runs through the Strasbourg jurisprudence relating to positive obligations generally, namely, that such obligations must be interpreted in a way that strikes a balance between the needs of the individual and the needs of the community. It has been suggested that "there must now be some prospect of overturning" the decision of the Court of Appeal in

---

[27] App no 22492/93, judgment dated 28 March 2000, at para. 77.
[28] For an English example, see *R* v. *Cambridgeshire District Health authority, ex parte B* [1995] 1 WLR 898.

R v. *Cambridgeshire Health Authority, ex parte B*[29] to uphold the health authority's refusal to fund further expensive treatment for a child who was terminally ill with an aggressive form of leukaemia.[30] It will be appreciated that this is probably an overly optimistic view, given the reluctance of Strasbourg to engage in issues which may have a bearing on resources and wider implications for macro-economic policy. The test as indicated by *Kilic* is what are *reasonable* measures: provided a health authority has asked itself the right questions and has arrived at a defensible conclusion it seems unlikely that Strasbourg would upset that decision. It might of course be different where it is alleged that the health authority has acted in a discriminatory fashion contrary to Article 14, read in conjunction with Article 2.[31]

Article 3: freedom from torture or inhuman or degrading treatment or punishment

The Article 3 prohibition on certain forms of treatment enshrines an absolute right from which no derogation under Article 15 is permitted.

In *Ireland* v. *United Kingdom*,[32] the Court defined torture as "deliberate inhuman treatment causing very serious and cruel suffering". In this case, the Court disagreed with the Commission view that the "five techniques"[33] used in the interrogation of IRA internees amounted to torture: although the five techniques undoubtedly amounted to inhuman and degrading treatment, "they did not occasion suffering of the particular intensity and cruelty implied by the word torture as so understood".[34] It was also held by both the Commission and the Court in *Ireland* v. *United Kingdom* that ill-treatment must attain a minimum level of severity if it is to fall within the scope of Article 3 and that such an assessment of the minimum is relative, depending upon all the circumstances of the case, "the duration of the treatment, its physical or mental effects and, in some cases, the sex, age and state of health of the victim".[35]

Article 3 may well prove to be fertile ground for claims which have traditionally been characterised as claims in negligence based on a breach of a duty of care by a public body. As with Article 2, Strasbourg has interpreted Article 3 as imposing a positive obligation on states to take appropriate steps to secure the

[29] *Ibid.*
[30] P Havers QC and N Sheldon, "The Impact of the Convention on Medical Law", in R English and P Havers QC (eds) *An Introduction to Human Rights and the Common Law* (Oxford, Hart Publishing, 2000) at 124.
[31] See discussion of Article 14, *infra.*
[32] Series A no 25 (1978).
[33] Wall-standing, hooding, subjection to noise, deprivation of sleep and deprivation of food and drink.
[34] *Supra* n.32 at para. 167.
[35] *Ibid.* at para 162. See M K Addo and N Grief, "Is There a Policy Behind the Decisions and Judgments relating to Article 3 of the European Convention on Human Rights?", (1995) 20 *European Law Review* 178.

right, in order to ensure that private individuals are prevented from committing acts that reach the level of severity contemplated by Article 3. The effect of bringing the Article 3 right "home" is that responsibility is attributed to the public authority for failing in its positive obligation to prevent the mistreatment. In *Z* v. *United Kingdom*,[36] the siblings who failed in their negligence action against the local authority in *X (Minors)* v. *Bedfordshire County Council* [37] petitioned Strasbourg on the basis, *inter alia*, that the failure of the local authority to remove the children from their parents into the care of the local authority amounted to a violation of Article 3. The question for the Commission was whether the state should be held responsible under Article 3 for the inhuman and degrading treatment inflicted on the children by their parents. The Commission referred to the decision of the Court in *A* v. *United Kingdom*,[38] where it was held that the obligation under Article 1 of the Convention, taken together with Article 3, requires states to ensure that individuals within the jurisdiction are not subjected to treatment contrary to Article 3, including such ill-treatment administered by private individuals and stated that:

"the protection of children who by reason of their age and vulnerability are not capable of protecting themselves requires not merely that the criminal law provides protection against Article 3 treatment but that, additionally, this provision will in appropriate circumstances imply a positive obligation on the authorities to take preventive measures to protect a child who is at risk from another individual".

In this case the Commission was satisfied that the authorities were aware of the very serious abuse the children were suffering and failed "despite the means reasonably available to them, to take any effective steps to bring it to an end". The placing of a known sexual abuser as a foster child with a family the members of which are subsequently assaulted would presumably fulfil the criteria for establishing liability under Article 3, particularly where a family had specified that they would not accept such a child for placement in view of the obvious risk.[39] In *Z*, the Commission also found that the decision to strike out the negligence claim in *X (Minors)* v. *Bedfordshire* was a violation of the Article 6 right of access to a court.

At the time of writing, the decision of the Strasbourg Court in these proceedings is awaited, but it is of interest to note that the United Kingdom government has conceded that there was a violation of Article 3, but is contesting the claim under Article 6. This issue is discussed in detail in Chapter 4. However, the interesting question for tort lawyers is how precisely will the English courts adapt to the developing jurisprudence regarding positive obligations. The question which was raised at the conclusion of Chapter 2 is: will the English courts feel constrained to develop the tort of negligence to accommodate such claims,

[36] (1999) 28 EHRR CD 65.
[37] [1995] 2 AC 63.
[38] (1999) 27 EHRR 611.
[39] *W* v. *Essex County Council* [2000] 2 All ER 237, see text accompanying n.108 in Chapter 4.

pursuant to their obligation under section 6(3) of the Human Rights Act to act compatibly with Convention rights? Or, as has been suggested may happen in Chapter 2,[40] will the courts confine such actions against public authorities to claims for compensation by way of proceedings against the public authority under section 7 of the Act. The decision to concede that Article 3 has been violated in the case of the Bedfordshire children may be a shrewd move on the part of the United Kingdom government, as an attempt to avoid a finding of violation of the Article 6 right of access to a court. The Court may indicate that in future, since claims for compensation may now be brought against the public authority under the Human Rights Act, the possibility of bringing an action in negligence at common law would be otiose. Clearly, proceedings under the Act were not available to the Bedfordshire siblings, but it is perhaps reasonable to expect that government legal argument before the Court will highlight the changed legal landscape since *Osman* v. *United Kingdom* was decided. The existence of a statutory obligation on a local authority under section 6(1) of the Act, together with the introduction of a remedy under section 8 of the Act may persuade the Court that in future a bar on the possibility of bringing a negligence action is not a disproportionate restriction on the right of access to a court under Article 6.[41] With the introduction of a remedy under the Act, at least in relation to public authorities, it is arguable that there is now an "effective remedy" as required by Article 13. One of the issues that concerned the Court in *Osman* v. *United Kingdom*[42] was the lack of accountability on the part of the police: the Human Rights Act now provides a vehicle through which that accountability may be provided.

The responsibility of the United Kingdom for compliance with Convention standards may also be engaged by acts or omissions that take place outside the jurisdiction. Thus, in *D* v. *United Kingdom*,[43] the Court held that deportation of an illegal immigrant in the terminal stages of AIDS would constitute inhuman and degrading treatment, because the level of medical care he would receive on return to St. Kitts, would be grievously inadequate. This is the first case where Strasbourg found that removal would be a violation of Article 3 even though the risk of the proscribed treatment would not engage the responsibility of the public authorities of the country of destination. In previous cases, the risk to an applicant in the country of destination would stem from the intentional act of a public authority. Extrapolating from this decision it must be arguable that to refuse medical treatment to someone in this condition would be inhuman and degrading treatment in the absence of reasonable justification.[44]

---

[40] See text accompanying n.116 in Chapter 2.
[41] Cf *Osman* v. *United Kingdom*, *supra* n.24. See Note on the Text.
[42] *Ibid.*
[43] (1997) 24 EHRR 423.
[44] See text accompanying n.23 *supra*.

Article 4: freedom from slavery and forced labour

Article 4(1), a non-derogable freedom, prohibits slavery or servitude and no violation has yet been found by Strasbourg. In *Van Droogenbroeck* v. *Belgium*, the applicant complained that he had been reduced to servitude by being required to work during imprisonment. The Commission[45] and the Court held that the applicant was not held in servitude: there was a limit of time and his position resulted from a criminal trial.

Article 4(2) prohibits forced or compulsory labour and Article 4(3) lists those categories of work that are not included within this category. Two categories may be relevant to tort law: neither "service exacted in case of emergency or calamity threatening the life or well-being of the community" (Article 4(3)(c)), nor "work or service which forms part of normal civic obligations" (Article 4(3)(d)) are included within the concepts of "forced or compulsory labour". Therefore, a positive obligation to rescue would not be within the definition, given that the European consensus is to impose such obligations, at least where the contemplated action poses no unreasonable risk to the rescuer.[46] In their commentary on Article 4, Gomien, Harris and Zwaak have observed that the main purpose of "normal civic obligations", "is to cover obligations which all citizens have, such as to assist someone who is helpless, to fill in official documents for tax purposes, to observe safety requirements, or other similar activities".[47]

Article 5: right to liberty and security

The aim of Article 5 is to protect the physical liberty of the person from arbitrary arrest or detention and to provide for a right to compensation where the provisions of this Article have been contravened. Most of the decided cases relate to arrest and detention as part of the criminal law process, but there are significant authorities also in the fields of mental health and immigration law.[48]

With the exception of the tort of false imprisonment Article 5 has little obvious relevance for tort law. This is a little used tort, the essential ingredient being that a person has been restrained without lawful justification. However, it is now incumbent on English courts to ensure that tort law principles are compatible with the Convention,[49] and Harris, O'Boyle and Warbrick must surely be right to argue that Article 5(1)(c) should be interpreted as imposing a positive obligation

---

[45] Series B no 44 (1980).
[46] See Chapter 5.
[47] D Gomien, D Harris and L Zwaak, *Law and Practice of the European Convention on Human Rights and the European Social Charter* (Strasbourg, Council of Europe Publishing, 1996) at 124.
[48] See generally, D J Harris, M O'Boyle and C Warbrick, *Law of the European Convention on Human Rights* (London, Butterworths, 1995), ch 5.
[49] Human Rights Act 1998, ss.6 (1) and (3).

on states to ensure that a citizen's arrest complies with this provision. Therefore, a citizen's arrest would be permitted by Article 5(1)(c) provided that there is "reasonable suspicion" of the person having committed an "offence". This power, though, will not be unlimited because "offence" bears an autonomous Convention meaning and Article 5(1)(c) "could be interpreted as setting limits to the seriousness of the offence for which a state may impose an arrest".[50]

Early twentieth century cases concerning the action for false imprisonment were examples where plaintiffs failed because it was found that the plaintiff had consented to the terms of his restraint and therefore there was no false imprisonment. It seems highly unlikely that such decisions would withstand Convention scrutiny today. For example, in *Herd* v. *Weardale Steel, Coal and Coke Co.*,[51] the plaintiffs were miners who, fearful that the work they were doing was unsafe, requested that they should be carried by the cage to the surface halfway through their shift. They were eventually taken to the surface several hours before the shift should have ended. The employers recovered five shillings for breach of contract and the claim by the miners that they had been falsely imprisoned failed because it was not false imprisonment to hold a person to the terms and conditions which he had accepted. It has been convincingly argued that just as consent can be freely given so it can be taken away.[52] Looked at from the perspective of Article 5, the question would be whether there had been a deprivation of liberty, and arguably such a deprivation would occur as soon as the consent to restraint had been withdrawn and the person effecting the restraint had the means and a reasonable opportunity to terminate the restraint. The latter point is important. Clearly, as Viscount Haldane LC stated in *Herd*, it would be invidious if a passenger on a train could withdraw their consent to travel before a scheduled stop and require to be free to disembark in order for the train company to avoid liability in an action for false imprisonment.

In *Robinson* v. *Balmain Ferry Co. Ltd*,[53] the defendants operated a ferry with turnstiles for payment on one side of the river only. The plaintiff paid to enter and then changed his mind, but he was unable to leave the wharf without paying a further penny, even though he had not used the ferry. The Privy Council held that the plaintiff had not been falsely imprisoned because he had agreed to leave by ferry and the requirement of payment to leave the wharf was a reasonable condition. As Jones has observed, both *Herd* and *Robinson* are "unsatisfactory to the extent that they appear to sanction extra-judicial detention for breach of contract".[54]

It will be noted that according to Article 5(1)(c), a person may be deprived of his liberty, "for the purpose of bringing him before the competent legal authority

---

[50] Harris, O'Boyle and Warbrick, *supra* n.2 at 115.

[51] [1915] AC 67. See generally M Jones, *Textbook on Torts* (London, Blackstone Press, 2000) at 473 *et seq.*

[52] Tan, "A Misconceived Issue in the Law of Tort", (1981) 44 MLR 166.

[53] [1910] AC 295.

[54] M Jones, *supra* n.51 at 475.

on reasonable suspicion of having committed an offence". In *Fox, Campbell and Hartley* v. *United Kingdom*,[55] the Strasbourg Court stated that "reasonable suspicion" supposes "the existence of facts or information which would satisfy an objective observer that the person concerned may have committed the offence". In *Elguzouli-Daf* v. *Commissioner of Metropolitan Police and another*,[56] the plaintiffs were arrested, charged and remanded in custody for periods of twenty-two and eighty-five days, respectively, after which the CPS decided not to proceed with prosecution. Thereupon, in an action for negligence against the CPS, the Court of Appeal upheld the judge's decision to strike out the claims. The Court of Appeal applied *Hill* v. *Chief Constable of West Yorkshire*,[57] and held that, in the absence of a voluntary assumption of responsibility to a particular defendant, the CPS owed no duty of care in the conduct of a prosecution. In this case, two plaintiffs claimed that the police were dilatory in concluding that prosecutions were bound to fail: in one case, it was alleged that the CPS was slow to process forensic evidence and in the other the plaintiff claimed that the information the CPS had in its possession should have enabled it to decide not to prosecute at a much earlier stage. If it can be shown that there is no "reasonable suspicion", as required by Article 5(1)(c), an enforceable right to compensation is required by Article 5(5). In future, in a case such as this the Human Rights Act may provide the claimants with a remedy. In the terminology of the Act, detention in the absence of such "reasonable suspicion" would mean that the CPS had acted incompatibly with Convention rights and proceedings for a remedy would lie directly against the CPS under sections 7 and 8 of the Act. It was acknowledged in *Elguzouli-Daf* that the CPS is a public body and amenable to judicial review: as a public body, proceedings will lie against it where it fails to comply with the obligation laid down in section 6(1) of the Human Rights Act to act compatibly with the Convention. Section 8 of the Act offers the possibility of recovering compensation for such a breach. Equally, it might be argued on the basis of *Osman* v. *United Kingdom*, that in a case such as this the court should consider the public policy arguments (fundamental rights are at stake, the gravity of the harm and the seriousness of the negligence involved) that speak in favour of a duty of care, rather than applying the exclusionary rule in *Hill*.[58]

Article 6: right to a fair trial

The right in Article 6 to a fair trial applies to both civil and criminal matters. Article 6 applies to the "determination of civil rights" and, in relation to these,

---

[55] Series A no 182 (1990) at para. 32, quoted by Harris, O'Boyle and Warbrick, *supra* n.2 at 118.

[56] [1995] QB 335.

[57] [1989] AC 53.

[58] On the duty of care arguments, see the discussion of *Osman* and *Z* in Chapter 4, and for consideration of the impact of the action under the Human Rights Act on the negligence action see text accompanying n.40 *supra* and text accompanying n.116 in Chapter 2. See also Note on the Text.

accords a right to a "fair and public hearing within a reasonable time by an independent and impartial tribunal established by law". The right includes a right of access to the court, in the words of the Strasbourg Court's *Golder* judgment:

"Article 6(1) secures to everyone the right to have any claim relating to his civil rights and obligations brought before a court or tribunal. In this way the Article embodies the 'right to a court', of which the right of access, that is the right to institute proceedings before courts in civil matters, constitutes one aspect only".[59]

However, as the Court has observed on a number of occasions, Article 6 of itself does not guarantee any particular *content* for civil rights and obligations. In *H* v. *Belgium*, the Court stated that the Article 6 guarantee extends to civil rights and obligations which can be said "at least on arguable grounds, to be recognised under domestic law".[60] Viewed from this perspective, Article 6 embodies a procedural right of access to a court to determine the effect of substantive national rules. The conclusion would follow, therefore, in relation to tort matters that Article 6 applies where English law recognises claims in tort. For example, in *Powell and Rayner* v. *United Kingdom*,[61] the applicants petitioned Strasbourg under various articles, including Article 6, in relation to aircraft noise and overflight at Heathrow Airport. The Court held that the statutory exclusion of actions for trespass and nuisance raised no issue under Article 6. However, recent Strasbourg jurisprudence has emphasised that a state cannot control the right of access to a court through the unrestricted use of procedural bars or the recognition of immunities. It would be contrary to the rule of law in a democratic society if such bars were unregulated. This line of jurisprudence led to the finding that the Court of Appeal decision in *Osman* v. *Ferguson* was a violation of Article 6. In *Fayed* v. *United Kingdom*, the Court stated that:

"Certainly the Convention enforcement bodies may not create by way of interpretation of Article 6(1) a substantive civil right which has no legal basis in the state concerned. However, it would not be consistent with the rule of law in a democratic society or with the basic principle underlying Article 6(1)—namely that civil claims must be capable of being submitted to a judge for adjudication—if, for example, a State could, without restraint or control by the Convention enforcement bodies, remove from the jurisdiction of the courts a whole range of civil claims or confer immunities from civil liability on large groups or categories of persons".[62]

The Court proceeded to reiterate the relevant principles in this area:

"(a) The right of access to the courts secured by Article 6(1) is not absolute but may be subject to limitations; these are permitted by implication since the right of access by its very nature calls for regulation by the State, regulation which may vary in time and place according to the needs and resources of the community and of individuals.

[59] Series A no 18 (1975) atpara. 36.
[60] Series A no 127-B (1987) at para. 40.
[61] Series A no 172 (1990).
[62] Series A no 242-B (1994) at para. 65.

(b) . . . the Contracting States enjoy a certain margin of appreciation but [the Court] must be satisfied that the limitations applied do not restrict or reduce the access to the individual in such a way or to such an extent that the very essence of the right is impaired.

(c) . . . a limitation will not be compatible with Article 6(1) if it does not pursue a legitimate aim and if there is not a reasonable relationship of proportionality between the means employed and the aim sought to be achieved".

The applicants in *Fayed* complained that their personal and commercial reputations had been sullied by the report of inspectors appointed under section 432 of the Companies Act 1985 to investigate the circumstances surrounding their take-over of the House of Fraser. The fact that the report was privileged meant that libel proceedings could not be instituted and the applicants argued that restriction on the right to bring proceedings constituted a violation of Article 6 . The Court did not consider it necessary to rule on whether the defence of privilege is, as the government had argued, a matter relating to the content of a right, rather than a procedural issue, because the same issues of legitimate aim and proportionality would be raised if the complaint were treated as raising a substantive complaint under Article 8. The defence was found to pursue a legitimate aim, namely the furtherance of the public interest in the proper conduct of the affairs of public companies and the remedy of judicial review was available to challenge the appointment of the inspectors making the report, its contents or publication if there had been unfairness or a breach of the rules of natural justice.

While the Fayed brothers failed in their claim, it is the development of Strasbourg case law in this area that has been the subject of much criticism by the English judiciary,[63] because the finding of a violation of Article 6 in *Osman* v. *United Kingdom*,[64] was perceived as an attack upon, and an attempt to influence, the content of substantive rules of English tort law. The ruling of the Strasbourg Court in *Osman* is discussed in detail in Chapter 4, but in view of its significance an outline will be drawn here.

It will be recalled that the applicants, the widow and son of a murder victim, had been victims of a sustained campaign of harassment and intimidation by a schoolteacher, which was brought to the attention of the police over a period of several months. The Court of Appeal applied the *obiter* views of the House of Lords in *Hill* v. *Chief Constable of West Yorkshire*[65] and struck out the negligence action against the police on the ground that public policy required that the police should be immune from suit in relation to the investigation and suppression of crime.[66] The Strasbourg Court held that the exclusionary rule applied by

---

[63] See Rt. Hon. Lord Hoffmann, "Human Rights and the House of Lords", (1999) 62 *MLR* 159 and the speech of Lord Browne-Wilkinson in *Barrett* v. *Enfield London Borough Council* [1999] 3 WLR 628. See Note on the Text.

[64] *Supra* n.24. See Chapter 4.

[65] [1988] 2 All ER 238.

[66] *Osman* v. *Ferguson, supra* n.25.

the Court of Appeal constituted a restriction on the Article 6 right of access to a court. The Court referred to the criteria employed to determine whether an action in negligence will lie and stated that the applicants must be taken to have had a right, derived from the law of negligence, to seek an adjudication on the admissibility and merits of an arguable claim that they were in a relationship of proximity to the police, that the harm caused was foreseeable and that in the circumstances it was fair, just and reasonable not to apply the exclusionary rule applied in *Hill*. The Court found that the Court of Appeal decision in *Osman* failed the test of proportionality because there had been no consideration of public interest arguments that pull in the opposite direction, such as the fundamental rights involved, the gravity of the harm suffered by the victims and the degree of negligence involved.[67] In the Court's view such issues should be examined on the merits and consequently, a striking out of the claim was a disproportionate interference with the right of access to a court under Article 6. The Strasbourg Court was particularly concerned (as was the Commission in Z) that there was no vehicle other than the negligence action through which the applicants could seek redress and render the defendants accountable. As will be seen, English courts, while confessing difficulty with the Strasbourg ruling, have responded by allowing negligence claims to go to full trial which would almost certainly have been struck out previously.[68]

Article 7: no punishment without law

This Article embodies the well-established principle of non-retroactivity: a person cannot be convicted of a criminal offence save in accordance with a law extant at the time the offence was committed. The importance of this right is demonstrated by the fact that it cannot be derogated from—Article 15(2) prohibits derogation in time of war or public emergency. It is a little used provision and while some torts may also constitute criminal offences, for example criminal libel, it is likely to be of little relevance in the field of tort generally.

Article 8: right to respect for private and family life, the home and correspondence

Article 8 has generated a very substantial body of case law, but the jurisprudence may fairly be described as a list of instances where the reasoning of the Court and the Commission is not underpinned by a secure theoretical foundation. Harris, O'Boyle and Warbrick could not be more apposite in their assessment:

[67] See Chapter 4.
[68] See Chapter 4. But see Note on the Text for an analysis of the potential impact of the Court's decision in Z v. *United Kingdom* (10 May 2001) on the use of the strike out procedure.

"Both the Commission and the Court have avoided laying down general under-
standings of what each of the items covers and, in some cases, they have utilised the
co-terminacy of them to avoid spelling out precisely which is or are implicated . . .
This has allowed them to take advantage of the lack of precision of Article 8(1) to
develop the case-law to take into account social and technical developments. The
disadvantage is the absence of a theoretical conspectus, which makes an account
of the jurisprudence inevitably descriptive and prediction about its likely progress
hazardous".[69]

Not only is the range of interests caught by the four "umbrella" headings
diverse, imprecise and continually expanding, predictive difficulties are exacerbated by the development of the "margin of appreciation" doctrine and the
recognition of positive obligations upon the part of states. Moreover, the application of margin doctrine in the realm of positive obligations compounds the
uncertainties, because it has been stated repeatedly by the Strasbourg organs
that especially as far as positive obligations are concerned the notion of
"respect" is not clear-cut.[70] The discussion in this section will focus on the
"interests" recognised as deserving of protection under Article 8 and which are
relevant to tort law and discussion of "margin doctrine" and positive obligations is reserved for the concluding section of this chapter.

In *Botta* v. *Italy*, the Court stated that:

"Private life, in the Court's view, includes a person's physical and psychological
integrity; the guarantee afforded by Article 8 of the Convention is primarily intended
to ensure the development, without outside interference, of the personality of each
individual in his relations with other human beings".[71]

This observation relates to the content of the core concept of private life and
this, coupled with the fact that a state may have positive obligations to protect an
individual's physical and psychological integrity, means that a wide range of
activities may be protected and a number of positive steps may be required by
states. A state must put in place laws to protect the physical and psychological
well-being of a person from the criminal acts of others. In *X and Y* v. *The
Nertherlands*,[72] the state was in violation of Article 8 where owing to a lacuna in
the criminal law, a rapist could not be prosecuted because the victim was a minor
and mentally handicapped. Where it is argued that domestic law gives inadequate
protection to the physical well-being of the individual, it is likely that a claim will
be pleaded as both a violation of Article 3 (inhuman and degrading treatment), as
well as Article 8, even where the actual ill-treatment is inflicted by private non-
state actors.[73] There are signs that the Strasbourg Court is becoming increasingly

---

[69] *Supra* n.2 at 303.
[70] *Johnston* v. *Ireland* Series A no 112 (1986) at para. 112.
[71] (1998) 26 EHRR 241 at para. 32. The applicant complained of the failure of the Italian authorities to ensure that private beaches were equipped with facilities for the disabled. See text accompanying n.57 in Chapter 5.
[72] Series A no 91 (1986).
[73] See, for example, *X and Y* v. *The Netherlands*, *ibid.*; *A* v. *United Kingdom supra* n.5 and *Z* v.
United Kingdom, *supra* n.36.

vigilant to guard the physical well-being of vulnerable members of society, by finding violations of Article 3, rather than Article 8. It will be recalled that Article 3 is a non-derogable right and therefore deserving of the highest degree of protection. In *X and Y*, decided in 1985, the Court preferred to approach the case under Article 8 and having found a violation stated that it therefore did not consider that it had to examine the case under Article 3. The Commission had found, by fifteen votes to one, that there had been no violation of Article 3. In contrast, in *A. v. United Kingdom*,[74] the Court having found a violation of Article 3, considered it unnecessary to examine whether the impugned ill-treatment (a jury acquitted a stepfather of assault after he pleaded "reasonable chastisement" of his stepson) constituted also a violation of Article 8. Similarly, in *Z and others*, the Commission, having found a violation of Article 3, did not go on to consider the Article 8 complaint. This increasing willingness to evaluate the state's actions by reference to the weightier Convention obligation betokens an increasing confidence on the part of Strasbourg. Feldman has analysed the process by which international human rights law obligations and supervisory bodies gain authority and achieve a pull towards compliance on the part of Contracting States. The substantive content of human rights law is developed through a process of dialogue between states which builds confidence on the part of states in the supervising institutions and it is not surprising that there is now an increasing tendency on the part of Strasbourg to recognise violations of Articles 2 and 3.[75]

The physical and psychological well-being of a person are affected by the state of the environment and a number of claims brought under Article 8 have facts which are analogous to claims in nuisance in English law. Environmental standards and the consequences of these for the tort of nuisance are considered in detail in Chapter 8. The important difference, though, between, English tort law and Convention jurisprudence is that it is not necessary to have any interest in property in order to complain under Article 8.[76] Thus, in *Lopez Ostra v. Spain*,[77] the applicants complained that the operation of a waste-treatment plant caused noise, fumes and smells and that this affected their private and family life, although without seriously endangering the applicants' health. The authorities had not created the emissions, but they had permitted the plant to be built on their land, with the assistance of government funding. The Court found a violation of Article 8, but considered that although the conditions created by the plant made life difficult, they did not reach the level of seriousness contemplated by Article 3 so that there was no degrading treatment.

The right to respect for private life is engaged in cases concerning consent to medical treatment. In *Herczegfalvy v. Austria*,[78] the applicant complained that

---

[74] *Supra* n.5.
[75] D Feldman, "Human Rights Treaties, Nation States and Conflicting Moralities", (1995) 1 *Contemporary Issues in Law* 61.
[76] Cf *Hunter* v. *Canary Wharf Ltd* [1997] 2 All ER 426: see Chapter 8.
[77] Series A no 303 (1995).
[78] Series A no 242-B (1992).

he had been force-fed and forcibly administered drugs. It was found that he had been lawfully detained as a person of unsound mind under Article 5(1)(e) of the Convention and the Court held that there was no violation of Article 8, because there was no evidence to disprove the authority's view that the applicant did not have capacity. Thus, where no valid consent is obtained from a competent patient there will at the very least be a violation of Article 8 (and possibly Article 3). Under English law, the action for battery will lie in the absence of consent. Grubb has observed that, "it is the medieval tort that the courts have used to allow them to recognise a patient's so-called 'right of self-determination' ".[79]

More problematic is the quality of information given to a patient; where it is argued that there has been insufficient disclosure of risk, for example, the action will sound in negligence, not battery, provided that the patient has been informed "in broad terms of the nature of the procedure which is intended" and has consented.[80] Exceptionally, a claim in battery may succeed where it can be shown that there was no "real" consent because the patient was not aware of what had been done or where consent has been procured by fraud. Grubb cites *Appleton* v. *Garrett*,[81] where a dentist undertook expensive and unnecessary work purely for financial gain, as a rare example of a case where the quality of information was in issue. The claim in battery succeeded, because the patient was unaware of "the nature of what was being done and thus her consent was not 'real' ". Where a claimant brings an action in negligence for failure to disclose a risk inherent in treatment there are two hurdles to surmount: first, the failure to disclose the risk must be a breach of duty; secondly, the claimant must establish causation by showing that had the risk been disclosed, the patient would not have proceeded with the treatment. The author is not aware of any Strasbourg decision directly on the issue of disclosure of risk in medical treatment. However, the right to respect for private life is clearly engaged in situations concerning disclosure of information that will enable individuals to make decisions that may have an impact on their health. In *Guerra* v. *Italy*,[82] the state was found to have violated Article 8 where a factory emitted toxic substances and there was a failure to make available information that would have enabled those living in the locality to assess the risks to their health if they remained living there. It was not necessary for the victims to prove causation by showing they would have moved away if they had known of the risk. The Strasbourg Court held that the applicants had suffered non-pecuniary damage and made an award to each of them. Arguing by analogy from this case, the issue of whether there should be disclosure of risk in medical treatment should, in cases brought under the Act, be determined by the court (as opposed to members of the medical profession under the

---

[79] A Grubb, "Problems of Medical Law", in B S Markesinis and S Deakin, *Tort Law*, 4th edn (Oxford, Oxford University Press, 1998) at 239.

[80] *Chatterton* v. *Gerson* [1981] QB 432 approved by the Court of Appeal in *Sidaway* v. *Bethlem Royal Hospital Governors* [1984] 1 All ER 1018.

[81] [1997] 8 Med LR 75; Grubb, *supra* n.79.

[82] (1998) 26 EHRR 357.

Bolam standard) and causation becomes an irrelevance in relation to the duty to disclose information in order to comply with Convention standards. Proceedings against a health authority under the Human Rights Act may therefore be a welcome option for a claimant as well as trying to surmount the technicalities of the negligence action.

A person's right to "privacy" in the sense of the right to be let alone against unreasonable intrusion by others and the right to prevent the dissemination of private information is contemplated by Article 8,[83] and this issue is discussed in detail in Chapter 7.

Private life encompasses sexual orientation,[84] and gender identity.[85] In *Dudgeon* v. *United Kingdom*, the applicant challenged successfully the total ban on homosexual relationships which existed in Northern Ireland (unlike the rest of the United Kingdom, there was then in Northern Ireland a complete ban on homosexual sex, rather than a threshold age of twenty-one years). A number of cases have been brought by transsexuals who have argued that domestic laws have been insufficiently flexible in their recognition of gender identity. In *Sheffield and Horsham*, the applicant, a male to female transsexual who had undergone gender reassignment surgery, challenged the refusal of English law to permit the gender of a person to be changed on a birth certificate. The Court was satisfied that the United Kingdom was acting within its margin of appreciation since for practical purposes a birth certificate is required to be produced on very few occasions and other documents such as driving licences will display the chosen gender.

The notion of family life has been interpreted to include relationships between parent and child, both legitimate and illegitimate,[86] as well as more extended family relationships.[87] The Court has held that, "[the] mutual enjoyment by parent and child of each other's company constitutes a fundamental element of family life".[88] Many of the claims brought before Strasbourg have related to procedures employed by states when taking children into care. This interest was invoked by the mother and child in *TP and KM* v. *United Kingdom*,[89] (the English proceedings were *M (A Minor)* v. *Newham London Borough Council*, appeal consolidated with *Bedfordshire*)[90] where a mother and child alleged that the London Borough of Newham was negligent in its removal of the child into the care of the local authority. The Article 8 claim

[83] See *Malone* v. *United Kingdom* Series A no 82 (1984), *Winer* v. *United Kingdom* (1986) D&R 154 and *Spencer* v. *United Kingdom* (1998) 25 EHRR 105.

[84] *Dudgeon* v. *UK* Series A no 45 (1981); *Smith and Grady* v. *United Kingdom* [1999] IRLR 734.

[85] *Rees* v. *United Kingdom* Series A no 106 (1986), *Cossey* v. *United Kingdom* Series A no 184 (1990) and *Sheffield and Horsham* v. *United Kingdom supra* n.16.

[86] *Marckx* v. *Belgium* Series A no 31 (1979).

[87] See, for example, *Boyle* v. *United Kingdom* Series A no 282-B (1994) where the applicant challenged the fact that as the law stood prior to the Children Act 1989 entering into force, there was no possibility for him to apply for access to his nephew after he had been taken into care.

[88] *Olsson* v. *Sweden* Series A no 130 (1988) at para. 59.

[89] Application no. 28945/95, Report of the Commission adopted on 10 September 1999.

[90] *Supra* n.37.

can be contrasted with the claim brought under Article 6: the Article 6 point centred on the argument that the House of Lords' decision in *Newham* was an improper conferment of immunity on the local authority, while the Article 8 claim related to the wrongful interference with a substantive interest protected by Article 8. In its Report, the Commission found that there was a violation of Article 8 because the local authority had failed to implement fair procedures after the second applicant had been taken into care. This failure (delay in a court hearing and delayed access to videotape evidence) had resulted in the first applicant's boyfriend being identified erroneously as the second applicant's abuser for a period of over one year. In future on analogous facts, proceedings will lie against the local authority under section 7 of the Human Rights Act on the basis that the local authority has acted incompatibly with Article 8 of the Convention and therefore unlawfully under the Act. As we have seen, the court itself must also act compatibly with Article 6 of the Convention in its development of the common law. The Commission in *TP and KM* also found that the decision of the House of Lords in *Newham* was a disproportionate restriction on the right of access to a court and therefore a violation of Article 6 in relation to the child but not her mother.

The decision of the Court of Appeal in *F* v. *Wirral Metropolitan Borough Council*[91] is of interest in this context. In *F*, the Court of Appeal held that a parent has no right at common law to seek damages for the tort of interference with parental rights. Strasbourg has clearly recognised that such rights are encompassed by family life and a violation of Article 8 may give rise to claims for just satisfaction under Article 41. It might, therefore, be argued that a common law duty of care should be recognised by the court in order to fulfil its obligation under section 6 of the Act, although, in the light of the availability of remedies under section 8, this argument may be rejected.[92] In *F*, the Court of Appeal held that the only remedies available were public law remedies to protect the child and, for parents, the tort of misfeasance in public office. This tort is of extremely limited scope, confined to cases where a claimant can show that a public officer has acted in bad faith, either by intending to injure the claimant or with reckless indifference to the illegality of his act and in the knowledge of or with reckless indifference to the probability of causing damage to the claimant.[93] The standard of care laid down by this tort would not be sufficient to meet the demands of Article 8, where the Strasbourg Court has held that when care orders are made, the Court's review is "not limited to ascertaining whether the State acted reasonably, carefully and in good faith". Strasbourg will examine whether impugned decisions (as to care orders, access etc) are justified by "relevant and sufficient" reasons. In practice this standard is that of the reasonable man in negligence. In *Olsson*, the Court having reviewed the evidence, concluded that there

[91] [1999] 2 All ER 648.

[92] See text accompanying n.116 in Chapter 2 and Note on the Text.

[93] *Three Rivers District Council* v. *Governor and Company of the Bank of England* [2000] 3 All ER 1.

were sufficient reasons to take the children into care: the "Swedish authorities were reasonably entitled to think having regard to the margin of appreciation that it was necessary to take the children into care".[94]

There is relatively little case law regarding the notion of "home" under Article 8. In the context of tort law, this interest is most likely to be invoked in the fields of privacy, as generally understood, and also where facts are analogous to those arising in the tort of nuisance.[95] It is clear that what is one's home is a question of fact and it is unnecessary to establish a proprietary interest in order to invoke this right.[96] In *Mentes* v. *Turkey*,[97] it was held that the applicant's home extended to a village she visited every year to which she had emotional ties and where she spent significant periods of time. It has been held that the notion of home may extend to business premises.[98]

Similarly, there is little discussion in the Strasbourg jurisprudence of the meaning to be attributed to correspondence. It is clear that "correspondence" includes telephone conversations,[99] as well as written communications.[100]

Article 9: freedom of thought, conscience and religion

There are two aspects to Article 9: the right to freedom of thought, conscience and religion (including the right to change that religion or belief) and the right to manifest one's religion or belief. Limitations on the right under Article 9(2) are permitted only in relation to the manifestation of religion or belief.

Like freedom of speech, which is protected under Article 10, freedom of thought, conscience and religion has been described as one of the essential foundations of a democratic society:

> "It is, in its religious dimension, one of the most vital elements that go to make up the identity of believers and their conception of life, but it is also a precious asset for atheists, agnostics, sceptics and the unconcerned. The pluralism indissociable from a democratic society, which has been dearly won over the centuries, depends on it".[101]

Article 9 is unlikely to feature as an argument in tort cases, because the facts that are typical of tortious situations fit more appositely under alternative articles. Thus, an obvious example, is the case of public protest: whether such action constitutes a public nuisance would more appropriately be considered in conjunction with Article 11 (freedom of assembly and association), rather than Article 9. Cases which arise in relation to allegedly defective educational

---

[94] *Supra* n.88 at para. 74.
[95] See Chapter 8.
[96] See *Lopez Ostra* v. *Spain* Series A no 303-C (1994) and see text accompanying n.25 in Chapter 8.
[97] (1998) 26 EHRR 595.
[98] *Niemitz* v. *Germany* Series A no 251-B (1992).
[99] *Klass* v. *Germany* Series A no 28 (1978) and *Halford* v. *United Kingdom* (1997) 24 EHRR 523.
[100] *Silver* v. *UK* Series A no 61 (1983).
[101] *Kokkinakis* v. *Greece* Series A no 260-A (1994) at para. 31.

provision may raise issues under Article 2 of Protocol 1 (the right of parents for their children to be educated in conformity with their own religious and philosophical convictions).

Article 10: freedom of expression

Article 10 guarantees the right to freedom of expression, which includes freedom to hold opinions and to receive and impart information and ideas without interference by public authority and regardless of frontiers. An extensive jurisprudence in relation to various types of speech (political,[102] including debate on matters of "public" interest,[103] commercial,[104] artistic)[105] has developed under this article and it is necessary to ensure that incompatibility between English law and Convention jurisprudence is eliminated. What emerges is that political speech is accorded the highest degree of protection so that a state's margin of appreciation to assess the necessity of any limitation upon the right is more restricted than is the case with commercial or artistic expression. The two areas of English law that appear particularly susceptible to attack on the ground of incompatibility are defamation and privacy (depending upon the relevant relationship between the Article 8 right to respect for private life and Article 10) and these issues are fully discussed in Chapters 6 and 7, respectively.

Article 11: freedom of assembly and association

The Strasbourg Court has acknowledged the special affinity of Article 11 with freedom of expression, describing Article 11 as *lex specialis* in relation to the *lex generalis* of Article 10. It will be recalled that the right of peaceful demonstration is protected by Article 11. In *Plattform "Ärzte für das Leben" v. Austria*,[106] the Court held that this right may give rise to a positive obligation upon the state to protect those who wish to demonstrate against violence from counter-demonstrators.

   If a state restricts the right on one of the grounds stated in Article 11(2), it must show that the restriction pursued a legitimate aim and that it was "necessary in a democratic society" to impose a restriction.[107] This requirement for any restriction to be convincingly justified should in future be applied in a case such as the leading English authority of *Hubbard* v. *Pitt*.[108] Here, the defendants objected to the progressive rise in the number of middle class families living in

---

[102] *Lingens* v. *Austria* Series A no 103 (1986).
[103] *Hertel* v. *Switzerland* (1999) 28 EHRR 534.
[104] *Markt. Intern and Beerman* v. *Germany* Series A no 164 (1989).
[105] *Müller and others* v. *Switzerland* Series A no 133 (1988).
[106] Series A no 139 (1988).
[107] See discussion of the margin of appreciation, *infra*.
[108] [1976] QB 142.

Islington and the associated driving out of the traditional working class population, which they attributed to the activities of property developers and local
estate agents. Therefore, they organised as the "Islington Tenants Campaign"
and picketed peacefully at the office of the plaintiff estate agents. An injunction
was granted by Forbes J on the ground that the picketing on the public highway
was a public nuisance, save where in pursuance of a trade dispute. The injunction was maintained by the Court of Appeal on the grounds that there was a
serious issue to be tried, namely whether the defendants were committing the
tort of private nuisance. Denning LJ dissented, remarking that the police inspector had thanked the pickets for ensuring that nothing unlawful was done and
none of the usual "nuisance" factors was present:

> "no obstruction, no violence, no intimidation, no molestation, no noise, no smells,
> nothing except a group of six or seven people standing about with placards and leaflets
> . . . all orderly and well-behaved".[109]

Forbes J dismissed the relevance of Article 11 because he said that it does not
give a "right to assemble anywhere the conveners of a public meeting choose,
and in particular does not give a right to assemble on the highway". This observation demonstrates a misunderstanding of the Strasbourg approach which
requires that any restriction on the right under Article 11, as in a case like
Hubbard, should be justified according to criteria set out in paragraph 2 of
Article 11. Equally, the enactment of the Human Rights Act means that a case
like *Thomas* v. *NUM*,[110] where Scott J injuncted striking miners on the basis of
"unreasonable harassment", should no longer be decided without the court
ensuring that it is acting compatibly with Article 11.

Article 12: the right to marry

Very few cases have been taken to Strasbourg under this Article and it seems
unlikely that the right to marry and found a family would be invoked in the context of a tort action.

Article 14: prohibition of discrimination

Article 14 requires states to secure the enjoyment of the rights and freedoms set
out in the Convention without discrimination on any ground and the Convention
sets out a non-exhaustive list of possible grounds of discrimination. Thus the
right under Article 14 is parasitic in that the obligation not to discriminate exists
only in relation to Convention rights. In contrast, Article 26 of the International
Covenant on Civil and Political Rights affords more extensive protection to the

---

[109] *Ibid.* at 177. See generally F Klug, K Starmer and S Weir, *The Three Pillars of Liberty*
(London, Routledge, 1996) at 192.
[110] [1985] 2 All ER 1.

individual because it is a general non-discrimination provision.[111] The Council of Europe recently opened Protocol No 12, which prohibits discrimination in the enjoyment of any right set forth by law, for signature. At the time of writing the United Kingdom government has no plans to sign this Protocol.

In order to come within Article 14, the applicant must first establish that the facts in question fall within the "ambit" of a Convention right. Thus, the applicant will argue that he has suffered discrimination in the enjoyment of one or more of the rights such as life, liberty, freedom of expression set out in Articles 2 to 13 or the Protocols to the Convention. It is not necessary for the applicant to show that another Convention article has been violated in order for there to be a violation of Article 14:

> "a measure which in itself is in conformity with the requirements of the Article enshrining the right or freedom in question may however infringe this Article when read in conjunction with Article 14 for the reason that it is of a discriminatory nature".[112]

Conversely, in practice, where a violation of another right is found, the Strasbourg organs are unlikely to consider Article 14, unless a "clear inequality of treatment in the enjoyment of the right in question is a fundamental aspect of the case".[113] So, for example, in *Dudgeon* v. *United Kingdom*, the applicant's complaint alleged that the criminalisation of all adult, private male homosexual acts was a breach of the Article 8 right to respect for private life as well as Article 14 in conjunction with Article 8. The Court, having found a violation of Article 8, decided that there was "no useful purpose" in addressing the Article 14 complaint.[114]

It is important to note that the "ambit" of a Convention right extends not only to state obligations under the various obligations of the Convention, but also to steps that a state may take *voluntarily* to further enhance the enjoyment of a Convention right. If a state chooses to take steps to implement a right, for example, the provision of mother-tongue education (not a right under Article 2 of Protocol 1),[115] then it must do so on a non-discriminatory basis.[116] In this

---

[111] Article 26 provides that: "All persons are equal before the law and are entitled without any discrimination to the equal protection of the law. In this respect, the law shall prohibit any discrimination and guarantee to all persons equal and effective protection against discrimination on any ground such as race, colour, sex, language, religion, political or other opinion, national or social origin, property, birth or other status".

[112] Case relating to *Certain Aspects of the Laws on the Use of Languages in Education in Belgium* (hereafter the "*Belgian Linguistics*" case) Series A no 6 (1968). See also *Abdulaziz, Cabales and Balkalandi* v. *United Kingdom* Series A no 94 (1985).

[113] *Airey* v. *Ireland* Series A no 32 (1979) at para. 30.

[114] Series A no 45 (1979) at para. 69.

[115] Article 2 of Protocol 1: "No person shall be denied the right to education. In the exercise of any functions which it assumes in relation to education and teaching, the State shall respect the right of parents to ensure such teaching in conformity with their own religious and philosophical convictions".

[116] *Belgian Linguistics*, *supra* n.112. See also *Gaygusuz* v. *Austria* (1996) 23 EHRR 364: state not required by any Convention right to make emergency assistance payments to the unemployed, but any such payments must be made without discrimination.

way, although the Convention embodies primarily civil and political rights, a state may find itself subject to demands for the implementation of economic and social rights.[117]

The applicant must then demonstrate that he has been treated differently from others in analogous situations. In *Stubbings* v. *United Kingdom*,[118] the applicants complained that as the victims of intentional harm (sexual abuse in childhood) they were treated less favourably by the English rules on the limitation of actions than those who suffered negligently inflicted harm. The Commission found violations of Article 14 taken together with Article 6(1). However, the Court stated that:

> "not every difference in treatment will amount to a violation of [Article 14]. Instead, it must be established that other persons in analogous or relevantly similar situation enjoy preferential treatment, and that there is no reasonable or objective justification for this distinction".

The Court concluded that the situation of the applicants was not analogous to the victims of negligent behaviour. However, flaws in the approach of the Court are apparent: whether analogy can be drawn between an applicant and others who are arguably more favourably treated depends upon which question the Court asks itself. In *Van der Mussele* v. *Belgium*, the applicant complained of a violation of Article 4 in conjunction with Article 14 because he was required to provide legal services on a *pro bono* basis as part of his training. He complained that Belgian *avocats* are subject to less favourable treatment than a whole range of professions. Trainee professionals in other fields were not expected to provide services free of charge. The Court referred to the fact that Article 14 safeguards individuals in analogous situations from discrimination and held that there was no similarity between the disparate situations as to legal status, conditions for entry to the profession and the nature of the functions involved etc.[119] The Court could have asked itself questions that would focus on commonality between groups: the fact that young people engaged in professional training were treated differently for example. Clearly, the impact of upholding the requirement is that the less well off may effectively be excluded from the profession.

The requirement of analogy may be subsumed by the arguments put forward by the state to justify a difference in treatment. In *Rasmussen* v. *Denmark*,[120] the applicant complained of a violation of Article 14 (in conjunction with Article 8) because he was prevented by the relevant limitation period from contesting the paternity of a child borne by his wife. However, the wife could apply for such a test at any time before the child reached the age of majority. The Court assumed that the husband and wife were in analogous situations and found the difference

---

[117] See discussion of positive obligations, Chapter 5.
[118] (1996) 23 EHRR 213.
[119] Series A no 70 (1983).
[120] Series A no 87 (1984).

in treatment justified, relying on the state's margin of appreciation:[121] the aim of the legislation was to protect the child's interests and to promote legal certainty.

It is for the applicant to identify the ground upon which he has been treated differently. One of the grounds listed in Article 14 is "property" and differential treatment on the grounds of disparity in wealth has been raised in a number of cases. The paradox implicit in recognising this ground of discrimination has been highlighted by Harris, O'Boyle and Warbrick who have observed that,

> "it seems quite wrong that the enjoyment of fundamental rights should depend on financial resources. On the other hand, in capitalist societies at least, the acceptance of even wide inequalities based on wealth is a central characteristic of a market system".[122]

Perhaps, not surprisingly, the Strasbourg Court has shown a reluctance to address this issue, and has preferred to find a violation of another substantive provision.[123] This ground of discrimination might have implications for the development of common law obligations. For example, in *McFarlane* v. *Tayside Health Board*,[124] the House of Lords has recently ruled that the birth of a healthy child following a failure to advise of the possible spontaneous reversal of a vasectomy procedure was pure economic loss and not recoverable. In contrast, where parents have claimed damages in contract after the medical team implanted three embryos, rather than two, general damages have been recovered. In the former case, the classification of the damage in tort as pure economic loss undermined the claim. Putting it at its simplest, these cases are consistent with the traditional view that warranties of quality arise only in contract law and if you want such a guarantee you must bargain for it.[125] In practical terms, though, the consequence is that those who can afford private medicine and therefore have a contractual relationship with a doctor will have a remedy while those to whom only a duty of care in tort is owed will not. According to Lord Steyn, the real reason for rejecting the claim lies in distributive justice: people on the London Underground would be shocked to learn that a couple received damages for the birth of a healthy baby they did not want, when so many go to inordinate trouble and expense to have a baby. One ventures to suspect that the bystanders on the London Underground would not be so sympathetic to appeals to distributive justice if they were told that those who could afford private medicine would receive damages. The couple in *McFarlane* could argue that the effect of the House of Lords' decision is that they have suffered discrimination in the enjoyment of their right to respect for family life on the grounds of property.

---

[121] See discussion of margin of appreciation in connection with Article 14, *infra*.
[122] *Supra* n.2 at 473.
[123] *Airey* v. *Ireland*, *supra* n.113.
[124] [1999] 3 WLR 1301. See T Weir, "The Unwanted Child", [2000] *CLJ* 238.
[125] By analogy with *Murphy* v. *Brentwood District Council* [1991] AC 398.

However, not every difference in treatment of persons in analogous situations will amount to discrimination contrary to Article 14. In order for a state to uphold any differential treatment, it must demonstrate that such treatment has a reasonable and objective justification in that the action pursues a legitimate aim and the means employed are proportionate to the end sought to be achieved. A "margin of appreciation" is conceded to states when they are making the judgment as to whether treatment is proportionate to the aim. In *Stubbings*, in addition to the fact that the applicants were considered not to be analogous to the victims of negligently inflicted harm, the Court found that the creation of separate regimes of limitation fell within the state's margin of appreciation:

> "It is quite reasonable, and falls within the margin of appreciation afforded to [states] in these matters to create separate regimes for the limitation of actions based on deliberately inflicted harm and negligence, since, for example, the existence of a civil claim might be less obvious to victims of the latter type of injury".

In *Belgian Linguistics*,[126] the Court also stated that any differences in treatment must "strike a fair balance between the protection of the interests of the community and respect for the rights and freedoms safeguarded by the Convention".

Article 1, Protocol 1: protection of property

This Article is concerned with the protection of ownership and enjoyment of property and there is an extensive jurisprudence which is likely to be of only peripheral relevance for tort principles.[127] In *Powell* v. *United Kingdom* it was held that:

> "This provision is mainly concerned with the arbitrary confiscation of property and does not in principle guarantee a right to the peaceful enjoyment of possession in a pleasant environment".[128]

Thus, it is unlikely that this article would be invoked in an action for nuisance: as we have seen, the most appropriate article would be Article 8. However, in *Powell*, it was observed that where a nuisance caused a diminution in property value, that interference could amount to a partial taking of property.

Article 2, Protocol 1: right to education

The leading authority in relation to the right to education is the *Belgian Linguistics* case.[129] The gist of the complaint was that the children of French

---

[126] *Supra* n.112.

[127] For a comprehensive analysis see Harris, O'Boyle and Warbrick, *supra* n.2, ch 18. A legal claim must be "sufficiently established" to constitute a "possession" within this Article: *National and Provincial Building Society and others* v. *United Kingdom* (1998) 25 EHRR 127.

[128] (1987) 9 EHRR 241, quoted by S Farran, *The UK Before the European Court of Human Rights* (London, Blackstone Press, 1996) at 353.

[129] *Supra* n.112.

speakers did not have access to mother-tongue education unless they travelled a considerable distance from their homes. The main challenge failed and the case laid down the basic principle that a person has the right to avail himself or herself of the system of education that has been put in place by the state. There is no right under the Convention to demand a particular form of education, except that to the extent that the state does make provision, such provision should not be made on a discriminatory basis, contrary to Article 14.

A number of applications have been made by the parents of children with special educational needs, but these have not been successful, Strasbourg refusing to interfere with the assessments made by the state.[130] Thus, a claim by parents of a severely disabled child for a place in a mainstream school was denied.[131] The Commission held that, notwithstanding that a parent's claim was based on their philosophical convictions, the local education authority "had a discretion on financial grounds to refuse to provide special facilities . . . in a mainstream school".[132] Similarly, the parent of a dyslexic child could not insist on special, rather than mainstream, schooling.[133]

Finally, it should be noted that the United Kingdom has entered a reservation to Article 2, to the effect that:

> "the principle affirmed in the second sentence of Article 2 is accepted . . . only in so far as it is compatible with the provision of efficient instruction and training, and the avoidance of unreasonable public expenditure".[134]

The legal effect of this reservation is within the jurisdiction of Strasbourg and it should be noted that under the Convention, Article 57 (formerly Article 64) permits reservations on signing the Convention to the extent that any law "then in force in [the state's] territory" is not in conformity with the provision. It is thus a transitional provision. However, in view of the weak nature of the case law under this article, it seems unlikely that objection would be taken to the reservation.

LIMITATIONS AND THE MARGIN OF APPRECIATION DOCTRINE

Articles 8 to 11 have been drafted in such a way that the first paragraph sets out the right to be secured and the second, or qualifying paragraph, enumerates the grounds upon which the right may be limited or subject to interference by the state. The structure of the qualifying paragraphs is identical, although there are differences in detail. It is through the interpretation of the qualifying paragraphs that Strasbourg has sought to achieve a balance between rights that may on

---

[130] For a review of the authorities see A Bradley, "Scope for Review: The Convention Right to Education and the Human Rights Act 1998", [1999] *EHRLR* 395 at 396.

[131] *PD* v. *United Kingdom* (1989) 62 D & R 292.

[132] Bradley, *supra* n.130 at 404.

[133] *Simpson* v. *United Kingdom* (1989) 64 D & R 188, cited by Bradley, *ibid.*

[134] Bradley, *ibid.* at 398.

occasion conflict,[135] and also between the needs of the individual and the needs of the wider community.[136] Although originally applied in the context of derogations under Article 15, it is in connection with permitted limitations on the rights set out in Articles 8 to 11 that Strasbourg has developed a substantial "margin of appreciation" jurisprudence. This means that in certain circumstances the Court and Commission have deferred to the state's assessment of the necessity for interfering with a Convention right, while insisting that Strasbourg nevertheless retains a supervisory jurisdiction over state activity (or non-activity). Although Strasbourg itself has always stressed that legal rules should be sufficiently clear that individuals can adjust their behaviour appropriately, the margin of appreciation doctrine, while arguably leading to a flexible and nuanced application of the Convention, tends to promote uncertainty; this uncertainty may be even more acute in the context of "positive obligations". The scope of the margin of appreciation allowed to the state is variable depending upon the nature of the interest at stake and the grounds for interfering with that interest. The doctrine makes it very difficult to predict outcomes. Janis, Kay and Bradley have observed that:

> "The numerous factors surveyed which have the capacity to widen or narrow the margin of appreciation may appear in multiple combinations with unpredictable results".[137]

They cite as an example the Court's decision in *Smith and Grady* v. *United Kingdom*,[138] where the applicants challenged the policy of excluding homosexuals from the armed forces. There were two forces pulling in opposite directions: on the one hand it is well-established that a state is accorded a wide margin of appreciation in matters of national security; on the other, the application concerned a most intimate aspect of private life and particularly serious reasons by way of justification are required.[139] What the Court did was to state "these two opposite influences" and then "make an *ad hoc* evaluation of the strength of each of the state's claimed justifications".[140]

The following discussion will take the reader through the steps taken in order to assess whether a limitation on a right is consistent with Convention obligations. In order for a state to establish that a limitation is permitted under the Convention three things must be established:

---

[135] For example, the Article 10 right to freedom of expression may have to give way to the Article 9 right to freedom of religion. In *Otto-Preminger Institut* v. *Austria* Series A no 295A (1994), the applicant cinema club failed in their complaint that the seizure of a film violated Article 10: the Court held that it was necessary in a democratic society to seize the film in order to protect the religious feelings of others (Roman Catholics in the Tyrol area) under Article 9.

[136] *Powell and Rayner* v. *United Kingdom* Series A no 172 (1990).

[137] M Janis, R Kay and A Bradley, *European Human Rights Law Text and Materials*, 2nd edn (Oxford, Oxford University Press 2000) at 163.

[138] *Supra* n.84.

[139] *Dudgeon* v. *United Kingdom*, *supra* n.15.

[140] Janis, Kay and Bradley, *supra* n.137.

(1) the limitation is "in accordance with" (Article 8) or "prescribed by" (Articles 9, 10 and 11) law;
(2) the limitation pursues a legitimate aim; and
(3) the limitation is "necessary in a democratic society".

With regard to (1), although there is a difference in drafting between Article 8 and the other personal freedom articles, in *Malone v. United Kingdom*,[141] the Court stated that both formulations should be given the same interpretation. For an interference to be "in accordance with the law", it is necessary that there should be legal provision, which may be contained in either written or unwritten law.[142] In *Sunday Times v. United Kingdom*, the Court held that "prescribed by law" means that:

"First, the law must be adequately accessible: the citizen must be able to have an indication that is adequate in the circumstances of the legal rules applicable to a given case. Secondly, a norm cannot be regarded as 'law' unless it is formulated with sufficient precision to enable the citizen to regulate his conduct: he must be able—if need be with appropriate advice—to foresee, to a degree that is reasonable in the circumstances, the consequences which a given action may entail. Those consequences need not be foreseeable with absolute certainty: experience shows this to be unattainable. Again, whilst certainty is highly desirable, it may bring in its train excessive rigidity and the law must be able to keep pace with changing circumstances. Accordingly, many laws are inevitably couched in terms which, to a greater or lesser extent, are vague and whose interpretation and application are questions of practice".[143]

In the *Sunday Times* case, the Court found that the common law offence of contempt of court was formulated with sufficient precision[144] to enable the applicants to make an assessment of the consequences that publication in violation of an injunction would entail. However, the injunction to prevent the *Sunday Times* from publishing an article concerning the research, testing, manufacture and marketing of the drug Thalidomide by Distillers was found to violate the Article 10 right to freedom of expression because it was disproportionate to the aim pursued. In *Malone v. United Kingdom*, the Court addressed the quality of domestic law, stating that the law:

"should be compatible with the rule of law, which is expressly mentioned in the Preamble to the Convention. The phrase thus implies—and this follows from the object and purpose of Article 8—that there must be a measure of legal protection in domestic law against arbitrary interferences by public authorities with the rights safeguarded by paragraph 1".[145]

---

[141] *Supra* n.83.
[142] *Sunday Times v. United Kingdom, supra* n.2.
[143] *Ibid.* at para. 49.
[144] Although the Phillimore Report had acknowledged that there was "a lack of clear definition of the kind of statement, criticism or comment that will be held to amount to contempt" (Cmnd. 5794, 1974).
[145] *Malone, supra* n.83 at para. 67.

The second hurdle that the state must surmount is that of demonstrating that any limitation on a right pursues one of the aims laid down in the second paragraphs of Articles 8 to 11. In this regard, the test applied by Strasbourg appears to be subjective: did the relevant authority at the date of the interference intend to pursue a particular aim. Unless there is anything to suggest that another purpose was pursued the government's explanation will be accepted. Whether in fact the aim of action taken to limit a Convention right is supportable is in any event implicitly assessed at the third stage of the Court's inquiry: whether the action taken was necessary in a democratic society.

In order for the state to satisfy the third requirement of "necessary in a democratic society" it must satisfy two conditions: first, the interference complained of must correspond to a "pressing social need" and, secondly, the interference must be proportionate to the aim pursued.[146] It is in relation principally to the first of these requirements that Strasbourg has developed its margin of appreciation doctrine, and the degree of the margin available will depend upon the particular aim in question. Two examples from the jurisprudence will illustrate the point.

In *Handyside* v. *United Kingdom*,[147] the applicant was the publisher and distributor of *The Little Red Schoolbook*, which contained advice aimed at teen-aged schoolchildren, including advice on matters sexual and drugs-related. The book had been prepared with the help of children and schoolteachers and had been distributed widely in Western Europe, having first been published in Denmark. Upon publication in England, the applicant was convicted of violating the Obscene Publications Act 1959, as amended by the Obscene Publication Act 1964, and he then petitioned the European Commission of Human Rights alleging, *inter alia*, a breach of the Article 10 right to freedom of expression. The UK government argued that the interference with Mr Handyside's freedom of expression was justified in accordance with Article 10(2) on the grounds that it was necessary in a democratic society for the "protection of morals". The Court noted that the machinery of protection established by the Convention is subsidiary to the national systems safeguarding human rights, stating:

> "The Convention leaves to each Contracting State, in the first place, the task of securing the rights and freedoms it enshrines. The institutions created by it make their own contribution to this task but they become involved only through contentious proceedings and once all domestic remedies have been exhausted (Article 35).[148] These observations apply, notably, to Article 10(2). In particular, it is not possible to find in the domestic law of the various Contracting States a uniform European conception of morals. The view taken by their respective laws of the requirements of morals varies from time to time and from place to place, especially in our era which is characterised by a rapid and far-reaching evolution of opinions on the subject. By reason of their direct and continuous contact with the vital forces of their countries, State authorities

[146] *Olsson* v. *Sweden, supra* n.88.
[147] Series A no 24 (1976).
[148] Article 35 was substituted by Protocol 11 for former Article 26.

are in principle in a better position than the international judge to give an opinion on the exact content of these requirements as well as on the 'necessity' of a 'restriction or penalty' intended to meet them. . . . 'necessary' is not synonymous with 'indispensable', neither has it the flexibility of such expressions as 'admissible', 'ordinary', 'useful', 'reasonable' or 'desirable' . . . it is for the national authorities to make the initial assessment of the reality of the pressing social need implied by the notion of 'necessity' in this context. Consequently, Article 10(2) leaves to the Contracting States a margin of appreciation".

The Court, however, went on to say that such a margin is not unlimited: indeed, if it were any protection offered by the Convention would be illusory. The final ruling as to whether a restriction or penalty is reconcilable with Convention rights is made by Strasbourg. In *Handyside*, having regard to the state's margin of appreciation, the fact that the book had circulated freely within other Contracting States did not mean that the criminal conviction in England was a violation of Article 10. Each state had fashioned their approach in the light of different views prevailing about the demands of the protection of morals. In *Handyside*, we see that a wide margin of appreciation was given to the state when making its assessment of the need to protect morals and that the state was acting within that margin when it seized the offending book.

A different conclusion was reached by the Court in the *Sunday Times* case, where the government sought to justify the imposition of an injunction to prevent publication of a newspaper article on the subject of the Thalidomide drug at a time when it was held by the House of Lords that the relevant litigation was not dormant. The government argued that the aim of the restriction under Article 10(2) was "maintaining the authority and impartiality of the judiciary". The Court examined the House of Lords' decision (*inter alia*, that by 'prejudging' the issue of negligence, publication would have led to disrespect for the processes of the law or interfered with the administration of justice, it would subject Distillers to pressure and the prejudices of prejudgment of the issues in the litigation, the danger of 'trial by newspaper') and concluded that the aim of the injunction was legitimate. However, this case was distinguishable from *Handyside* in relation to the margin of appreciation, because unlike the issue of morals, the domestic practice of Contracting States revealed a "fairly substantial measure of common ground in this area. This is reflected in a number of provisions of the Convention, including Article 6, which have no equivalent as far as 'morals' are concerned. Accordingly, here a more extensive European supervision corresponds to a less discretionary power of appreciation".[149]

The Court found that the injunction was disproportionate to the aim pursued. What we see in the *Sunday Times* case is the idea that where there is consensus between states upon a particular issue, the margin of appreciation left

---

[149] *Supra* n.2 at para. 59.

to the state will be more restricted than in cases where there is a diversity of opinion.[150]

A margin of appreciation which appears to be of an even vaguer scope is also allowed to the state in connection with the implementation of "positive obligations" which may arise under the various articles and this issue is discussed in the following section.

POSITIVE OBLIGATIONS

There is an extensive jurisprudence in relation to positive obligations upon the state and this case law was touched upon in the previous chapters[151] and is discussed in detail in Chapter 5. In a line of cases, particularly under Article 8, Strasbourg has recognised that states may have an obligation to take positive steps to make real and effective the enjoyment of the rights set out in the Convention, to the extent of regulating the conduct of non-state actors *inter se*. A right to privacy that can be asserted against a private body would derive from a positive obligation on the state to regulate the conduct of the media, for example. The issue of privacy is discussed in Chapter 7.

Strasbourg has held that in relation to certain positive obligations (including those arising under the Article 8 right to respect for private life) states enjoy a wide margin of appreciation in determining the steps a state should take to ensure compliance with the Convention.

The margin of appreciation doctrine, whether arising in connection with an "interference" with rights, or the steps required to implement positive obligations, applies to states. As *Handyside* demonstrates, the justification for the doctrine is that in certain circumstances the national authorities are best placed to assess the necessity for restrictions and limitations on rights. The margin doctrine is applied by Strasbourg to evaluate the action/inaction of the state for compliance with the Convention. As Grosz, Beatson and Duffy have stated,[152] it is not, therefore, a doctrine that can be transposed into the domestic context. However, the fact is that the application of margin doctrine has shaped the content of state obligations and to that extent the margin doctrine will impact on English courts when they take account of Strasbourg jurisprudence under section 2 of the Act. In *R v. Stafford Justices, ex parte Imbert*, Buxton LJ stated that "the doctrine of the margin of appreciation would appear to be solely a matter for the Strasbourg Court" so that "the English judge cannot therefore himself apply or have recourse to the doctrine of the margin of appreciation as implemented by the Strasbourg Court. He must, however, recognise the impact of that doctrine

---

[150] See, for example, *Sheffield and Horsham, supra* n.16, where the Strasbourg Court advised the UK government to keep under review laws relating to gender reassignment in order to keep pace with any emerging consensus.

[151] See text accompanying n.16 in Chapter 1 and nn.62–69 in Chapter 2.

[152] S Grosz, J Beatson and P Duffy, *Human Rights: The 1998 Act and the European Convention* (London, Sweet & Maxwell, 2000) at 18.

upon the Strasbourg Court's analysis of the meaning and implications of the broad terms of the Convention provisions".[153] Thus, although the margin of appreciation doctrine has no direct application in English law, when the courts adjudicate claims under section 7 of the Act, or consider the development of the common law, the doctrine will inform their reasoning. The Convention is in the nature of a Code, a statement of principles, which can only be rendered meaningful through the Strasbourg jurisprudence in which margin doctrine has had a substantial role to play.

CONCLUSION

The foregoing discussion has highlighted key principles developed by Strasbourg. English courts must seek to "bring home" these principles through the Act. As we have seen the Act creates a new remedy against public authorities, as well as preserving the right to bring other proceedings, so that claimants may seek redress with regard to the violation of Convention rights through both the statute and common law. Any possibility of double recovery is prevented by section 8(3) of the Act which requires the court to take account of any other relief or remedy granted and states that damages can only be awarded where "necessary" to afford just satisfaction. The effect of the Act is that courts and claimants are forced to adopt a bifurcated approach to the law. On the one hand, courts are obliged to act compatibly with Convention rights in their development of common law principles, and on the other Convention rights will be enforced directly against public authorities.

When this manuscript was delivered for publication, it seems that there had been little argument in English tort litigation that centred upon the substantive rights protected by the Convention, other than Articles 6 and 10. The finding of a violation of the Article 6 right of access to a court in *Osman* v. *United Kingdom* as a result of the Court of Appeal's decision to strike out the Osmans' claim has had a significant impact on recent negligence authority and the following chapter analyses the Strasbourg jurisprudence together with the reaction of English courts to it. A consistent pattern of refusal to strike out claims in negligence has emerged, notwithstanding that those claims may not have engaged Convention rights, other than Article 6. In this respect English courts overreacted to *Osman*.

The Court of Human Rights in its judgment in *Z* v. *United Kingdom* delivered on 10 May 2001 found that the decision of the House of Lords in *X* v. *Bedfordshire County Council* did not amount to a violation of Article 6. The reader's attention is therefore directed to Note on the Text where the decision in *Z* is discussed and its potential impact assessed. In future the attention of English courts will be drawn to the entire range of rights protected by the Convention as they grapple with their own obligation under section 6 of the Act.

---

[153] [1999] 2 Cr App R 276, quoted by Grosz, Beatson and Duffy, *ibid.* at 20.

4

The Duty of Care and Compatibility with Article 6 of the Convention

INTRODUCTION

THE ENGLISH LEGAL system has cast the tort of negligence in a demanding role, constituting a vehicle through which the careless behaviour of a wide range of actors may be redressed. The gatekeeper of liability is the duty of care and it is little wonder that the tort has creaked under the load. A number of problematic issues can be readily identified. English tort law has been bedevilled particularly by the fact that there has been no separate coherent system of public law. Until the advent of the Human Rights Act 1998, a claimant was required to use the tort of negligence in order to seek compensation for damage caused by the negligence of a public body. In principle, proceedings could be brought in negligence against any defendant, public or private.[1] However, the judiciary has considered that one of its primary tasks is to keep public spending within appropriate bounds and we see that many pages of the law reports have been devoted to the development of ever more elaborate devices in order to restrain the scope for recovery of compensation. Where technical legal devices have not been sufficient to contain liability, the courts have had recourse to their own notions of the dictates of public policy.

The decision of the House of Lords in *X (Minors)* v. *Bedfordshire County Council*[2] (*"Bedfordshire"*) is a good example and mirrors in terms of structure the decision of the Court of Appeal in *Osman* v. *Ferguson*.[3] In both these cases, the courts adverted to legal devices as a means of restricting liability: in *Bedfordshire*, the public law test of *Wednesbury* unreasonableness was grafted onto the tripartite *Caparo* elements of the negligence action, thus creating an additional hurdle for the plaintiff. That, however, did not assure the public body defendant of an immunity from suit, so the House of Lords decided that as a matter of policy no direct duty of care was owed by the local authority to the children. Similarly, in *Osman*, a majority in the Court of Appeal decided that there was proximity of relationship, but as a matter of policy it was decided that the police were immune from suit in negligence in relation to the investigation of crime. Those policy arguments, once recognised and given legal force by

---

[1] See text accompanying n.4 in Chapter 1.

[2] [1995] 2 AC 633.

[3] [1993] 4 All ER 344.

the higher courts, were unanswerable. Unsurprisingly, in both cases the defeated parties took their complaints to Strasbourg and the European Court of Human Rights subsequently handed down its decision in *Osman* v. *United Kingdom*[4] and the Commission has recently adopted Reports in relation to the *Bedfordshire* plaintiffs.[5]

Features of English negligence law which have caused problems for the courts have included the time-honoured common law distinction between misfeasance and nonfeasance. In principle, the tort of negligence does not compensate for failures to act/failures to confer a benefit: such rights should be negotiated for by contract. But there are exceptions, including the area of negligent misstatements, where the identification of an assumption of responsibility is crucial. Once certain claims are admitted, how then to retain intellectual coherence in tort law? The continued refusal to recognise mental distress short of injury as a legitimate head of damage in negligence is also causing difficulty for English law. All these issues, as well as the interplay between the action in negligence and other remedies, require re-evaluation in the light of the Human Rights Act and Strasbourg jurisprudence.

Consideration of the duty of care from a Convention perspective is especially mandated in the light of the important decision of the Court in *Osman*, as well as the jurisprudence which is emerging in relation to the immunity of local authorities in the proceedings before Strasbourg by the *Bedfordshire* children. It was to be expected following *Osman* that established immunities would be susceptible to attack as potential violations of Article 6 of the Convention and, unsurprisingly, in *Arthur J. S. Hall* v. *Simons*,[6] the House of Lords overturned the anachronistic immunity for advocates.

In many negligence actions the Convention will be relevant in two ways: first, the courts are responsible for delimiting the criteria for recognition of a duty of care so that, by virtue of the court's obligation under section 6 of the Act, the Article 6 right of access to a court is engaged; secondly, the damage complained of may amount to the violation of one of the other substantive rights and freedoms set out in the Convention. The remedy or remedies available in relation to any such violation will depend upon whether the defendant is a public or private defendant. If a claimant is unable to establish that a duty of care is owed because policy considerations so dictate, there may be a violation of Article 6 by the United Kingdom, brought about through the activity of the courts,[6a] as well as a violation of other substantive articles, brought about through the activity of other bodies for which the United Kingdom is responsible. It is axiomatic that it is only the state that can violate treaty obligations under the Convention. However, as we have seen,[7] a failure by the state to

---

[4] [1999] 1 FLR 193.
[5] (1999) 28 EHRR CD 65.
[6] [2000] 3 All ER 673.
[6a] But see now Note on the Text.
[7] See text accompanying nn.17–19 in Chapter 1, and Chapter 5.

control private parties in their relations *inter se* may amount to a violation of individual rights and freedoms where the relevant article casts upon the state a positive obligation to control the acts of such parties. The Human Rights Act imposes obligations upon public authorities,[8] and the definition of "public authority" includes the court.[9] This means that a claimant will have different remedies depending upon the public/non-public character of the defendant. Where a negligence action is brought against a private body/person, the claimant will argue that the courts are obliged, by virtue of section 6(1), to develop the common law to achieve compatibility with the Convention. This means that Clapham's observation (prior to the Act) regarding the impact of the Convention has even greater force:

> "private bodies may have a duty to behave in conformity with European norms as developed through the decisions of the European supranational organs. The very strength of the Convention is its ability to straddle the national and international dimensions, synthesising the international standards with national enforcement procedures".[10]

Against a public body defendant the claimant will have two arguments: first, that the relevant body has itself breached section 6(1) with the possibility of attendant liability in damages under section 8,[11] and, secondly, as in the case of the private defendant, that the court should develop principles of tort law to be compatible with the Convention. There is an important difference between the two in that the Convention does not mandate that the negligence action should be the means of achieving state compliance with Convention articles, other than Article 6, so that other effective remedies may legitimately be invoked by the courts as the means of satisfying the requirement of compatibility. As against the private defendant, there is of course no remedy available under the Act itself.

The foregoing has set out the context for discussion in the present chapter. Within this context, the analysis in the next section aims to address the following elements: (1) the decision of the Strasbourg Court in *Osman* v. *United Kingdom* and its potential impact upon the constituent elements of the duty of care; (2) the reaction of English courts to the *Osman* decision; and (3) the impact of the Convention and the Human Rights Act on heads of damage currently recognised by the tort of negligence. Thereafter, attention is drawn to Note on the Text for analysis of the repercussions flowing from *Z* v. *United Kingdom*.

BACKGROUND TO *OSMAN V. UNITED KINGDOM*

Writing in 1953, Fleming described remoteness and the duty of care as the control devices in the tort of negligence.[12] It seems incontestable that the boundaries

---

[8] Section 6, see text accompanying nn.25–49 in Chapter 2.

[9] Section 6(3), see discussion *ibid*.

[10] A Clapham, *Human Rights in the Private Sphere* (Oxford, Clarendon Press, 1993) at 9.

[11] See text accompanying n.79 in Chapter 2.

[12] J G Fleming, "Remoteness and Duty: The Control Devices in Liability for Negligence", (1953) 471 *Can BR* 31.

of negligence are now circumscribed almost entirely by the concept of the duty of care,[13] which seems in recent years to have assumed monolithic importance. If a claimant is to bring a negligence action she must first demonstrate that she was owed a duty of care by this *category* of defendant in relation to the *type* of damage suffered. It is not enough that harm has been caused to the claimant by the careless conduct of the defendant: the harm must be of such a type that is recognised by the tort of negligence and the defendant must be recognised by the law of tort as owing a duty of care. In addition, not only is the type of harm important, the manner of its occurrence (quite independent of traditional notions of causation, for example, the proximity criteria for secondary victims who suffer psychiatric damage) may also be crucial to the existence of a duty of care. Thus, despite the fact that all law students begin their studies of negligence with Lord Atkin's "general conception of relations giving rise to a duty of care",[14] the position in English law now is that there is a web of "duty-specific" rules to which reference must be made in any case to determine the existence of a duty of care. It is noteworthy that from 1985 onwards one of the most frequently cited dicta in negligence cases is the statement by Brennan J in the High Court of Australia in *Sutherland Shire Council* v. *Heyman*:

> "It is preferable, in my view, that the law should develop novel categories of negligence incrementally and by analogy with established categories, rather than by a massive extension of a prima facie duty of care restrained only by indefinable 'considerations which ought to negative, or to reduce or limit the scope of the duty or the class of person to whom it is owed' ".[15]

This approach signalled the final nail in the coffin to the application of Lord Wilberforce's statement of general principle in *Anns* v. *London Borough of Merton*.[16] The main preoccupation of the English courts in the years following *Junior Books* v. *Veitchi*[17] has been the containment of liability. The spectre of the American tort crisis[18] seems to have hovered over the English courts, albeit silent and unacknowledged.

The position has now been reached that there is no statement of general principle to determine the existence of a duty of care which is applicable to all fact situations. As is well-known, Lord Bridge having surveyed the leading authorities post-*Junior Books*[19] enunciated a three-stage evaluation for the existence of

---

[13] This is not to underestimate the important roles attributed to breach of duty and causation, particularly in the action for medical negligence: *Bolitho* v. *Hackney* [1998] AC 232 and *Wilsher* v. *Essex Area Health Authority* [1987] QB 730.

[14] *Donoghue* v. *Stevenson* [1932] AC 562 at 580.

[15] (1985) 60 ALR 1 at 43–44.

[16] [1978] AC 728.

[17] [1983] 1 AC 520.

[18] J G Fleming, *The American Tort Process* (Oxford, Clarendon, 1988).

[19] *Governors of Peabody Donation Fund* v. *Sir Lindsay Parkinson & Co. Ltd* [1985] AC 210, 239F–241C; *Yuen Kun Yeu* v. *Attorney General of Hong Kong* [1988] AC 175, 190E–194F; *Rowling* v. *Takaro Properties Ltd* [1988] AC 473, 501 D–G and *Hill* v. *Chief Constable of West Yorkshire* [1989] AC 53, 60B–D.

a duty of care in *Caparo* v. *Dickman*:[20] (1) there should be forseeability of damage, (2) proximity of relationship between the claimant and the defendant and (3) the situation should be one where the court considers it "fair, just and reasonable" to impose a duty of care. He went on to say that concepts of proximity and fairness:

> "are not susceptible of any such precise definition as would be necessary to give them utility as practical tests, but amount in effect to little more than convenient labels to attach to the features of different specific situations which, on a detailed examination of all the circumstances, the law recognises pragmatically as giving rise to a duty of care of a given scope".[21]

Much judicial thinking in cases decided subsequent to *Caparo* has focused upon the development of principles which should be applied in relation to certain categories of damage, in particular, psychiatric damage suffered by secondary victims and victims of loss which is "pure economic" not consequential upon physical injury. During the 1980s, the leading cases regarding the duty of care were very largely monopolised by pure economic loss issues; during the 1990s issues of governmental liability, particularly in the context of social welfare and education, came to the fore. During the last decade, the higher courts have revisited the issue of whether liability may attach to the negligent acts/omissions of public bodies and it is this sphere of liability which has particularly vexed the courts. A rash of cases has been brought against bodies charged with the exercise of statutory powers and duties, which were enacted in order to protect particular groups within society: thus, cases have been brought by a variety of plaintiffs in relation to the negligence of social workers, educational psychologists, teachers and the police force. Activity in the courts has been echoed by extensive work undertaken by the academic community. What is so striking about the emergence of authority prior to the decision of the Court in *Osman* v. *United Kingdom*[22] is that, despite the encouraging words of Balcombe LJ in *Derbyshire County Council* v. *Times Newspapers*,[23] the development of the law has taken place without any reference to the Convention, neither in terms of Article 6 compliance nor by reference to argument under other articles. It is as if, notwithstanding the fact that the defendants were extremely powerful public bodies and that, quite clearly, various human rights were in issue, judicial reasoning was conducted in a human rights law vacuum. Not only that, the cases which had provided the template for analysis were those in which "principles" to guide the recovery of compensation for pure economic loss had been developed, arguably an inappropriate model for claims brought against local authorities by abused children. The author has argued previously

[20] [1990] 2 AC 605.
[21] *Ibid.*
[22] *Supra* n.4.
[23] Balcome LJ stated that the Convention could be used when the common law, including the doctrines of equity, is uncertain and even where the common law was certain the courts would still, when appropriate, consider the Convention: [1992] 3 All ER 65 at 77–8.

that it would have been appropriate to consider the standards laid down by Strasbourg under the third head of *Caparo*, to determine in cases like *Bedfordshire*, whether it would be fair, just and reasonable to recognise a duty of care.[24] In his study of the "Relevance of the ECHR in UK Courts", Clapham has suggested that the blame for the sporadic and erratic use of the Convention by English courts could be laid upon the bar and Parliament. He castigated the lack of a Human Rights Commission, a lack of familiarity with the European dimension and a lurking xenophobia on the part of the English lawyer.[25] The Human Rights Act, should ensure that, in future, the human rights dimension is not overlooked.

The significance of *Osman* lay in its impact on the power of English courts to recognise immunity from suit in negligence. The next section will, therefore, examine the *Osman* decision and evaluate the reaction of English courts to it before moving on to consider the wider implications of Convention jurisprudence for the tort of negligence, as well as the function of the Human Rights Act in a negligence context.

Despite *Z v. United Kingdom*, *Osman* is a decision of unparalleled influence in recent English authority. Ironically, it was indeed this influence that indirectly enabled the Court of Human Rights to undertake its reassessment of English tort law in *Z*. According to the Court, the potential opening up of tort liability in the wake of *Osman*, meant that the court was wrong in *Osman* itself. These intellectual gymnastics and the streak of disingenuity running through *Z* are addressed in Note on the Text.

THE *OSMAN* CASE

The decision of the Court in *Osman v. United Kingdom* had its genesis in the bizarre behaviour of a schoolteacher, Paget-Lewis, who developed an obsession for a pupil, Ahmet Osman. Paget-Lewis subjected Ahmet and his family to an escalating campaign of harassment and intimidation over a period of a year which culminated in the tragic shooting and death of Ali Osman, Ahmet's father, and the wounding of Ahmet himself. A number of those incidents will be detailed in order to convey the progressive fear which built up in the Osman family and the information upon which the police could act. Prior to the shooting Paget-Lewis locked Ahmet in the classroom on the pretext of seeking instruction in Turkish; he followed the boy home from school in his car; graffiti appeared alleging a sexual relationship between Ahmet and his friend, Leslie Green, but Paget-Lewis denied responsibility; Paget-Lewis changed his name to Paul Ahmet Yildirim Osman. The police were informed of these events. Later a brick was thrown through the Osmans' window, the windscreen of Ali Osman's

---

[24] J Wright, "Local Authorities, the Duty of Care and the European Convention on Human Rights", (1998) *OJLS* 1.

[25] Clapham, *supra* n.10 at 27.

car was smashed and dog excrement was smeared on the doorstep. In December 1987, Paget-Lewis rammed a van in which Leslie Green was travelling as a passenger. Also in December 1987, when interviewed by the police, one officer later recalled that Paget-Lewis had said that he was going to do something that would be "a sort of Hungerford". There were further incidents, including the theft of a shotgun, although, at the time, that was not traced to Paget-Lewis. Finally, on 7 March 1988, Ali Osman was shot and killed and Ahmet was injured. Paget-Lewis then drove to the deputy headmaster's house and shot and injured the deputy headmaster and killed his son.

The Osmans instituted proceedings against the police force in negligence. On appeal by the Metropolitan Police Commissioner, the Court of Appeal struck out the claim as disclosing no reasonable cause of action.[26] Although a majority in the Court of Appeal (McCowan and Simon Brown LJJ) considered that the plaintiffs had an arguable case that "there existed a very close degree of proximity amounting to a special relationship", the action was struck out unanimously on the grounds of public policy which had been elaborated by Lord Keith in *Hill* v. *Chief Constable of West Yorkshire*:[27] the imposition of liability could lead to the exercise of the police function of investigation and suppression of crime being carried on in a detrimentally defensive frame of mind and there could be a significant diversion of manpower and financial resources in defending such actions, all of which would distract attention from the most important function of suppressing crime. It was, of course, unnecessary for Lord Keith to have articulated the public policy arguments, as he saw them, given that the Hill action failed for want of proximity in any event. As Tregilgas-Harvey has observed,[28] the effect of *Osman* v. *Ferguson* was to elevate the status of Lord Keith's remarks in *Hill* from *obiter* to *ratio*. Having been refused leave to appeal to the House of Lords, the Osman family petitioned the Strasbourg organs, alleging violations by the United Kingdom of Articles 2, 6 and 8 of the Convention.

The Court, after acknowledging that Article 2 obliges states not only to refrain from taking life, but also to take appropriate steps to safeguard those within the jurisdiction, found that in relation to positive obligations:

> "it must be established . . . that the authorities knew or ought to have known at the time of a real and immediate risk to the life of an identified individual or individuals from the criminal acts of a third party and that they failed to take measures within the scope of their powers which, judged reasonably, might have been expected to avoid that risk".[29]

On the facts, the Court held, by seventeen votes to three, that there was no decisive stage in the series of events when the police knew, or ought to have known, that there was a real and immediate risk to the Osman family: thus,

---

[26] *Osman* v. *Ferguson, supra* n.3.

[27] [1989] AC 53.

[28] M Tregilgas-Harvey, "*Osman* v. *Metropolitan Police Commissioner*: The Cost of Police Protectionism", (1993) 56 MLR 732.

[29] *Supra* n.4 at para. 116.

there was no violation of Article 2. The dissenting opinion of the minority on this point is trenchant. Some harm had occurred prior to the fatal attacks and by December 1997 "[the police] could have had hardly any doubts that further, more serious harm was to be foreseen".[30] Much more significantly for the development of the tort of negligence, and the duty of care in particular, the Court did find a violation of Article 6.

It will be recalled that Article 6 provides that: "In the determination of his civil rights and obligations, . . . everyone is entitled to a . . . hearing by [a] . . . tribunal". The Court recalled that Article 6 embodies the "right to a court", but that right is not absolute and may be subject to limitations, described in the following frequently-used formula:

> "these are permitted by implication since the right of access by its very nature calls for regulation by the State . . . [the Court] must be satisfied that the limitations applied do not restrict or reduce the access left to the individual in such a way or to such an extent that the very essence of the right is impaired. Furthermore, a limitation will not be compatible with Art 6(1) if it does not pursue a legitimate aim and if there is not a reasonable relationship of proportionality between the means employed and the aim sought to be achieved".[31]

The Court found that Article 6 was applicable, because it accepted the government's argument that the principle of *Hill* did not automatically doom to failure a civil action against the police for negligent conduct in the investigation or suppression of crime. Therefore, the applicants must be taken to have had a right, derived from the law of negligence, to seek an adjudication on the admissibility and merits of an arguable claim (that the duty of care criteria laid down in *Caparo* were satisfied).[32] The Court then proceeded to consider whether the restriction (the strike out procedure) was lawful.

The Court found that the restriction pursued a legitimate aim, namely, "that the interests of the community as a whole are best served by a police service whose efficiency and effectiveness . . . are not jeopardised by the constant risk of exposure to tortious liability".[33] However, the Court was less sanguine on the issue of proportionality, taking the view that the Court of Appeal had proceeded on the basis that the exclusionary rule of *Hill* provided a watertight defence to the police and that the conferment of immunity, without inquiry into public policy arguments which pull in the other direction, amounted to an unjustifiable restriction on the applicant's right to have a determination on the merits of his

---

[30] Partly dissenting, partly concurring opinion of Judge de Meyer, joined by Judges Lopes Rocha and Casadevall who found that Articles 2 and Article 8 had been violated by the failure of the authorities "to do what they should have done". See also the Court of Appeal decision, *supra* n.3, regarding the reference to the meeting at which a police officer recalled the threat by Paget-Lewis to "do a Hungerford". The Commission in its fact-finding capacity stated that it preferred to place greater weight on the contemporaneous notes of the relevant meeting, where it was reported that Paget-Lewis had stated that he would not do a Hungerford: *Osman, supra* n.4 at para. 70 .

[31] Citing *Tinnelly & Sons Ltd and McElduff v. United Kingdom* (1998) 27 EHRR 249.

[32] *Osman, supra* n.4 at para. 139.

[33] *Ibid.* at paras 149–50.

or her claim in deserving cases. The requirement of proportionality meant that the Court should examine the scope of the rule as applied in the specific factual context. The Court considered that the fact that the applicants were claiming: an alleged failure to protect the life of a child, that the failure was the result of a catalogue of acts and omissions which amounted to grave negligence as opposed to minor acts of incompetence, that the police had assumed responsibility for their safety and that the harm sustained was most serious, meant that there must be a hearing on the merits.[34] If such competing policy considerations are not considered "there will be no distinction made between degrees of negligence or of harm suffered or any consideration of the justice of a particular case".[35] The need to balance individual and community interests is a constant thread which runs through all Convention jurisprudence: in *Fayed* v. *United Kingdom*, the Court described its task as that of "striking a fair balance between the demands of the general interest of the community and the requirements of the protection of the individual's fundamental rights".[36]

The Court's decision, as predictable though it was from a reading of that Court's previous jurisprudence, was not greeted with unalloyed pleasure by the English judiciary. In his essay on "Human Rights and the House of Lords", Lord Hoffmann railed against the submersion of "our own hierarchy of moral values, our own culturally-determined sense of what is fair and unfair . . . under a pan-European jurisprudence of human rights".[37] Perhaps not surprisingly, given the tone of English authority on governmental liability at that time, Lord Hoffmann located the Court of Appeal decision in *Osman* v. *Ferguson* with other decisions in which the courts have denied a duty of care on the ground that a failure to receive a benefit should not entitle a person to compensation which will be borne by the public purse and he declared:

> "The social justification for such a rule is that, on the one hand, the person who has failed to receive the benefit is no worse off than if it had not been provided in the first place, and on the other hand, the budgetary and efficiency grounds discussed in *Hill* v. *Chief Constable of West Yorkshire*".[38]

There are two problems with Lord Hoffmann's analysis. First, whilst his reasoning reflects the traditional stance of the common law that there can be no liability for omissions, such an approach is at odds with Strasbourg jurisprudence which admits of "positive obligations" upon states. In *Osman* v. *United Kingdom*, the applicants' arguments before Strasbourg proceeded on the basis that the United Kingdom had failed in its obligation to protect the life of Mr Osman and his son. The Court noted that the first sentence of Article 2(1)[39]

---

[34] *Ibid.* at paras 152–3.

[35] *Ibid.* at para. 151.

[36] Series A no 294-B (1994) at para. 65.

[37] See Rt Hon Lord Hoffmann, "Human Rights and the House of Lords", (1999) 62 *MLR* 159 at 165 and Lord Browne-Wilkinson in *Barrett* v. *Enfield London Borough Council* [1999] 3 WLR 79 at 84.

[38] Lord Hoffmann, *ibid.* at 163.

[39] "Everyone's right to life shall be protected by law . . .".

"enjoins the State not only to refrain from the intentional and unlawful taking of life, but also to take appropriate steps to safeguard the lives of those within its jurisdiction (see the *LCB* v. *UK* judgment of 9 June 1998)".[40] This duty may in "well-defined circumstances" extend beyond the provision of effective criminal laws to "preventive operational measures to protect an individual whose life is at risk from the criminal acts of another".[41] States are required to take steps to secure the rights and freedoms set out in the Convention and effective implementation of those rights and freedoms may in some instances require positive action by states in relation to conduct by non-state parties. A failure to take positive steps may constitute a violation of the relevant substantive article, as well as Article 13 (the right to an effective remedy). There is, arguably, a fundamental tension between the individualism of the common law and the values of the Convention, which are premised upon the basis that some people may need protection from the actions of others and it is the duty of the state in some circumstances to ensure that they get the protection they need.[42] The next chapter examines the general principle of tort law that there can be no liability for an omission for its compatibility with the Convention and related jurisprudence.

Secondly, to group all cases which have been brought against public authorities together, as Lord Hoffmann does, to speak of *X (Minors)* v. *Bedfordshire County Council* and *Murphy* v. *Brentwood London Borough Council*[43] in the same breath, and without making any distinction between them, loses sight of the fact that the harm suffered by the respective plaintiffs was of a very different type, ranging from damage to bodily and mental integrity to pure economic loss. The nature of the statutory responsibility imposed on the defendants in each case was different also. In the *Bedfordshire* example, the local authority was charged with procuring the welfare of the most vulnerable members of society. It is this insensitivity to the interests of claimants and the degrees of culpability of defendants which offends Strasbourg principles. The importance of considering each case on its own facts and examining claims through the lens of proportionality, rather than applying arbitrary rules which are not fact sensitive, has been emphasised by the Commission on Human Rights in its Report on the application by the Bedfordshire children to Strasbourg. The Commission's Report is discussed below.

Although causing something of a furore, the decision in *Osman* was readily to be predicted[44] in the light of a trilogy of earlier decisions: *Ashingdane* v. *United Kingdom*,[45] *Fayed* v. *United Kingdom*[46] and *Tinnelly & Sons Ltd and McElduff* v. *United Kingdom*.[47] In *Ashingdane*, the applicant wished to

[40] *Supra* n.4 at para. 115.

[41] *Ibid.*

[42] See for example *Lopez Ostra* v. *Spain* Series A no 303-C (1995); *X and Y* v. *The Netherlands* Series A no 91 (1985); text accompanying n.56 in Chapter 5.

[43] [1991] 1 AC 398.

[44] See, generally, Wright, *supra* n.24.

[45] Series A no 93 (1985).

[46] *Supra* n.36.

[47] *Supra* n.31.

complain in the English courts of the failure of the Secretary of State and health authority to provide appropriate hospital care for his mental health (hospital staff at the most suitable hospital did not consider that they had the necessary resources to care for this category of offender). He was prevented from bringing an action against the Department of Health and Social Security and the local health authority by section 141 of the Mental Health Act 1959, which afforded immunity from suit, unless an act was done in bad faith or without reasonable care. Thus, the right of access to a court guaranteed by Article 6 was restricted. The Court accepted that section 141 pursued a legitimate aim, namely, to avoid the risk of those responsible for the care of mental patients being unfairly harassed by litigation. However, while that was legitimate for individuals, closer scrutiny was required regarding the immunity of the Department of Health and Social Security and the local health authority.[48] The Court found that the restriction on access to a court was not disproportionate and did not impair the very essence of the right to a court: section 141 did not prevent the applicant from bringing an action alleging negligence or bad faith. The Court was yet more explicit on the question of immunity in *Fayed*.

The context which gave rise to the *Fayed* application was the bitterly contested take-over battle for House of Fraser waged between Tiny Rowland of Lonrho Plc and the Fayed brothers, the ultimate victors. After much pressure upon the government by Lonrho, the then Secretary of State for Trade appointed inspectors[49] to investigate the affairs of the brothers and the circumstances surrounding the acquisition of the shares in House of Fraser. The inspectors concluded that the Fayed brothers had lied to the competition authorities at the time of the merger. The DTI Report was published and its findings made known throughout the UK media. The Fayeds argued that their Article 6 right of access to a court was violated because they were prevented from challenging the condemnatory findings in the Report in defamation proceedings as a result of the common law principle of privilege.

The Court addressed the requirement that a person should have a "civil right" susceptible of determination for Article 6 to be engaged. As the Commission had observed in *Ashingdane*,[50] whether a person has a civil right may depend not only upon substantive law, but also upon procedural bars. In a judgment that clearly prefigures *Osman*, the Court said:

> "Whether a person has an actionable domestic claim may depend not only on the substantive content, properly speaking, of the relevant civil right as defined under national law but also on the existence of procedural bars preventing or limiting the possibilities of bringing potential claims to court. In the latter kind of case Article 6(1) may have a degree of applicability. Certainly the Convention enforcement bodies may not create by way of interpretation of Article 6(1) a substantive civil right which has no legal basis in the state concerned. However, it would not be consistent with the rule of law in a

---

[48] *Supra* n.45 at paras 57 and 58.
[49] Under Companies Act 1985, s. 432(2).
[50] *Supra* n.45 at para. 93.

democratic society or with the basic principle underlying Article 6(1)—namely that civil claims must be capable of being submitted to a judge for adjudication—if, for example, a State could, without restraint or control by the Convention enforcement bodies, remove from the jurisdiction of the courts a whole range of civil claims or confer immunities from civil liability on large groups or categories of persons".[51]

The Court commented that it is not always easy to trace the division between substance and procedure. This difficulty is exacerbated in a system like the English common law which has been dominated by the forms of action. The Court found that the restriction on bringing a defamation action should be examined in the context of the protection of the public interest which was served by the effective supervision of public companies. The rationale for the defence of privilege was, adopting the words of Lord Denning in *Re Pergamon Press Ltd*,[52] that "Inspectors should make their report with courage and frankness".[53] Therefore, the restriction on access to a court fulfilled a legitimate aim. In relation to proportionality, the Court found that having regard to the existence of a number of procedural safeguards (the possibility of judicial review and the applicability of the rules of natural justice), there was a reasonable relationship of proportionality between the aim of protecting the public interest and the freedom to report.

Whilst there has been judicial disappointment with *Osman*, it may be ventured that *Tinnelly* is a decision that would receive judicial approval. Here, it was the action of the executive, rather than the courts, which had the effect of erecting a complete bar on access to the court. The applicants, who had been led to believe that they would be awarded certain construction contracts, complained that they were victims of discrimination on the grounds of religious belief and/or political opinion which was declared unlawful by the Fair Employment (Northern Ireland) Act 1976. In both cases the Secretary of State for Northern Ireland had issued certificates pursuant to section 42(2) of the 1976 Act to the effect that the various actions of which the applicants complained were done for the purposes of safeguarding national security. The effect of the certificates was to prevent a tribunal from determining the complaints. The Strasbourg Court acknowledged the importance of security considerations and of the need to "display the utmost vigilance in the award of contracts for work involving access to vital power supplies or public buildings",[54] but said that having regard to the principles developed by the court, the issuing of the certificates must be scrutinised to check the proportionality of this response to the concerns for national security. The Court concluded that the certificates were a disproportionate restriction on the right of access to a court: the right guaranteed "cannot be displaced by the *ipse dixit* of the executive".[55] The Court noted that

[51] *Supra* n.45 at para. 65.
[52] [1971] 1 Ch 388.
[53] *Supra* n.45 at para. 70.
[54] *Supra* n.31.
[55] *Ibid.* at para. 77.

in other contexts the means had been found to protect national security whilst according procedural justice to the individual.[56] The decision in *Tinnelly* is analogous to the decision of the European Court of Justice in *Johnston* v. *Chief Constable of the Royal Ulster Constabulary*,[57] where the ECJ had regard to Article 6 of the Convention in holding that the certification provisions of the Sex Discrimination Act 1976 infringed Community law. The first instance judge in *Tinnelly* was clearly unhappy with the proceedings and was unable to "dispel his own doubts about certain features of the *Tinnelly* case", but his hands were tied by the conclusive nature of the certificate. Unlike *Osman*, this decision has not been criticised by the English judiciary, the views expressed by the Court echoing the discomfiture felt by English judges in the field of administrative law, prior to the Human Rights Act. It is noteworthy that such thinking has not penetrated the field of tort despite the "public law" nature of so many recent cases.

The message for English courts from *Osman* was that in order to comply with Article 6, Convention arguments both for and against the imposition of a duty of care should be considered and given their due weight. It was no longer an option for English courts merely to toll the mantra of public policy and public finance constraints in order to deny any possibility of liability. The decision of the Court in *Osman* did not decide that the Osman family were owed a duty of care by the police; rather, that the Court of Appeal was in error in failing to give due consideration to arguments that would speak in favour of a duty of care. However, the author's view is that the inescapable conclusion is that a duty of care should have been recognised on facts such as these: it was not an untenable case and the damage complained of was extremely serious.[58] The Court intimated that liability should be confined to cases where the police "have caused serious loss through truly negligent actions".[59] There are echoes here of the "sufficiently serious" test for state liability for breach of EC law.[60] The conceptual framework employed by the Strasbourg Court is cast in terms of causation and breach: this is not surprising in view of the fact that the civil law world has recourse to these concepts in determining liability for tortious behaviour.[61]

The Commission applied the *Osman* ruling in *Z* v. *United Kingdom* (the application to Strasbourg by the abused children in *Bedfordshire*) and *TP* v. *United Kingdom* (the application to Strasbourg by the plaintiffs in

---

[56] For example, in *Johnston* v. *Chief Constable of RUC* [1986] ECR 1633, following the preliminary ruling of the European Court of Justice, the industrial tribunal took evidence from a witness in camera.

[57] *Ibid.*

[58] *Supra* n.4 at para. 142.

[59] *Ibid.*

[60] See the discussion of the appropriate threshhold for liability of public authorities by M Andenas and D Fairgrieve, "Judicial Restraint in Tortious Liability of Public Authorities and the European Influence", in M Andenas, *English Public Law and the Common Law of Europe* (London, Key Haven Publications PLC, 1998) at 285 *et seq.*

[61] See B S Markesinis and S F Deakin, *Tort Law* (Oxford, Clarendon Press 1999) at 72 *et seq* and for an interesting comparative discussion see the dissenting judgment of La Forest in *Canadian National Railway* v. *Norsk Pacific Steamship Co.* (1992) DLR 289.

M (a minor) v. *Newham London Borough Council* ("*Newham*") (appeal consolidated with *Bedfordshire*)[62] emphasising that the scrutiny of immunities
would be particularly close where what it described as the "fundamental rights"
of the applicant are involved. In relation to the exclusionary rule applied in
Bedfordshire (and *Newham*) the Commission Reports in both cases stated:

> "The Commission accepts that this restriction pursued a legitimate aim, namely, to
> preserve the efficiency of a vital sector of public service . . . However, it is not satisfied
> that it was proportionate to that aim. It notes that the exclusionary rule gave no con-
> sideration to the seriousness or otherwise of the damage or the nature or degree of
> the negligence alleged or the fundamental rights of the applicants' which were
> involved".[63]

The implications of this dictum for courts in their determination of whether
a duty of care should be recognised on particular facts is that they should consider the nature of the interest in respect of which compensation is sought, as
well as the degree of culpability of the defendant. The general approach of
English courts has been to focus on the defendant, its role and responsibility,
whether statutory or otherwise, so that where a decision to recognise a duty of
care would have an impact on public funds the courts have rejected liability. In
some cases, classification of the nature of damage has been determinative,[64] in
others the existence of policy factors argued against a duty of care.[65] Claims
brought against local government bodies over the last twenty years have concerned different types of interest, but the tendency has been to group them
together as Lord Hoffmann does in his essay. The reasoning of the House of
Lords did not address the fact that fundamental rights were at stake. The
requirement of proportionality requires courts to be sensitive to the nature of
the claim: property damage is different from inhuman and degrading treatment
and pure economic loss is different from personal injury. If human rights standards are to be observed, rules should be sensitive to those differences, particularly where a public body has a statutory responsibility to protect the vulnerable
within society. *Osman* v. *United Kingdom* did not decide that the existence of a
duty of care can never be denied on the grounds of policy; rather, a court must
consider all the policy arguments, both for and against liability. *Z* and *TP* took
the matter further by making it explicit that consideration of fundamental rights

---

[62]   *Supra* n.2.

[63]   Application no 29392/95, *supra* n.5, and Application no 28945/95, Reports of the Commission
adopted 10 September 1999 at paras 114 and 91 respectively. The Commission decided that there
had been violations of Article 6 in both *Z* and *TP* (only in relation to the child), but there was a significant difference in the voting numbers in each case. In the *Bedfordshire* application there was a
unanimous vote that Article 6 was violated, whereas in *Newham* the conclusion of a violation was
by only ten votes to nine. The difference is explicable, taking account of the proportionality arguments described above, by the fact that in *Bedfordshire* the Commission concluded unanimously
that the United Kingdom had failed in its positive obligation under Article 3 of the Convention to
provide adequate protection against inhuman and degrading treatment.

[64]   *Murphy* v. *Brentwood London Borough Council*, *supra* n.43.

[65]   See Lord Browne-Wilkinson in *Bedfordshire*, *supra* n.2 and Wright, *supra* n.24.

is essential for the requirements of Article 6 to be satisfied. In other words, denial of a duty of care and a decision to strike out a pure economic loss claim on *Caparo* type facts is more unlikely to fail the proportionality test. The Strasbourg jurisprudence (prior to judgment in *Z*) did not say that strike out orders could never be made; rather, courts should be sensitive to the interests damaged and the rights (other than Article 6) engaged. Each case should be scrutinised on its particular facts to strike a fair balance between the demands of the general interest of the community and the requirements of the individual's fundamental rights.

In considering the adequacy of alternative remedies, the Commission held that:

> "the possibility of applying for an investigation by the ombudsman does not provide the applicants with adequate, alternative means of obtaining redress in respect of their claims. It does not provide any enforceable right to compensation in respect of the damage suffered, the ombudsman having only recommendatory powers. As held in [*Osman* v. *United Kingdom*] the applicants were entitled to have the local authority account for its acts and omissions in adversarial proceedings".[66]

In contrast, it will be recalled that in *Ashingdane*, where the Court did not find against the United Kingdom under Article 6, the applicant could have brought a negligence action against the mental health authority concerned. Thus, the restriction on access to the court was not disproportionate and did not therefore impair the very "essence of the right". At the time that these proceedings were argued before Strasbourg, there was no cause of action, other than negligence, by which an enforceable right to compensation could be obtained. This has now changed, by virtue of section 8 of the Human Rights Act, which provides an alternative vehicle through which compensation may be sought and through which the public authority can be required to account for its actions. It might reasonably be anticipated that in future, the government, if defending similar applications under Article 6 in Strasbourg, and public authority defendants in domestic negligence proceedings, will argue that to recognise a common law duty of care would be otiose.[67]

In the light of the previous discussion, it was to be expected that other areas of immunity would be scrutinised closely in order to avoid a breach of the standards developed by Strasbourg under Article 6. As we have seen, to comply with Article 6, any restriction on the right of access to a court must pursue a legitimate aim and the means employed to do so must be proportionate to that aim. One of the most obvious areas of tort law which called for Convention scrutiny was the immunity of advocates,[68] and this issue is addressed in the following

---

[66] *TP* v. *United Kingdom, supra* n.63 at para. 92 and *Z* v. *UK, supra* n.63 at 115. Likewise, see Lord Slynn in *Barrett* v. *Enfield London Borough Council* [1999] 3 WLR 79 at 94 who said: "Nor do I think that the remedies accepted to be available in *Bedfordshire* . . . are likely to be as efficacious as the recognition by the court that a duty of care is owed at common law".

[67] See text accompanying n.116 in Chapter 2.

[68] See also Courts and Legal Services Act, s. 62 which extended the immunity to non-barrister advocates.

section which evaluates the reaction of English courts to *Osman* in negligence actions more generally.

THE IMPACT OF *OSMAN* ON ENGLISH COURTS

What *Osman* has done is to change the climate of negligence litigation, which until the Strasbourg Court's decision had been pro-public body defendant, at the expense of individualised justice. This view is supported by a general emerging trend in recent House of Lords' decisions in negligence (admittedly, largely, but by no means always, in the context of strike-out applications) that suggests that the boundaries of negligence may be about to expand, both in terms of recognised harms and also defendants susceptible to positive findings of liability. Broadly, it may be said that for the first time since the era of *Junior Books* v. *Veitchi*, the House of Lords is adopting a more pro-claimant stance, with Lord Slynn being particularly influential. On the other hand, some members of the Court of Appeal appear to have engaged in a rearguard action to fend off the inevitable consequences of *Osman*, through the deployment of the proximity element, as opposed to utilising policy considerations under the umbrella requirement of "fair, just and reasonableness". As the following discussion demonstrates, though, the House of Lords has not been amenable to these arguments and has favoured the possibility for claimants to take their arguments through to full trial. All of the decisions discussed in the next section were handed down during the period between judgment in *Osman* v. *United Kingdom*, and 2 October 2000, the date the Human Rights Act came into force. The impact of the Act on the availability of the negligence action as a remedy against a public authority can, therefore, only be a matter of conjecture.[69]

While commonly attributed to the House of Lords decision in *Rondel* v. *Worsley*,[70] advocates enjoyed immunity for their conduct in performing their duties in court for more than two centuries.[71] In *Saif Ali* v. *Sydney Mitchell*, Lord Diplock emphasised two reasons for the immunity (he rejected the argument put forward in *Rondel* that in the absence of immunity there would be a potential conflict of interest between the advocate's duty to the court and his duty to the client): first, barrister's immunity is part of the immunity from civil liability which attaches to all persons who participate in judicial proceeding in the interests of public policy to ensure that trial are conducted without avoidable stress and tensions of alarm and fear; secondly, there is the need to maintain the integrity of public justice which requires that there should not be collateral attacks on the correctness of a subsisting judgment by retrial of the same issue.

---

[69] See text accompanying n.116 *et seq* in Chapter 2. See Note on the Text.
[70] [1969] 1 AC 191.
[71] S Williams, "Immunity in Retreat", (1999) 2 *PN* 15.

The House of Lords finally despatched the immunity of advocates in both civil and criminal proceedings in *Arthur J. S. Hall* v. *Simons*.[72] The decision is to be welcomed, for there can be no justification for singling out one professional body and giving it special treatment to the detriment of those using the service. The principal cogent argument used to support the immunity is that it is needed to prevent collateral attacks on decisions in civil and criminal cases, but the House was satisfied that this aim is served by the existing jurisdiction to strike out a civil challenge to a criminal conviction as an abuse of process. Likewise, the principles of *res judicata*, issue estoppel and abuse of process satisfied concerns regarding collateral attacks on civil proceedings. The effect of removing the immunity is that public policy will not a bar a negligence claim where a person has succeeded in having a criminal conviction set aside.

The House was much influenced by empirical evidence from Canada, which had rejected the immunity,[73] and which demonstrated that fears that the possibility of actions in negligence against barristers would tend to undermine the public interest are unnecessarily pessimistic. It will be recalled from the discussion in Chapter 2 that the compatibility of immunity with Article 6 was considered only by two of the three Law Lords who dissented. Thus, Lord Hope and Lord Hutton, who both decided that the core immunity in criminal cases should remain, recognised that any continuation of immunity should satisfy the demands of Article 6. Lord Hobhouse considered that the question of advocate immunity must be examined for compatibility with Article 6 as interpreted in *Ashingdane*, since that case concerned a true immunity, rather than the public policy limitation on the scope of the duty of care which led to the complaint in *Osman* v. *United Kingdom*. This statement is puzzling since the standards against which either an immunity or a limitation on the duty of care are measured are the same: as demonstrated above, *Osman* v. *United Kingdom* is an application of the *Ashingdane* principles. However, he concluded that these criteria are "similar to and no more rigorous than those applied under English law", namely the immunity must pursue a legitimate aim and satisfy the proportionality principle.

Lord Hope spoke of the risk that the advocate's independent judgement would be influenced by the fear of litigation to the detriment of the efficient administration of justice and that removal of the immunity would be bound to "to have some effect on the performance of their functions by advocates". He expressed concern in particular that advocates would adopt a defensive approach. Regarding proportionality, there are various mechanisms available to redress miscarriages of justice: the availability of compensation under section 133 of the Criminal Justice Act 1988 and advocates are subject to professional disciplinary procedures. Therefore, Lord Hope concluded that the immunity in criminal cases did not significantly disadvantage the client. Lord Hutton spoke

---

[72] *Supra* n.6.
[73] *Demarco* v. *Ungaro* (1979) 95 DLR (3d) 385.

of his "perception" that counsel who defend in criminal proceedings "are at a greater risk of harassment from vexatious actions than counsel who appear in civil proceedings because the 'unpleasant, unreasonable and disreputable persons' [described by Lord Pearce in in *Rondel* v. *Worsley*] are more likely to be defendants in criminal cases than civil cases".[74] For Lord Hobhouse, it would be invidious to single out one of the participants at trial, when all others are in the public interest immune. The appropriate way of disputing a criminal conviction is through the appeal process itself.

Lord Millett, alone of the majority, stated that a blanket professional immunity would be hard to defend in terms of the Convention and that he could find no compelling reasons to support it "based on more than instinct or intuition".[75] That really is the nub of the problem with the minority speeches; they contain much opinion, based on matters of impression, and what is required is evidence to support that opinion. The problem for English law in seeking to uphold advocate immunity is that other Council of Europe states do not operate such a rule, so while the aim is likely to be legitimate in all probability it would be regarded as a disproportionate device. It had been observed prior to *Arthur J. S. Hall* that:

> "The signs are that Strasbourg, again, may remind us that Continental European advocates are also subject to duties towards their courts and judges along with their duties to their clients. Their potential liability for negligent conduct has not caused them to be less honest, less forthright, or less effective than our barristers; and compulsory insurance has ensured they have not suffered financial ruination as a result of a liability rule".[76]

It might be argued that it is inapposite to compare the English position with countries which have an "inquisitorial" tradition of trial procedure, that it is necessary that the advocate who leads the case before the court should not be haunted by the spectre of liability. Two responses may be made: first, and principally, other common law systems function perfectly well without such protectionism and, secondly, we live in an age of legal convergence, an example of which is the Civil Procedure Rules 1998 which will lead to far greater involvement by the court in the active management of cases. Thus, we move closer to the inquisitorial model of procedure.

The influence of *Osman* on the decision of the House of Lords in *Barrett* v. *Enfield London Borough Council*[77] is manifest, if not always explicit. In *Barrett*, the plaintiff had been placed in the care of the local authority at the age of ten

---

[74] *Arthur J. S. Hall* v. *Simons, supra* n.6 at 732.
[75] *Ibid*. at 751.
[76] B S Markesinis, J-B Auby. D. Coester-Waltjen and S F Deakin, *Tortious Liability of Statutory Bodies* (Oxford, Hart Publishing, 1999) at 80; see also the Foreword by Sir Sydney Kentridge who castigated the rule, saying that, "the manner in which South African advocates have done their duty without the benefit of absolute immunity would show how hopelessly wide of the mark were the gloomy speculations of Brett MR [in *Munster* v. *Lamb* (1883)]".
[77] [1999] 3 WLR 79.

months and remained there until he was seventeen. He claimed damages for personal injury on the basis that, as a result of the mismanagement of his childhood by the local authority, he had reached adulthood with deep-seated psychological and psychiatric problems. By the time he was seventeen the plaintiff had had nine unsuccessful placements and he argued that if the defendants had not breached the duties which lay upon them, he would not "on the balance of probabilities have left the care of the local authority as a young man of 18 years with no family or attachments whatsoever, who had developed a psychiatric illness causing him to self-harm and who had been involved in criminal activities".[78] The House of Lords upheld the plaintiff's appeal against the Court of Appeal's decision to strike out the claim as disclosing no reasonable cause of action. The leading speech in *Barrett* was given by Lord Slynn, but Lord Browne-Wilkinson's views are highly significant because they articulate the influence of *Osman* and also because it was Lord Browne-Wilkinson who had given the leading speech, for a unanimous House, in *Bedfordshire*, where the possibility of liability was denied. It will be recalled that in *Bedfordshire*, the House of Lords held that five children who had been physically and psychologically abused by their parents were not owed a duty of care by the local authority responsible for their care. A range of policy arguments were arrayed including the fear of defensive practice and vexatious and costly litigation.

Lord Browne-Wilkinson remarked that there had been two developments since *Bedfordshire* that militated in favour of a different answer in *Barrett*. First, the Court of Appeal had denied in *Phelps* v. *Hillingdon London Borough Council*[79] that a plaintiff could recover damages from the local authority for the negligent failure of an educational psychologist to identify dyslexia. It will be recalled that in the *Dorset* case (appeal consolidated with *Bedfordshire*),[80] Lord Browne-Wilkinson had decided that the local authority did owe a duty of care to the plaintiff with regard to the provision of an educational psychology service. As His Lordship was at pains to point out in *Barrett*, this finding had been based upon a mistaken assumption of fact, namely, that such a psychology service was offered directly to the public in much the same way as a hospital opens its doors to the public. However, this error was corrected by the Court of Appeal in *Phelps* where the evidence proved that the psychology service was established to advise the local authority. What *Phelps* demonstrated was "how important it is to decide these cases on actual facts and not on mistaken hypotheticals".[81] The inference to be drawn is that where there is doubt a case should proceed to trial.

Secondly, the Strasbourg Court had decided *Osman*, and in view of that decision it was "difficult now to foretell what would be the result in the present case

[78] *Ibid.* at 87 per Lord Slynn.
[79] [1999] 1 WLR 500. The House of Lords' decision in *Phelps* is discussed *infra*, text accompanying n.106.
[80] *E (a minor)* v. Dorset *County Council* [1995] 2 AC 633.
[81] Per Lord Browne-Wilkinson, *supra* n.77 at 83.

if we were to uphold the striking out order. It seems to me that it is at least prob-able that the matter would then be taken to Strasbourg". Lord Browne-Wilkinson was clearly unhappy with the *Osman* decision, which he confessed he found difficult to understand, and, echoing the spirit of Lord Hoffmann,[82] he referred to the "present very unsatisfactory state of affairs". Whilst only Lord Browne-Wilkinson adverted to *Osman*, Lord Steyn and Lord Nolan agreed with his speech.

Barrett represents something of a *volte-face* for Lord Browne-Wilkinson. In *Bedfordshire*, the House of Lords had been confronted for the first time with the question of whether a local authority owed a duty of care to children at com-mon law, concurrent with statutory obligations, and a unanimous House had no doubt that the answer was negative. Lord Browne-Wilkinson attempted to clarify when a local authority may be liable in negligence where a case involves the exercise of a statutory discretion and he stated that it must first be shown that impugned decisions (in that case whether to take children into care) are *Wednesbury* unreasonable.[83] In *Bedfordshire*, however, the House of Lords held that, even if the plaintiffs could surmount this hurdle and establish that the decisions were so unreasonable, no reasonable authority could have taken them, the claim failed because it would not be fair, just and reasonable to impose a duty of care. Lord Browne-Wilkinson then proceeded to enumerate in detail the policy factors that militated against finding a duty (for example, fear of defen-sive social work, diversion of resources, the multi-disciplinary nature of the responsibility involved).[84]

In *Barrett*, Lord Slynn, with whom Lords Nolan and Steyn agreed, distin-guished the claim from *Bedfordshire*, on the narrow ground that the policy fac-tors described by Lord Browne-Wilkinson in *Bedfordshire* did not have the same force once a child has been taken into care. The true test for liability where a statutory power is given to a local authority is

"whether the particular issue is justiciable or whether the court should accept that it has no role to play. The two tests (discretion and policy/operational) . . . are guides. . . . The greater the element of policy involved, the wider the area of discretion accorded, the more likely it is that the matter is not justiciable so that no action in neg-ligence can be brought . . . A claim of negligence in the taking of a decision to exercise a statutory discretion is likely to be barred, unless it is wholly unreasonable so as not to be a real exercise of the discretion . . . acts done pursuant to the lawful exercise of discretion can, however, in my view be subject to a duty of care, even if some element of discretion is involved".[85]

Lord Slynn held that where a child has been taken into care the test to be adopted is the three stage test of *Caparo simpliciter*.

[82] See text accompanying n.37, *supra*.
[83] Are the decisions taken so unreasonable that no reasonable authority could have reached them: *Associated Picture Houses* v. *Wednesbury Corporation* [1948] 1 KB 223.
[84] For analysis see Wright, *supra* n.24.
[85] *Barrett*, *supra* n.77 at 97.

While Lord Slynn did not expressly allude to *Osman*, it is certain from *Barrett* that strike out applications will only succeed in the very clearest cases: according to Lord Slynn "the importance of seeing in each case whether what has been done is an act which is justiciable or whether it is an act done pursuant to the exercise or purported exercise of a statutory discretion which is not justiciable requires in this kind of matter, *except in the clearest cases*, an investigation of the facts".[86]

However, commentators have observed that there may be a fundamental tension between the requirements of *Osman* (which suggests that an inquiry into the merits of a claim, which is by its nature "exceedingly fact-sensitive", is mandated where fundamental rights are in issue), and the introduction of procedural reforms designed to ensure swifter (and cheaper) justice. The Woolf Reforms, in the shape of the Civil Procedure Rules 1998, envisage a wider use of summary judgment and strike-out orders, inherent in which is "potential fact-suppression".[87]

The 'proximity requirement' and *Osman*

The cases discussed so far are all cases where the English courts have been invited to strike out/have struck out claims under the third limb of *Caparo*, that it would not be "fair, just and reasonable" to impose a duty of care. *Hill* was a case where there was found to be no proximity of neighbourhood between the police and Peter Sutcliffe's last victim, but it was the *obiter* policy considerations of Lord Keith which were instrumental in formulating the Court of Appeal decision in *Osman* v. *Ferguson*. It was the third limb and the policy arguments in *Bedfordshire* which were determinative in those cases. *Barrett*, arguably in the light of the Strasbourg Court's *Osman*, decided that the plaintiff's claim should go to full trial. It might, therefore, be tempting for defendants to shift their focus from using overt policy arguments under the third limb of *Caparo* to the second limb of "proximity", which could afford a more covert means of achieving immunity for some conduct. The question then raised is whether such a strategy may amount to the denial of access to a court and, therefore, a violation of Article 6. This debate is of more than academic interest as the following discussion will demonstrate.

As Deakin and Markesinis have observed, the notion of proximity itself is "inevitably bound up with policy issues".[88] There is no neat dividing line between the second and third limbs of *Caparo*. The factors which the courts have delineated as being requisite to fulfil the criterion of proximity are on one view indicators of the fact that it is "fair, just and reasonable" to impose a duty

---

[86] *Barrett*, *supra* n.77 at 99.

[87] A Sprince and J Cooke, "Article 6 and Immunity in Tort: Let the Facts Speak for Themselves", (1999) 15 *PN* 4.

[88] B S Markesinis and S F Deakin, *Tort Law* (Oxford, Oxford University Press, 1998) at 95.

of care. In *Elguzouli-Daf* v. *Commissioner of Police for the Metropolis*, Steyn LJ observed that "these considerations . . . inevitably . . . shade into each other".[89] Judge LJ in the Court of Appeal in *W* v. *Essex County Council* referred to the impracticality of separating out the ingredients of the duty of care and treating them as discrete compartments:

> "The continuing process of analysis and increasing refinement of these concepts can sometimes obscure the practical realities. In my judgment the question whether it would be 'just and reasonable' to impose a duty on the council and the evaluation of the claim for immunity could not properly be decided without reference to the assurances [that no child suspected of being a sexual abuser would be placed with the family]".[90]

The language used may obfuscate issues of immunity/quasi-immunity from suit, but the construction of proximity criteria frequently constitute no less of a hurdle to a plaintiff. In this regard, the classification of the damage will be crucial for a claimant: the rules developed to establish "proximity" vary depending upon whether damage is physical, psychiatric or pure economic and if the damage suffered is, in fact, grief, distress and upset there will be no claim in negligence. Therein lies the interest of the Court of Appeal decision in *Phelps* for in this decision the classification of the damage as pure economic loss was effectively determinative of the outcome. The House of Lords, in the education appeals which were consolidated with *Bedfordshire*, had not considered the nature of the damage.

In *Phelps*, the plaintiff sought damages in respect of the failure of an educational psychologist to diagnose dyslexia. Stuart-Smith LJ gave the leading judgment and the first question he sought to answer was what precisely was the nature of the damage suffered by Pamela Phelps? The trial judge had found that the claim for psychiatric injury was not made out and that claims for loss of confidence, low self-esteem, embarrassment and social unease were not matters that sounded in damages. However, he was prepared to regard the failure to mitigate the consequences of a congenital defect as "injury" which sounded in damages. Stuart-Smith LJ did not agree:

> "Dyslexia is not itself an injury and I do not see how failure to ameliorate or mitigate its effects can be an injury . . . But in my judgment . . . that is not conclusive of the fact that damages are irrecoverable. Damages for economic loss are recoverable in tort provided there has been an assumption of responsibility to protect the plaintiff from the type of loss sustained".[91]

On the facts, there was no such assumption of responsibility: the educational psychologist was retained to advise the school and the local education authority. The fact that the plaintiff was the object of that advice did not amount to such an assumption. Mr and Mrs Phelps had not apparently met the educational

[89] [1995] QB 335 at 349.
[90] [1998] 3 WLR 535 at 559.
[91] *Supra* n.79 at 433.

psychologist and she was discharging her duty to the defendants. Stuart-Smith LJ went on to hold that in any event it would not be fair, just or reasonable to impose a duty of care on the educational psychologist for the same reasons that the House of Lords denied any direct duty of care owed by the local education authority in *Bedfordshire*. Stuart-Smith LJ was particularly concerned that the decision in *Bedfordshire* should not be circumvented by the device of vicarious liability. It may be observed, though, that Lord Browne-Wilkinson took the view in *Bedfordshire* that "in almost every case . . . there will be an alternative remedy by way of a claim against the authority on the grounds of its vicarious liability for the negligent advice on the basis of which it exercises its discretion".[92]

In terms of compliance with the Convention, it could be argued that matters not whether a restriction on access to the court through a refusal to recognise a duty of care is achieved through the means of the "proximity" requirement, by the setting of highly restrictive criteria, for example, or by way of answering the question of whether it is "fair, just and reasonable" to impose a duty of care in the negative. It may be that "policy" factors that supposedly argue in favour of immunity will be given more explicit consideration[93] under the third head of *Caparo*, but it will be recalled that the proximity criteria first shaped by Lord Wilberforce in *McLoughlin* v. *O'Brien*,[94] were designed to stem the perceived flood of claims that might eventuate in the absence of strict guidelines regarding which secondary victims could claim damages for nervous shock. The same considerations prompted the development of proximity criteria in relation to pure economic loss claims.

In *G* v. *Bromley London Borough Council*,[95] the plaintiff appealed against the judge's decision to strike out his claim that the defendant was vicariously liable for the negligent conduct of the headteacher and teachers of a special school for disabled pupils. The plaintiff suffered from Duchenne Muscular Dystrophy, a progressively degenerative disease affecting speech and movement. His case was that the teaching staff were professionally incompetent and that he had not been provided with appropriate computer teaching or aids to enable him to learn and socialise. Auld LJ giving judgment (Aldous and Gage LJJ concurring) noted that the all important thing with this disease is that as far as possible the means of communication should be preserved. The appeal was allowed, the Court of Appeal relying upon the decision of the House Lords in *Hampshire County Council* v. *Keating*[96] in which the House held that a claim against the education authority for vicarious liability in respect of the negligence of a headteacher who failed to refer a pupil for assessment of special educational needs was justiciable.

---

[92] *Bedfordshire*, *supra* n.2 at 762: see also D Fairgrieve and M Andenas, "Tort Liability For Educational Malpractice: the *Phelps* Case", (1999) 10 *KCLJ* 210.

[93] As was the case in *Bedfordshire*.

[94] [1983] 1 AC 410.

[95] *The Times*, 28 October 1999 and LEXIS transcript.

[96] Appeal consolidated with *Bedfordshire*, *supra* n.2.

More significant for the present discussion is the fact that Auld LJ acknowledged that the *Osman* decision could strike at the proximity requirement:

> "And if, as Lord Browne-Wilkinson considered in *Barrett*, at 199j–200b, the effect of *Osman* is uncertain, say in that it may also apply to the ingredient of proximity, that is a further and equally powerful reason for concluding that it is not a clear and obvious case for a striking out order".

In contrast, the Court of Appeal in *Palmer* v. *Tees Health Authority*,[97] had rejected the argument that the notion of proximity was liable to attack on the basis of *Osman* and *Barrett*. Stuart-Smith LJ interpreted *Osman* as authority for the view that it is appropriate to strike out actions on the grounds that in law proximity is not established. With respect, Stuart-Smith LJ did not quite catch the nuance of the Strasbourg Court's judgment. The Court had accepted the applicants'submission that the "combined effect of the strict tests of proximity and forseeability provided limitation enough to prevent untenable cases ever reaching a hearing"[98] and the Court went on to describe the proximity test as "a threshold requirement which is in itself sufficiently rigid [to narrow the number of negligence cases against the police]".[99] It is suggested that epithets such as "strict" and "rigid" do not sit happily with Strasbourg jurisprudence under Article 6, the effect of which is to reject arbitrary rules[100] in favour of proportionality. What the Court did not do in *Osman* is to say that the concept of proximity itself should *never* require evaluation for compliance with Article 6.[100a]

The Court of Appeal continued its restrictive approach in *Jarvis* v. *Hampshire County Council*,[101] where the plaintiff, who was described as having had "a catastrophe of an education", sought damages from the defendant local education authority for its failure to provide him with an education appropriate to his needs. The statement of claim alleged that the educational psychologist employed by the defendant owed the plaintiff a duty of care and that the defendant was vicariously liable for breaches of duty. The Court of Appeal adopted the analysis of Stuart-Smith LJ in *Phelps* and held that the failure to diagnose or ameliorate the condition of dyslexia is a claim for pure economic loss, in relation to which an assumption of responsibility towards the plaintiff must be found if a claim is to succeed. The Court of Appeal relied upon *Palmer* to the effect that "it was implicit in *Osman* v. *United Kingdom* that the court might strike out claims where in law proximity could not be established".[102] So, if proximity is to be the linchpin of the action, when would such an assumption of responsibility be demonstrated? *Jarvis* could have been distinguished from *Phelps*: in *Phelps*, neither parent could recall

---

[97] [1999] Lloyd's Rep Med 351, *The Times*, 6 July 1999.
[98] *Supra* n.4 at para. 142.
[99] *Ibid.* para. 151.
[100] See, generally, *Osman, Ashingdane, Golder, Fayed, Tinnelly, supra.*
[100a] *cf Bromiley* v. *United Kingdom* (unrep'd) and *Powell* v. *United Kingdom* (unrep'd).
[101] *The Times*, 23 November 1999.
[102] *Ibid.* at para. 57, *per* Morritt LJ.

ever having met the educational psychologist and this clearly weighed in Stuart-Smith LJ's judgment. In *Jarvis*, on the other hand, Morritt LJ acknowledged that:

"[the educational psychologist] was bound by regulation 8 to discuss Marcus's problems with his mother and ascertain her views. Once again, in accordance with the principle established in *Phelps*, I regard the allegations relied on as incapable of amounting to the assumption of responsibility alleged".[103]

It is difficult to resist the conclusion that the Court of Appeal attempted to mount an attack on *Osman* through proximity. *Jarvis* and *Phelps* were claims in relation to a failure properly to educate children with dyslexia; *Palmer*, a case of the sexual assault and murder of the plaintiff's four-year-old daughter by a known psychopath. The facts of *Palmer* were broadly analogous to *Hill*, save that the offender was known to the defendants as a patient suffering from personality disorder or psychopathic personality. Like *Hill*, though, there was nothing on the facts to single out the child as likely victim, from the general population. The effect of the Court of Appeal's view in *Jarvis* and *Phelps* is that it would be difficult to envisage circumstances in which an educational psychologist, employed by a local authority, would assume responsibility to a pupil. What factor(s) would make a difference, if meeting and discussing the child's needs with the parent does not lead to an assumption of responsibility? Stuart-Smith LJ recognised, implicitly, the difficulty in the construction of what is a de facto immunity.

In conclusion, while the *Osman* decision seemed to have "weighed heavily"[104] on the House of Lords decision in *Barrett*, the Court of Appeal evinced a scepticism that was out of tune with the changing legal culture brought about by *Osman* and the (impending) Human Rights Act. It will be recalled that both *Barrett* and *Arthur J. S. Hall & Co* were decided before the Act came into force, but both were clearly influenced by the Convention dimension. Unsurprisingly, the sceptical approach was however rejected by the House of Lords when judgment in the consolidated appeals of *Phelps*, *Jarvis* and *G*[105] was handed down.

Phelps in the House of Lords

It will be recalled that the issue in all the cases was whether a local education authority could be directly or vicariously liable for the failure to provide appropriate educational services. *Phelps* was the only case in which there had been a trial and the House of Lords reversed the Court of Appeal's decision and upheld the first instance judge's award of damages. It was held in *Jarvis* and *G* that both matters should proceed to trial.

---

[103] *Ibid.* at para. 43, *per* Morritt LJ.
[104] Pill LJ in *Palmer*, *supra* n.97.
[105] *Phelps* v. *Hillingdon London Borough Council* [2000] 3 WLR 776.

Lord Slynn and Lord Clyde gave separate speeches with which the five other members of a specially constituted House agreed. In relation to *Phelps*, Lord Slynn began by approving Auld LJ's "valuable" analysis in *G*, and his observation that "the law is on the move and much remains uncertain" and he stressed the importance of considering actual rather than assumed facts. Applying *Barrett*, he held that there was no ground for holding that Pamela Phelps's claim was not justiciable and that ordinary *Caparo* principles should be applied to determine whether there was a duty of care. Where an educational psychologist is requested to advise in relation to a particular child and it is clear that parents and teachers will follow that advice, then *prima facie* a duty of care will arise. A casual remark and an isolated act would not create sufficient nexus. Lord Slynn implicitly rejected the approach of Stuart-Smith LJ regarding assumption of responsibility and in a view reminiscent of Lord Griffiths in *Smith* v. *Eric S. Bush*,[106] he observed that, the phrase simply means that: "the law recognises a duty of care. It is not so much that responsibility is assumed as that it is recognised or imposed by the law".[107] In Lord Slynn's view, damage in the nature of loss of employment or wages through a failure to diagnose dyslexia can constitute damage recognised by the common law, even if difficult questions of causation and quantum have to be addressed.

In *G*, Lord Slynn approved the views of Auld LJ in the Court of Appeal that it would be wrong to strike out the claim because Stuart-Smith LJ's views must now be read in the light of *Barrett* and the claim in *Jarvis* should, by analogy with the reasoning in *Phelps*, proceed to trial.

Lord Clyde alone considered *Osman* explicitly, highlighting the fact that broader considerations alone of policy may not be determinative of the duty issue: regard is to be had, *inter alia*, to the gravity of the negligence and the seriousness of harm. In the instant appeals there were not sufficient grounds to exclude liability on public policy grounds alone and he took the same view as Lord Slynn that there was quite clearly proximity in *Phelps*; the appeal in *Jarvis* must accordingly be allowed.

Psychiatric damage post-*Osman*

It is noteworthy that the recent decision of the House of Lords in *W* v. *Essex County Council*,[108] also evinced a willingness to reconsider the circumstances in which a duty of care will arise, this time in the context of psychiatric damage suffered by secondary victims. The leading speech was given by Lord Slynn who omitted any reference to *Osman* and it is hard not to resist the conclusion, to adopt Craig and Fairgrieve's simile, that *Osman* was hovering over this decision "rather like Banquo's ghost".[109] It is a decision that calls into question principles

---

[106]   [1990] AC 473.
[107]   *Supra* n.105 at 791.
[108]   [2000] 2 All ER 237.
[109]   P Craig and D Fairgrieve, "Barrett, Negligence and Discretionary Powers", [1999] *PL* 626.

which have been reiterated and refined for almost twenty years, in particular by *McLoughlin* v. *O'Brien*[110] and *Alcock* v. *Chief Constable of South Yorkshire*.[111] In *W* v. *Essex*, the plaintiff parents were appealing against the decision of the Court of Appeal to uphold the first instance judge's decision to strike out their claim for damages for psychiatric injury. They had been approved as foster parents and told the council and a social worker that they were not prepared to foster any child who was known to be, or suspected of being, a sexual abuser. Despite that stipulation a fifteen-year-old boy who had been cautioned for indecent assault on his sister and who was being investigated for rape was placed with the parents. These facts were known to the council and the social worker. Within one month of placement the boy had sexually assaulted all the plaintiffs' children. When they discovered these facts the plaintiffs suffered psychiatric damage. It is apparent that these plaintiffs do not fulfil the criteria hitherto laid down for secondary victims. As Lord Slynn observed:

> " Here the parents had the necessary ties of love for their children but they were neither near enough in time or space to the acts of abuse and they did not have direct visual or oral perception of the incident or its aftermath as the House, agreeing with the speech of Lord Oliver, required that they would have to have in order to claim . . . The parents only knew about the incidents after they had happened".[112]

However, Lord Slynn proceeded to describe the complete destruction of what had been a very happy marriage and family life and observed that "the categorisation of those claiming to be included as primary or secondary victims is not as I read the cases finally closed".[113] He left open the question whether the plaintiffs might be able to establish that they were either primary or secondary victims. The influence of *Osman* is implicit when Lord Slynn describes the caution which should attend any decision to strike out: "in *Barrett* Lord Browne-Wilkinson repeated what he said in *X (Minors)* and . . . added that the development of the law should be on the basis of actual facts found at trial 'not on hypothetical facts assumed (possibly wrongly) to be true' ".

Heads of damage in negligence in the light of the Act

A case like *W* v. *Essex* highlights a particular facet of the tort of negligence which may well prove problematic in the light of the Human Rights Act and this is the refusal of the common law to grant compensation for injury which is unrelated to physical damage, except in limited circumstances. Restrictive criteria have been developed to cover secondary victims of negligence who suffer psychiatric damage, but grief, distress and what might be described as a ruined

---

[110] [1983] AC 410.
[111] [1992] 1 AC 310.
[112] *Supra* n.108 at 241.
[113] *Ibid.* at 243.

life[113a] are beyond the purview of negligence. In their seminal article in 1890, Warren and Brandeis traced the recognition by the common law and equity of a range of intangible interests.[114] Their aim, of course, was to demonstrate that the time had finally come to make explicit what had for long been implicit: that the common law recognised a right to be "let alone" or a right of privacy. Their call was heeded by American courts but fell on deaf ears as far as England was concerned. Thus, despite the fact that concepts like goodwill, confidence and reputation are recognised and protected by the common law, one's moral well-being, in the absence of actual illness or injury, is not.

It would be helpful to illustrate this discussion by looking in detail at the *Newham* case. Here, a child was removed from her mother following the erroneous assessment that she had been abused by her mother's boyfriend. This meant that both child and mother were deprived of each other's companionship for over one year, quite needlessly. However, the obvious upset and grief this would cause would not in, the absence of psychiatric injury, ground a cause of action in negligence.[115] Damage/injury to family relationships does not afford a cause of action.[116] The House of Lords denied that any duty of care was owed to either the child or her mother by the social worker and the psychiatrist to the child on two grounds: first, "the social workers and the psychiatrists were retained by the local authority to advise the local authority, not the plaintiffs . . . the fact that the carrying out of the retainer involves contact and relationship with the child cannot alter the extent of the duty owed by the professionals under the retainer from the local authority"; and, secondly, the same policy considerations that applied in the case of the five sibling *Bedfordshire* children "apply with at least equal force to the question whether it would be just and reasonable to impose such a duty of care on the individual social worker and the psychiatrist".

The applicants complained to Strasbourg that their rights under Articles 6 (access to a court), 8 (respect for family life) and 13 (right to an effective remedy) had been violated.

In relation to Article 6, the Commission concluded that the exclusionary rule applied by the House of Lords in *Bedfordshire* constituted a disproportionate restriction on the child's right of access to the court. As in the case of *Osman* and *Bedfordshire*, the applicant was entitled to have the local authority account for its actions in adversarial proceedings.

With regard to Article 8, the Commission recalled that "according to the Court's well-established case-law, 'the mutual enjoyment by parent and child of each other's company constitutes a fundamental element of family life' and domestic

---

[113a]   *cf Phelps, supra* n.105, failure to ameliorate dyslexia can constitute damage.

[114]   S D Warren and L D Brandeis, "The Right to Privacy", (1890) 4 *Harv L Rev* 193.

[115]   In fact both mother and child claimed damages for psychiatric injury. Only Sir Thomas Bingham MR in the Court of Appeal considered the problems raised for the plaintiffs by the restrictive heads of damage recognised by the tort of negligence.

[116]   The Court of Appeal held in *F v. Wirral Metropolitan Borough Council* [1991] 2 WLR 1132 that there is no tort of interference with parental rights.

measures hindering such enjoyment amount to interference with the right protected by Article 8".[117] There had been an interference with the applicants' rights
by the removal of the child from her home. However, the interference pursued a
legitimate aim, safeguarding the second applicant's health and rights (Article 8(2)).

The United Kingdom then had to show that the interference was "necessary
in a democratic society": to do this it must be shown that the interference corresponded to a pressing social need and that it was proportionate to the aim pursued. The Commission cautioned governments: "while there are no explicit
procedural requirements contained in Article 8, the case-law establishes that
where decisions may have a drastic effect on the relations between parent and
child and may become irreversible, there is a particular need for protection
against arbitrary interferences".[118] The Commission found that the initial
removal of the child was within the margin of appreciation afforded to the
authorities. However, the conduct of the authorities subsequent to the removal
of the child amounted to a violation of Article 8: the place of safety order meant
that there was a delay of one month before the mother's interests could be represented in court and there was a failure to make available information (in this
case video evidence) which would have given the mother the opportunity to
clarify the true position. The Commission concluded that "the first applicant
was not provided with a proper, fair or adequate opportunity to participate in
the decision-making procedures following the removal of the second applicant .
. . [this amounted to] a lack of respect for the family life of both applicants".[119]

In relation to Article 13, the Commission rejected the government's argument
that complaint lay to the local authority ombudsman and that a claim for criminal injuries compensation would lie: the former has power only to make recommendations and the latter would not address the failures of the local
authority. The Commission discussed the discretion which is afforded to states
in the manner that they conform to Article 13. The "scope of the obligation
under Article 13 varies depending on the nature of the applicant's complaint".[120] The more serious the allegation, the more likely that compensation
should be available. In this case, having regard to the fundamental right of
parent and child to enjoy each other's company, "the Commission [found] that
the first applicant should have been afforded the opportunity of applying for
compensation for the alleged psychiatric illness that resulted".[121]

The question then posed is: should the applicants in *Newham* seek compensation for their injuries by way of a common law claim? They do not fulfil the
criteria laid down in *Alcock*,[122] and we know from *F v. Wirral* that there is no

---

[117] *Supra* n.2 at para. 67.

[118] *Ibid.* at para. 70.

[119] *Ibid.* at para. 77. For the Court's decision, see Note on the Text.

[120] *Ibid.* at para. 99.

[121] *Ibid.* at para. 102. The second applicant's complaint under Article 13 was absorbed by the
Commission's finding of a violation of Article 6.

[122] But, see now the House of Lords' refusal to strike out the parents' claim in *W v. Essex, supra*
n.108.

tort of interference with parental rights. It will be recalled that the existence of physical/psychiatric damage is not a prerequisite for the award of compensation under the Convention.[123] Rather, it is the gravity of the interference with the right itself to which weight attaches. In a similar case, *McMichael* v. *United Kingdom*,[124] where parents were not afforded access to reports regarding their child in child care proceedings, the Court awarded compensation, notwithstanding the fact that there was no injury cognisable in English law.

The failure of English law to recognise grief/distress as a head of damage in negligence was considered recently by the Commission in *Keenan* v. *United Kingdom*.[125] The applicant's son had a history of mental illness and was serving a sentence of imprisonment. He had assaulted a police officer while in prison and as a result was put in solitary confinement in a segregation block. He committed suicide and his mother claimed a violation of Articles 2 (right to life), 3 (inhuman and degrading treatment) and 13 (no effective remedy). Her claim related to the failure of the authorities to take the appropriate steps to protect his life. This case is unusual in that there had been no litigation in the English courts. Counsel had advised that no claim lay in English law for mental distress short of injury and, therefore, no claim lay for the son under the Law Reform Miscellaneous Provisions Act 1934 and there was no cause of action open to the applicant herself. The limitations of English law were discussed by the Commission: having referred to the Law Reform Act 1934, the Commission stated that:

> "It appears that this would not have covered any claims that her son had suffered inhuman or degrading treatment insofar as this related to mental distress [as opposed to injury or aggravation to his mental illness] resulting from the conditions of his detention or that these conditions caused his death by suicide . . . the Commission considers that these proceedings, which would not have recognised any non-pecuniary damage suffered by the applicant or her son, short of physical or psychiatric injury, as founding an appropriate award of damages, did not afford effective redress in respect of her complaints".[126]

It is trite to observe that human rights law and tort law are conceptualised differently. Human rights law is about vindicating rights, the violation of which leads to harm; English tort law is about compensation for damage. The starting point is different in both spheres. In negligence the first question is whether there is a duty of care on the part of the relevant defendant in relation to the relevant harm; in the case of Convention rights the starting point is the identification of the right and consideration as to whether it has been violated. It is hardly surprising therefore that there is no equivalence between tort remedies and Convention rights.

---

[123] See text accompanying nn.107–111 in Chapter 2.
[124] Series A no 307-B (1995).
[125] Application no 27229/95, Report of the Commission adopted 6 September 1999. The Court found violations of Article 3 (inhuman and degrading treatment) and Article 13 (the right to an effective remedy), see text accompanying n.18 in Chapter 2.
[126] *Ibid.* at paras 99 and 100.

As far as the Convention is concerned, though, we have seen in Chapter 2 that there may be a violation of a human right giving rise to injury which would not be recognised as "injury" by the tort of negligence and such breach may require payment of compensation to the injured party in order to accord "just satisfaction" in accordance with Article 41 of the Convention. Article 41 of the Convention has not been given further effect by the Human Rights Act under section 1, but section 8 of the Act, which provides for the payment of damages in respect of breaches of section 6 (unlawful acts of public authorities), requires the court "to take into account the principles applied by the European Court of Human Rights in relation to the award of compensation under Article 41 of the Convention".

As outlined in Chapter 2, the effect of the Act is that English courts are required to develop the common law so that it is compatible with the Convention. The dilemma which the courts will face will be whether to restrict the tort claim so that it continues to develop within established boundaries, so that claims for harms that are compensated by Strasbourg, but unrecognised by tort law continue to be denied by the common law. This approach may be justified where there exist alternative remedies which will satisfy the obligations of Article 13 (the right to an effective remedy). This dilemma will not apply with the same force where a damages claim can be brought against a defendant under the Act, ie an action is brought against a public body for failure to comply with the Act.[127] The issue, though, has now been thrown into sharp relief by the Court's decision in *Z* v. *United Kingdom*. For there will be claims for many years to come by claimants whose Convention rights have arguably been violated, but who cannot proceed under the Human Rights Act, because the impugned conduct occured before 2 October 2000 (section 22(4)).[127a]

CONCLUSION

The driving sentiment of the Strasbourg Court's judgment in *Osman* and the Commission's Reports in *Bedfordshire* and *Newham*, is that public bodies should be made accountable for their actions, especially where fundamental rights are involved. At the time that the English proceedings were determined, there was no (realistic) possibility of seeking compensation and requiring those public bodies to account for their actions apart from the action in negligence. The response of English courts to the *Osman* decision was to refuse to strike out cases, preferring instead that they should go to full trial, where argument on the merits can take place and proper consideration can be given to the public policy arguments that "pull in the other direction" (ie in favour of liability). The

---

[127] As opposed to a claim against a private body/person where the claimant's argument is that the court must act in a manner compatible with the Convention through the appropriate development of the common law.

[127a] See Note on the Text.

author is not aware of any case since *Barrett* where a decision to strike out has been upheld by the higher courts. In *L v. Chief Constable of Thames Valley Police*,[128] the Court of Appeal refused to strike out a claim in negligence against the police force by a father who had been wrongly accused of sexually abusing his child. It was held that the case should go to trial to determine whether there had been an assumption of responsibility by the police force to the claimant. The Court of Appeal had no doubt that, but for *Osman* and *Barrett*, it would be appropriate to strike out the claim.

It has been observed that the legal landscape has changed immeasurably since the decision in *Osman v. United Kingdom*. There is now the availability of a remedy against a public authority under the Act. Proceedings under the Act are less advantageous to a claimant in view of the limitation period and it remains to seen how large damages awards will be. However, in principle, there is now a remedy for the type of violation that occurred in *Bedfordshire*. It seems highly likely that in appropriate cases, public authority defendants will argue that any liability should be confined to the Act, in the hope that damages awards will be modest,[129] as well as the fact that claimants are potentially disadvantaged by the shorter limitation period.

In view of the fact also that a major preoccupation of English courts has been the containment of the floodgates of liability, confining claimants to actions under the Act may prove an attractive alternative to the possible expansion of negligence liability.[130]

---

[128] [2000] EWCA Civ 346, LEXIS transcript.
[129] See text accompanying n.122 in Chapter 2. See, however, Note on the Text.
[130] See text accompanying n.116 in Chapter 2. See, however, Note on the Text.

5

Positive Obligations, Omissions and the Convention: Should English Law Recognise a Duty to Rescue/Warn?

INTRODUCTION

T HE EUROPEAN CONVENTION on Human Rights (the "Convention") can broadly be described as enshrining the obligation of states to accord to their citizens full enjoyment of their *civil and political rights*, as opposed to economic, social and cultural rights. Civil and political rights are essentially those rights which guarantee the liberty of the citizen against unlawful and arbitrary interference from the state and the right to participate in a democratic polity. These are the rights which emerged from the natural rights discourse of the Enlightenment. Economic, social and cultural rights (for example, the rights to food, housing and work), on the other hand were borne of the later struggle between the working classes and the dominant elites, and their realisation became central to the programmes of the socialist governments of the twentieth century.[1] In the European sphere, economic and social and cultural rights are recognised and protected by the European Social Charter. However, this sphere is a much weaker normative area: there is no equivalent of the Strasbourg machinery in relation to the Social Charter and the rights themselves are drafted in terms of aims rather than absolutes. While the 1993 Vienna Declaration of the World Conference on Human Rights declared that, "all human rights are universal, indivisible, and interdependent and interrelated", and that "it is the duty of states, regardless of political, economic and cultural systems to promote and protect all human rights and fundamental freedoms",[2] the fact remains, nevertheless, that economic and social rights occupy a weaker normative area than their civil and political cousins.[3]

---

[1] For general discussion, see D J Harris, M O'Boyle and C Warbrick, *Law of the European Convention on Human Rights* (London, Butterworths, 1995), ch 1.

[2] "World Conference on Human Rights: The Vienna Declaration and Programme of Action 1993" (1993) 14 *HRLJ* 352 at para. 5.

[3] This applies in both the European and the United Nations spheres: in relation to the International Covenant on Economic, Social and Cultural Rights there is no equivalent to the quasi-judicial Human Rights Committee which is the supervisory body under the International Covenant on Civil and Political Rights and has jurisdiction to receive individual complaints where states have ratified the Optional Protocol to the International Covenant on Civil and Political Rights.

Economic and social rights are frequently perceived as raising difficult issues for states because of their financial implications: if the rights to food, health and housing are to be implemented, states must put in place programmes to ensure that these goods are delivered to their peoples. Thus, economic and social rights impose potentially onerous, positive obligations on states. In contrast, civil and political rights are sometimes portrayed as the more readily realisable because in many instances they are negative in character: they require the state not to interfere with the liberty of the citizen. In this sense, they might be described as liberties or negative rights. But, civil and political rights cost money too. The Convention guarantee in Article 6 of the right to a fair trial requires states to expend large sums in the provision of courts, judges, interpreters and legal aid, for example. Equally, there are some rights in the Convention which straddle the civil and political/economic and social boundary, for example the right to property in Article 1 of Protocol 1 and the right to education in Article 2 of Protocol 1. However, notwithstanding the principally negative nature of the rights in the Convention, in the sense that the state is required to abstain from certain forms of treatment, the Strasbourg organs have developed a body of jurisprudence the essence of which is that the state may be required to take positive steps to secure the enjoyment of a right. Article 1 of the Convention requires states to "secure" to everyone within the jurisdiction the rights and freedoms set out. This obligation to take positive steps may extend beyond situations concerning the relationship between the individual and the state[4] into areas where the state is required to act to procure that third parties behave in such a way that other citizens can enjoy the rights and freedoms set out in the Convention.[5] Thus, the notion of positive obligations as recognised by Strasbourg, encompasses two ideas: first, the state may be required to expend resources in taking positive steps to ensure that rights are effectively protected and, secondly, the state may be required to regulate conduct between non-state actors so that the rights set out are secured. In relation to the former, an example might be the provision of a particular form of policing in the face of a known terrorist threat, while an example of the latter would include privacy laws to ensure that the right to private life is respected.

This chapter will examine, first, the extent to which positive obligations (in both of the senses described above) upon states have been recognised by Strasbourg and, secondly, analyse the possible implications for tort law of such obligations against the doctrinal backdrop of the general rule of English tort law that there can be no liability for an omission. In particular, the discussion will focus on the extent to which a duty to rescue on the part of public and private actors, respectively, is recognised by Strasbourg jurisprudence and consider how such obligations may be met by English law. While *Osman* v. *United Kingdom*

---

[4] See, for example, *Marckx* v. *Belgium* Series A no 31 (1979); *Airey* v. *Ireland* Series A no 32 (1979) and *Osman* v. *United Kingdom* [1999] 1 FLR 193.

[5] *Young, James and Webster* v. *United Kingdom* Series A no 44 (1989); *X and Y* v. *The Netherlands* Series A no 91 (1985); *Plattform "Ärtze für das Leben"* v. *Austria* Series A no 139 (1988).

had a direct impact on the approach that English courts should take to ensure compatibility with Article 6, there is, generally, no prescription by Strasbourg as to the means by which rights should be protected in terms of available legal mechanisms. Thus, to the extent that positive obligations inhere in the Convention, there may be a number of ways in which that protection may be secured, of which the doctrines of tort law are one. To take an example, the Commission has held that there is a positive obligation under Article 8 of the Convention to protect a person against harassment by a non-state actor in their home.[6] The Protection from Harassment Act 1997 would arguably fulfil that obligation rather than the common law.

In the context of both public authority and private liability, the reader's attention is drawn to the discussion in Chapter 2 regarding the framework of liability established by the Human Rights Act[7] and the potential development of the common law by the court by virtue of section 6(3) of the Act;[8] it will be appreciated that the same arguments apply, *mutatis mutandis*, to the Convention obligations which are the subject of present discussion.

POSITIVE OBLIGATIONS UNDER THE CONVENTION

The notion of positive obligations under the Convention is traceable to *Marckx* v. *Belgium*.[9] The complaint in *Marckx* related to the fact that according to Belgian law, birth did not create a legal bond between a child and its unmarried mother. Under the Civil Code the mother had to follow an affiliation procedure which would result in adoption of the child. Even then, Belgian law was such that the child was excluded from full participation in family life. For example, completion of the affiliation procedure had a limited effect on the rights of the child and his mother in matters of inheritance on intestacy and voluntary dispositions. The European Court of Human Rights declared that:

"As the Court stated in the *'Belgian Linguistic'* case, the object of [Article 8] is 'essentially' that of protecting the individual against arbitrary interference by the public authorities. Nevertheless, it does not merely compel the state to abstain from . . . interference: in addition to this primarily negative undertaking there may be positive obligations inherent in an effective 'respect' for family life. This means, amongst other things, that when the State determines in its domestic legal system the régime applicable to certain family ties such as those between an unmarried mother and her child, it must act in a manner calculated to allow those concerned to lead a normal family life".[10]

---

[6] *Whiteside* v. *United Kingdom* (1994) 18 EHRR CD 126.
[7] See text accompanying n.79 *et seq.* in Chapter 2.
[8] See text accompanying n.25 *et seq.* in Chapter 2.
[9] Series A no 31 (1979).
[10] *Ibid*. at para. 31.

Further, and more significantly for the civil/political//economic/social dicho-tomy, in *Airey* v. *Ireland*,[11] the Court held that the failure of the state to afford the applicant legal aid in order to seek a judicial separation amounted to a violation of Article 8: the failure of the state to afford an accessible remedy for marriage breakdown amounted to a failure to respect her family life. The Court reiterated that there may be a need for positive action on the part of the state and elaborated further by observing that there is no watertight distinction between economic/social rights and civil/political rights:

> "fulfilment of a duty under the Convention on occasion necessitates some positive action on the part of the State; in such circumstances the State cannot simply remain passive and 'there is . . . no room to distinguish between acts and omissions' (see, *mutatis mutandis*, . . . *Marckx* . . . and the *De Wilde, Ooms and Versyp* judgment) . . . While the Convention sets forth what are essentially civil and political rights, many of them have implications of a social and economic nature. The Court therefore consid-ers, like the Commission, that the mere fact that an interpretation of the Convention may extend into the sphere of social and economic rights should not be a decisive fac-tor against such an interpretation; there is no water-tight division separating that sphere from the field covered by the Convention".[12]

In *Passanante* v. *Italy*,[13] the Commission examined the applicant's complaint that a wait of five months in order to see a hospital specialist amounted to a vio-lation of Article 8 and considered that where the state has an obligation to pro-vide health care, an excessive delay in provision by the public health service which could have a serious impact on a patient's health might raise an issue under Article 8(1). In fact, the application was declared inadmissible because there was no proof or allegation that the delay had a serious impact on the applicant's health or psychological condition.

Thus, positive obligations on the part of the state to secure "respect for pri-vate and family life" may be inherent in Article 8(1) of the Convention. As we have seen, Article 8(2) permits *interference* with the exercise of the right enshrined in Article 8(1), provided that the three strand criteria laid down are fulfilled.[14] The question arises, then, as to what limitations or justifications may be invoked by the state against an allegation that it has not fulfilled a positive obligation under Article 8(1). In *Stjerna* v. *Finland*,[15] the Court stated that the boundaries between the state's positive and negative obligations are not suscep-tible of precise definition, but in both contexts "regard must be had to the fair balance that has to be struck between the competing interests of the individual and the community as a whole".[16] It is clear that in relation to positive obliga-tions the state enjoys a wide margin of appreciation:

---

[11] Series A no 32 (1979).
[12] *Ibid.* at para. 26.
[13] Application no 32647/96.
[14] See text accompanying n.140 *et seq.* in Chapter 3.
[15] Series A no 299-B (1994).
[16] *Ibid.* at para. 38, citing *Keegan* v. *Ireland*, Series A no 290 (1994).

"... especially as far as those positive obligations are concerned, the notion of 'respect' is not clear-cut: having regard to the diversity of the practices followed ... in the Contracting States, the notion's requirements will vary considerably from case to case ... Contracting Parties enjoy a wide margin of appreciation in determining the steps to be taken to ensure compliance with the Convention with due regard to the needs and resources of the community and individuals".[17]

It may be difficult to determine whether a complaint relates to a positive obligation under paragraph 8(1) or an interference with a right set out in Article 8(1), which must then be justified under paragraph 8(2).[18] The Court has stated that the aims mentioned in the second paragraph of Article 8 may be of a "certain relevance" in striking the fair balance between the community and individuals.[19] However, as Judge Wildhaber observed in his concurring opinion in *Stjerna*, the Court has only considered the three strand criteria in relation to interferences under 8(2). Moreover, as Judge Wildhaber pointed out, the same set of facts can be classified as either an interference, and therefore a breach of Article 8(2), or a breach of Article 8(1). For example, in *Gaskin* an adult who had spent his childhood in care sought access to records of that care. A failure to grant such access could be viewed as a negative interference, whereas the duty to provide such information could be perceived as a positive obligation. There could be a material difference in outcome, given the repeated assertion that the margin of appreciation under Article 8(1) is wide, in other words the state is allowed greater latitude where reasoning is confined to Article 8(1) rather than by reference to paragraph 8(1), read with paragraph 8(2). The methodological process applied by Strasbourg to the evaluation of interferences under Article 8(2) is clear, even if the outcomes may not easily be predicted. It is submitted that there is force, therefore, in Wildhaber's suggestion that the same formula should be applied to state action/inaction under Article 8(1) as Article 8(2). Where the state seeks to justify an interference with the right to respect for private life it must surmount the three-stage test, described in Chapter 3.[20] The state must set forth: (1) a legitimate aim for the interference and (2) demonstrate that the interference was necessary in a democratic society, by showing that there was a pressing social need and that any action taken was proportionate to the aim pursued.

Both *Marckx* and *Airey* are examples of positive steps being required on the part of the state to regulate the ordering of private relationships: in *Marckx*, the enactment of laws to regulate the status of illegitimate children and in *Airey*, the possibility of procuring a decree of judicial separation. Thus, these positive

---

[17] *Johnston* v. *Ireland* Series A no 112 (1986). See also, *Abdulaziz, Cabales and Balkalandi* v. *United Kingdom* Series A no 94 (1985).

[18] See M Janis, R Kay and A Bradley, *European Human Rights Law Text and Materials*, 2nd edn (Oxford, Oxford University Press, 2000) at 246.

[19] *Rees* v. *United Kingdom* Series A no 106 (1986) at para. 37; *Gaskin* v. *United Kingdom* Series A no 160 (1989) at para. 42 and *Powell and Rayner* v. *United Kingdom* Series A no 172 (1990) at para. 41.

[20] See text accompanying n.140 in Chapter 3.

steps would impact upon the relationships between private individuals in terms of their status *inter se* and the concomitant rights and obligations arising between them.

Positive obligations may also be found where, in order to secure the rights of the individual, steps must be taken by the state to prevent third parties from interfering with Convention rights. Thus, Convention rights where implemented properly by the state may require that private parties are prevented from behaving in a manner that infringes the rights of others. If the state fails to take those steps, it will be in violation of its obligations under the Convention, although at domestic level it is the behaviour of individuals which must be restrained or punished in order for state compliance with the Convention to be achieved. The most graphic example is afforded by *X and Y* v. *The Netherlands*,[21] where, owing to a *lacuna* in Dutch criminal law, there could be no criminal prosecution of the person who had sexually assaulted the applicant. The Strasbourg Court found that, although the essential object of Article 8 is the protection of the individual against arbitrary interference by public authorities, there may be positive obligations and these obligations "may involve the adoption of measures designed to secure respect for private life even in the sphere of the relations of individuals between themselves".[22] Accordingly, there had been a violation of Article 8. We have seen also that the right to demonstrate peacefully may engage state authorities in preventing others from interfering with that right through the disruption of peaceful protest.[23] The right to privacy, as generally understood to mean the right to prevent others from disseminating private information, is derived in the Convention from the positive obligations inherent in Article 8.[24]

All of the cases described above were decisions under Article 8. Latterly, the Court has elaborated positive obligations under Article 2, which guarantees the right to life. It was only very recently that the Court found a violation under Article 2 for the first time[25] and since then there have been a number of findings against states under this article. The first sentence of Article 2 provides that: "Everyone's right to life shall be protected by law". Clearly, the state is therefore enjoined to put in place measures to protect life and consequently has a positive obligation in this regard. The difficult question to determine is the extent to which a state should ensure the protection of life. It is incumbent upon the state to put in place laws which make the taking of life illegal. As Harris, O'Boyle and Warbrick observed: "The kind (criminal, civil) or degree (in criminal law, for murder, manslaughter, etc) of liability is not specified. The principle of proportionality suggests that what is required will vary with the

---

[21] Series A no 91 (1985).
[22] *Ibid.* at para. 23.
[23] *Plattform "Ärzte für das Leben"* v. *Austria* Series A no 139 (1988).
[24] See Chapter 7.
[25] *McCann and others* v. *United Kingdom* Series A no 324 (1995) (deaths of three members of an IRA active service unit in Gibraltar).

circumstances so that, for example, the negligent taking of life by careless driving may be treated less harshly than a premeditated case of poisoning".[26]

In *Osman* v. *United Kingdom*,[27] it was accepted by the UK government that the Article 2(1) obligation extends beyond the provision of effective criminal law provisions and "may also imply in certain well-defined circumstances a positive obligation on the authorities to take preventive operational measures to protect an individual whose life is at risk from the criminal acts of another individual".[28] The Court elaborated the nature of this positive obligation:

> "such an obligation must be interpreted in a way which does not impose an impossible or disproportionate burden on the authorities . . . In the opinion of the Court where there is an allegation that the authorities have violated their positive obligation to protect the right to life in the context of their above-mentioned duty to prevent and suppress offences against the person, it must be established to its satisfaction that the authorities knew or ought to have known at the time of the existence of a real and immediate risk to the life of an identified individual or individuals from the criminal acts of a third party and that they failed to take measures within the scope of their powers which, judged reasonably, might have been expected to avoid that risk. The Court does not accept the Government's view that the failure to perceive the risk to life in the circumstances known at the time or to take preventive measures to avoid that risk must be tantamount to gross negligence[29] or wilful disregard of the duty to protect life . . . For the Court, and having regard to the nature of the right protected by Art 2, a right fundamental in the scheme of the Convention, it is sufficient for an applicant to show that the authorities did not do all that could be reasonably expected of them to avoid a real and immediate risk to life of which they have or ought to have knowledge".[30]

On the facts the Court found that there was no decisive stage at which the police knew or ought to have known that there was a real and immediate risk to the lives of the Osman family. Thus, *Osman* is not a case that would found liability under the Human Rights Act.

The test of liability applied in *Osman*, namely knowledge of real and immediate risk to the applicant, was recently applied by the Commission in its Report in *Z and others* v. *United Kingdom*[31] (the petition by the abused children in *X (Minors)* v. *Bedfordshire County Council*)[32] in relation to an allegation that the UK government had violated Article 3. It will be recalled that the *Bedfordshire* children alleged that the United Kingdom had violated the Article 3 right not to be subjected to inhuman and degrading treatment by its failure to take the children into care in a timely fashion. The Commission considered that the local

---

[26] *Supra* n.1 at 38.

[27] *Supra* n.4.

[28] *Ibid.* at para. 115.

[29] Cf the Courts's observations as to the factors to be taken into account under Article 6, which include the degree of negligence, see text accompanying n.35 un Chapter 4.

[30] *Supra* n.4 at para. 116.

[31] (1999) 28 EHRR CD 65. See also Note on the Text.

[32] [1995] 2 AC 633.

authority was subject to "the positive obligation to take those steps that could reasonably be expected of them to avoid a real and immediate risk of ill-treatment contrary to Article 3 of which they knew or ought to have had knowledge (see . . . *Osman* . . .)".[33] The Commission held that the authorities were aware of the serious ill-treatment and neglect suffered by the applicants and failed to bring it to an end despite having the means reasonably available to do so.

THE SCOPE OF A DUTY TO RESCUE UNDER THE CONVENTION

Osman is a case which concerned danger to individuals from the homicidal acts of another. The more difficult question is whether a state may be subject to positive obligations under Article 2 where the danger to the individual comes from other causes: for example, can a person who is trapped in a burning building complain that the fire brigade failed to answer an emergency call or can the parents of a child who drowned while a champion swimmer walked by complain of the failure of the law to protect that child, in the absence of a recognised duty to rescue? These two examples illustrate the public/private dimension to this issue. *Osman* and *Z* are both cases that concern the liability of public authorities. Perhaps the more difficult question relates to the extent to which the state should require private individuals to act to protect life. In other words, should English law, in the light of its Convention obligations and the enactment of the Human Rights Act, now recognise a duty to rescue? If a duty to rescue is imminent, what type of liability should it attract? Another difficult question that arises in the context of positive obligations is, can a person complain that the state has an obligation to provide expensive health care in the form of surgical intervention (which might have little chance of success)? The next section will examine the scope of positive obligations recognised by Strasbourg under Articles 2 and 8 and will then juxtapose those principles with the precepts of the tort of negligence in order to elicit the areas of English law that might be susceptible to arguments for reform. As far as English law is concerned, there are two separate questions that require to be addressed: first, are established principles of English tort law compatible with the standards enshrined in the Convention and, secondly, if tort law does not accommodate those standards, is the common law an appropriate vehicle for achieving compliance? It is important to reiterate that while Convention case law may reveal to us positive obligations, they may be fulfilled by a variety of means.

Article 2

Osman v. *United Kingdom* demonstrates that in certain circumstances there will be an obligation upon a state to take "preventive operational measures to

---

[33] *Supra* n.31 at para. 94.

protect an individual whose life is at risk from the criminal acts of another". On the facts such an obligation did not arise because there was no decisive stage at which it could be said that the police knew or ought to have known of the risk to the Osman family. In contrast, in a series of cases brought against Turkey, the standard of this positive obligation has been applied and the actions of the state have been found wanting, which has resulted in findings of violations of both Articles 2[34] and 3.[35]

The background to the Turkish cases is the state of unrest in the south-eastern region of the country, where security forces have been attempting to deal with armed and violent attacks by the PKK and other groups. As the Court remarked in *Kilic*, the cases brought to Strasbourg concerning the region have resulted in numerous findings of "failures by the authorities to investigate allegations of wrongdoing by the security forces, both in the context of the procedural obligations under Article 2 of the Convention and the requirement for effective remedies imposed by Article 13".[36]

The central allegation in *Kilic* was that the authorities had failed to take steps to protect the life of a journalist, Kemal Kilic, who was shot dead by unknown gunmen following a request for protection less than two months earlier. Kilic worked for the *Özgür Gündem* newspaper which was described by the owners as seeking to reflect Turkish Kurdish opinion. In his request for protection, Kilic had maintained that persons working for the newspaper had been killed and attacked and that those involved in its distribution had been victims of assaults and arson. The Turkish government mounted a defence analogous to the proximity argument in *Hill* v. *Chief Constable of West Yorkshire Police*,[37] and argued that Kilic was at no more risk than any other person or journalist in south-east Turkey. The Court referred to its previous jurisprudence, in which it had found that those working for the paper were victims of a campaign, tolerated if not approved by state officials, and concluded that Kemal Kilic was at particular risk and that the risk was real and immediate.

The Court found that the state had failed to protect the life of Kilic in two ways. First, a series of findings against Turkey in relation to three issues demonstrated a lack of accountability which was not compatible with the rule of law and which therefore resulted in the removal of the protection Kemal Kilic should have received. These issues were: the fact that offences committed by state officials were investigated by administrative councils which did not provide an independent or impartial procedure; a failure to investigate complaints of wrongdoing by the security forces and, finally, the use of state Security Courts for the trial of those alleged to have committed terrorist crimes by the PKK. The

---

[34] *Kilic* v. *Turkey* App no 22492/93, judgment dated 28 March 2000.
[35] *Aksoy* v. *Turkey* (1996) 23 EHRR 553.
[36] *Supra* n.34 at para. 73.
[37] [1989] AC 53.

court found that these defects fostered a lack of accountability that was not compatible with the rule of law.[38]

More significantly for present discussion, however, the Court found that in addition to these defects, there was an absence of any *operational* measures of protection. As in *Osman*, the Court acknowledged that operational choices have to be made in terms of priorities and resources and that the scope of the positive obligation should not impose an impossible or disproportionate burden on the authorities. The government had disputed whether effective protection could have been provided but the Court was not convinced by government argument. There was a wide range of preventive measures available, including both steps for protection, by applying reasonable methods of protection, and investigation of the alleged risk to the employees of *Özgür Gündem*. Unfortunately, the Court did not elaborate on the nature of the operational measures that might have been reasonable, but presumably something in the nature of police protection or hired bodyguards would be appropriate. *Kilic* can be contrasted with *X v. Ireland*, where the applicant had been injured in an assassination attempt by the IRA and was given police protection for several years. He complained to Strasbourg of a violation of Article 2 when that protection was withdrawn. The Commission held that "Article 2 cannot be interpreted as imposing a duty on the state to give protection of this nature, at least not for an indefinite time".[39]

The implications of these positive obligations for English law are difficult to gauge, both in terms of the mechanisms which need to be in place to meet those obligations and the remedies which should be made available for a failure so to do. Clearly, though, English law should be scrutinised for compatibility with Strasbourg jurisprudence, since its effect is that there will in certain circumstances be a duty to rescue on the part of the state under Article 2. This issue is discussed below. More difficult to determine is the precise circumstances in which such a positive obligation to rescue will arise and the extent of steps to be taken to discharge the obligation. The situation in south-east Turkey is exceptional, one in which the very existence of the rule of law is seriously open to doubt. What is the position where an individual is hurt/killed through failures in the operation of rescue services, whether fire, ambulance or coastguard? What about failures to provide appropriate health care? Where the physical integrity of an individual is threatened through failures on the part of the state to afford appropriate protection, can an applicant allege that the state failed to provide reasonably expected operational measures?

While the full implications of the *Osman* and *Kilic* approach to positive obligations have yet to be worked out, it will be appreciated that the potential impact of this very important decision goes well beyond the duty of care/immunity issue that arises under Article 6. While it may be debatable whether it is appropriate for Article 6 of the Convention to be applied to affect the

---

[38] *Supra* n.34. at para. 75.
[39] Application no 6040/73, (1973) 16 Yearbook 388 at 392.

development of substantive principles by expanding the circumstances in which a duty of care is recognised, the difference is that the interpretation of Article 2 clearly has the potential to impinge upon the development of *substantive* principles of English law. Now that the Human Rights Act has given further effect to the Convention in English law and established a framework of remedies, where a public authority acts incompatibly with the positive obligation under Article 2, at the very least a victim can bring proceedings against that authority under section 7 of the Act. The courts may also consider that, in their duty under section 6, it is appropriate to develop the common law to embrace these principles.[40] The important point is that any positive obligation should be implemented, and any failure to do so should attract redress.

The question of whether a positive obligation under Article 2 to summon emergency medical help may arise came before the Commission in the somewhat bizarre case of *Hughes* v. *United Kingdom*.[41] The applicant's husband had collapsed at his place of work (a private school) and he was examined by a number of colleagues who assumed that he was dead and (presumably in view of that fact) there was a failure to call an ambulance immediately. He was left on the floor for almost two hours. His widow complained that not all necessary measures to save or prolong her husband's life were taken and that "British law appears to condone such negligence by not imposing a specific obligation to take prompt emergency steps in such circumstances and by not awarding compensation to the victims or their families".[42] The Commission declared that the application was incompatible *ratione personae* with the Convention within the meaning of [then] Article 27(2) of the Convention because the applicant was complaining of the conduct of members of a private school. According to Article 25, applications should relate to a failure by a Contracting Party ie the state. The Commission also found that the application was manifestly ill-founded because, according to the medical evidence, the existence of an express obligation to summon medical help would not have been to any avail. There was massive coronary damage and any ambulance summoned would not have arrived in time. Thus, any failure on the part of the state to have in place a rescue law was not a "but for" cause of death. However, it will be recalled that in *LCB* v. *United Kingdom*,[43] the Court did not rule out the possibility of a violation of Article 2, even where the applicant's health prospects would not have been affected by the provision of information (regarding the Christmas Island nuclear tests). In the light of its finding on causation, the Commission did not consider it necessary to decide whether English law should impose such an obligation.

Clapham has subjected this decision to robust criticism. He has suggested that the public/private dichotomy should not be used in this way:

---

[40] See text accompanying n.25 in Chapter 2. See also Note on the Text.
[41] Application no 11590/85, (1986) 48 DR 258.
[42] *Ibid.* at 259.
[43] (1998) 27 EHRR 212, text accompanying n.18 in Chapter 3.

"private schools are covered by a state regulatory framework, second, all private schools are to some extent subsidised by the state . . . through grants . . . tax relief . . . and third, the implication is that the Commission might impose a duty on state teachers whilst private teachers are bound by no 'good Samaritan' principle".[44]

He also suggested quite rightly that it would have been appropriate to consider first whether the Article 2 right *could* operate as between individuals so that the state would be under an obligation to require its citizens to take positive steps to protect the life of a third party. However, Clapham concludes that the phrasing of Article 2 "would not seem to impose positive obligations or responsibilities for omissions on private individuals".[45] He also goes on to suggest that even assuming that Article 2 did embody such an obligation it would have to be shown that "but for the government's lack of legislation this injury probably would have been avoided". Clapham was writing before the emergence of a number of substantive principles developed by Strasbourg, particularly in the Turkish cases, and it is submitted that this conclusion does not necessarily flow from the current Strasbourg jurisprudence. What is in issue under Article 2 is the existence of preventive/protective measures which are geared to the protection of life. It is the existence itself of various measures which "protect the right to life". It is the *right to* life which is to be protected, not life. Such measures may be constituted by the legal framework, for example, effective criminal laws (which might include the criminalisation of a failure to rescue),[46] or they may be operational measures, for example the deployment of police and security forces.[47] *Kilic* demonstrates that an applicant does not have to show that had such operational measures been deployed they would have prevented the loss of life in order to be successful.

It is, however, difficult to quarrel with Clapham's conclusion that Article 2 does not generate positive obligations on individuals to take steps to protect the lives of others. All the Strasbourg jurisprudence under Article 2 regarding positive obligations relates to positive obligations upon the state to take steps to prevent criminality aimed at taking the lives of others. Clapham has stated that:

"the special nature of the positive obligations on the State under Article 2 cannot simply be transferred to private individuals at the national level. Private bodies are not obliged to provide the sort of protection and preventive measures which the State can be called on to implement. In other words private persons are prohibited from torturing under Article 3 but are not obliged to provide armed protection or health care to secure the right to life".[48]

---

[44] A Clapham, *Human Rights in the Private Sphere* (Clarendon Press, Oxford, 1993). In *Costello-Roberts* v. *United Kingdom* Series A no 247-C (1993), the Court held, on the basis of a positive obligation under Article 2 of the First Protocol (the right to education), that state responsibility was engaged where corporal punishment was inflicted in private schools.

[45] Clapham, *supra* n.44 at 206.

[46] See discussion *infra*.

[47] *Kilic*, *supra* n.34, *Osman* v. *United Kingdom*, *supra* n.4.

[48] *Supra* n.44 at 205.

However, as in the case of privacy, it is perhaps difficult to draw conclusions as to whether Article 2 requires states to procure private individuals to take positive steps to rescue others, because English law is out of step with other European jurisdictions where such an obligation is recognised.[49] It is less likely, therefore, that such a matter will be litigated before Strasbourg.

Article 8

The Strasbourg jurisprudence as currently developed has not admitted of an explicit obligation upon the state to procure that private individuals take positive steps to protect another's right to life under Article 2. Under Article 8, however, the Strasbourg organs have stated on a number of occasions that the right enshrined in Article 8(1) to respect for private and family life, the home and correspondence may give rise to a positive obligation upon the state to "secure respect for private life even in the sphere of the relations of individuals between themselves".[50] As Clapham has observed, "this is the strongest indication so far that the European Court of Human Rights will intervene and hold States responsible for violations of rights where the actor involved was a private individual".[51] The notion of private life extends to the "physical and moral integrity of the person",[52] so it is essential to consider the extent of positive obligations under Article 8 in order to establish the extent of a duty to rescue, if any, under this article. There has not been a great number of cases the determination of which has hinged upon discovering a positive obligation and indeed it is difficult to discern any principle to guide future courts. What does seem tolerably clear is that all the cases which have been decided on the basis of such a positive obligation under Article 8 have been cases where the private actors have interfered in a positive manner with the enjoyment of another's Convention rights and freedoms. They are not cases where the impugned facts said to give rise to a state violation concern a failure to act, or in common law terms nonfeasance/an omission. Rather, the obligation upon the state has been to act to prevent individuals taking actions that interfere with others' private lives. Thus in *X and Y*, the private actor had sexually assaulted the mentally disabled girl, thereby interfering with her physical and moral integrity, both of which are inherent in the concept of private life. The Court held that the fact that no criminal proceedings could be brought amounted to a failure by the state to respect private life. In *Whiteside* v. *United Kingdom*,[53] the Commission held that government was under a positive obligation to provide an individual with a remedy against harassment by her former partner in and around her home.

[49] See discussion *infra*.
[50] *X and Y, supra* n.5.
[51] *Supra* n.44 at 214.
[52] *X and Y, supra* n.5 at 11.
[53] *Supra* n.6.

There have been a number of cases brought under Article 8 where the Court has held that the state was in violation as a result of the environmental pollution created by a non-state actor and the corresponding failure of the state to take positive steps to ameliorate the dangers created. In the recent decision of *Guerra* v. *Italy*,[54] the state's failure to protect the applicants' right to respect for their private and family life consisted in the failure to make available "essential information that would have enabled [the applicants] to assess the risks they and their families might run if they continued to live at Manfredonia, a town particularly exposed to danger in the event of an accident at the factory".[55] This case bears comparison with *Lopez Ostra* v. *Spain*,[56] where the Court held that, in permitting the establishment of a waste treatment plant that caused pollution, the state had not struck a fair balance between the economic well-being of the town and the applicant's right to respect for private life. The fact that the applicant had been rehoused by the authorities did not satisfy the obligations under Article 8. The tenor of the judgment in *Lopez Ostra* is very different from that in *Guerra*, in that the running of the plant itself led to a violation, whilst in *Guerra*, the omission lay in the failure to provide information which would have cast the onus on the applicants to move way, if they considered it necessary.

The Court has recently baulked at developing the scope of positive obligations under Article 8. In *Botta* v. *Italy*,[57] the applicant was disabled and complained that the Italian authorities had failed to ensure proper implementation of domestic laws designed to ensure that disabled persons had access to private beach establishments. The Commission considered that the case essentially concerned a "broad range of social relations" and that in this area compliance with domestic or international norms depended, *inter alia*, on financial considerations. Accordingly, the state should enjoy a wide margin of appreciation in achieving compliance and, insofar as the rights concerned are "primarily social rights", protection is more properly ensured through flexible monitoring such as that provided by the Social Charter. The Commission held that Article 14 was of no application since the facts did not fall within the ambit of Article 8. The Court reviewed its jurisprudence under Article 8 and concluded that positive obligations have been found where there is "a direct and immediate link between the measures sought by an applicant and the latter's private and/or family life".[58] In this case, "the right to gain access to the beach and the sea at a place distant from his normal place of residence during his holidays, concerns interpersonal relations of such broad and indeterminate scope that there can be no conceivable direct link between the measures the State was urged to take in

[54] (1998) 26 EHRR 357.

[55] *Ibid.* at para. 60. It is noteworthy that the operation of the factory in itself was not a violation of Article 8. See Chapter 8.

[56] (1995) 20 EHRR 277.

[57] (1998) 26 EHRR 255.

[58] *Ibid.* at para. 34, for example, the lack of legal aid to ensure equal access to a decree of judicial separation.

order to make good the omissions of the private bathing establishments and the applicant's private life". Therefore, Article 8 was not applicable.

If we compare the cases which fall either side of the line drawn by the European Court, with *Lopez Ostra* and *Guerra* on one side and *Botta* on the other, an argument can be made that in view of the pre-eminence accorded to the protection of physical integrity under Article 8 (*X and Y*), an obligation to rescue clearly has a "direct and immediate link" with a person's private life and it should make no difference that a third party has not created a danger in the manner exemplified by *Guerra* and *Lopez Ostra*. It seems arguable, therefore, that an obligation to rescue/warn on the part of private actors may be inferred from the general thrust of the jurisprudence. If a duty to rescue is cast in terms that the individual need only act to the extent that he/she is not exposed to personal danger the fair balance that needs to be struck between the interests of the individual and the wider community will be met. There is no case directly on point, but this is not surprising given that the United Kingdom is exceptional in failing to impose such an obligation upon individuals, either through criminal or civil law.[59]

ENGLISH LAW AND NON-LIABILITY FOR OMISSIONS

One of the first principles students of English tort law encounter is the general rule, that there can be no liability for a pure omission.[60] Thus, there is no obligation upon an individual to act in such a way that s/he confers a benefit upon a third party and there is no general duty of care to protect others from harm caused by third parties. Failure to act and failure to confer a benefit upon another do not ground an action in tort unless there has been an assumption of responsibility by the defendant to that person[61] or an affirmative duty of action is otherwise recognised as arising.[62] Looked at in terms of the constituent elements of the negligence action, policy arguments may militate against a duty of care (imposing positive obligations would restrict unduly the liberty of the individual and translate what is properly a moral obligation into a legal obligation), but the refusal to recognise a duty of care is further supported doctrinally by the lack of a direct causal link between

---

[59] Cf the paucity of Strasbourg jurisprudence regarding the right to privacy: other Council of Europe states recognise such a right so complaints in the nature of *Spencer* v. *UK* ((1998) 25 EHRR 105) are rare.

[60] *Smith* v. *Littlewoods Organisation Ltd* [1987] AC 241.

[61] For example, *Henderson* v. *Merrett Syndicates Ltd* [1995] 2 AC 145; *White* v. *Jones* [1995] 2 AC 207; *Williams* v. *Natural Life Health Foods Ltd* [1998] 1 WLR 830; *Barrett* v. *Ministry of Defence* [1995] 1 WLR 397 and *Phelps* v. *Hillingdon London Borough Council* [2000] 3 WLR 776.

[62] Examples of affirmative duties include the duty of an occupier to ensure that premises are safe for visitors and the duty of employers to provide a safe system of work: see, generally, B S Markesinis and S Deakin, *Tort Law* (Oxford, Clarendon Press, 1999) at 138. See, generally, T Honoré, "Are Omissions Less Culpable?", in P Cane and J Stapleton, *Essays for Patrick Atiyah* (Oxford, Clarendon Press, 1991).

any act of the defendant and the damage suffered by the claimant. There can be no liability because any damage suffered has not been caused directly by the defendant.

Parallels can be drawn between tort principles and Convention jurisprudence regarding positive obligations or to adopt the terminology of English courts, affirmative duties of action, in situations where a private actor can be said to have created a danger. Cases described above such as *Guerra* and *Lopez Ostra* are examples of situations where the state has permitted the private actor to create a source of danger and a positive obligation to rectify the situation therefore arises. They are not examples of a situation where altruistic behaviour is required of a private party.

It is commonly observed by commentators that an affirmative duty to act (frequently a duty to warn) will arise where a defendant creates a risk of harm and this affirmative duty is described as an exception to the common law exclusion of liability for an omission.[63] However, it is submitted that such cases are not examples of true omissions: rather, they are, to adopt the analysis of Weinrib, examples of pseudo-nonfeasance,[64] which can be distinguished from real nonfeasance by "transforming the but-for test so that it attends not to the actual injury but to the risk of injury". The question which should be asked is whether the relevant risk to the claimant existed independently of the defendant's presence or absence.[65] In the cases where English courts have recognised affirmative duties the activity of the defendant has been "a factual cause of the plaintiff's exposure to the risk of the injury that he suffered".[66] The main exception to this approach in English law is in the case of affirmative duties on landowners in relation to dangers on their land, in the creation of which the landowner took no part.[67] In such a case the duty to act affirmatively for the protection of others arises simply through occupation of the land.

As Weinrib has pointed out, a defendant who has the opportunity to come to someone's aid and prevent their suffering harm will always be a "but-for" cause of any actual injury suffered. But, in the case of a true omission, as opposed to "pseudo-nonfeasance", the putative defendant will have played no part in creating the risk of danger to which the plaintiff was exposed.

---

[63] See, for example, M Lunney and K Oliphant, *Tort Law Text and Materials* (Oxford, Oxford University Press, 2000) at 390 *et seq*; A Sprince and J Cooke, "Article 6 and Immunity in Tort: Let the Facts Speak for Themselves", (1999) 15 *PN* 4, and Lord Goff's speech in *Smith* v. *Littlewoods*, *supra* n.60 at 730.

[64] Weinrib borrowed this term from McNeice and Thornton, "Affirmative Duties in Tort", (1949) 58 *Yale LJ* 1272 and applied it to the conduct impugned in *Newton* v. *Ellis* 119 Eng. Rep. 424 (K. B. 1855) where the plaintiff suffered injuries after his carriage passed over a hole dug by the defendant and left unlit at night. The defendant attempted to argue, unsuccessfully, that the complaint of the plaintiff related to an omission, namely, failure to light the excavation.

[65] E Weinrib, "The Case for a Duty to Rescue", (1980) *Yale LJ* 247 *et seq*.

[66] *Ibid.* at 255.

[67] *Goldman* v. *Hargrave* [1967] 1 AC 645.

The distinction between acts and omissions may, in theoretical terms, be easy to grasp; it is much more difficult to apply it to a specific set of facts.[68] Nevertheless, it is a distinction which continues to pervade the tort of negligence, so that it is correct to say that, as a general rule, there can be no liability for an omission. Many of the leading tort cases brought against public bodies in the last twenty-five years have concerned attempts by plaintiffs to seek redress for damage suffered as a result of the failure of a governmental body to act to prevent damage occurring (either at the hands of a third party or through exposure to natural dangers). Thus, on one view the claims have related to omissions[69] rather than negligent acts. For the most part the reasoning in these authorities has not focused on the misfeasance/nonfeasance distinction, although it is clearly a lurking presence: the courts have repeatedly said in the case of public authority liability that great care should be taken before awarding compensation for others' wrongdoing. The unifying thread that does run through all the cases is the desire on the part of the courts to restrict liability with its consequential strain on the public purse. The devices employed by the courts have varied depending upon the nature of the responsibility attributable to the defendant.

In cases concerning the failure to exercise statutory powers *simpliciter*, the courts have adhered to the misfeasance/nonfeasance distinction: it was held by a three to two majority of the House of Lords in *Stovin* v. *Wise*,[70] that a claimant must satisfy two minimum pre-conditions: (1) it must have been irrational not to have exercised the power, so that there was in effect a public duty to act, and (2) there must be exceptional grounds for holding that the policy of the statute requires compensation to be paid to persons who suffer loss because the power was not exercised. Lord Hoffmann, indicated, however, that such liability would be extremely rare. These principles are likely to be challenged in the light of the decision of the House of Lords in *Barrett* v. *Enfield London Borough Council*,[71] where the House of Lords substituted the public law hurdle erected by Lord Browne-Wilkinson in *X (Minors)* v. *Bedfordshire County Council*, for a test of justiciability.[72] It should be noted also that *Stovin* was a majority decision, where the dissenting speech was given by Lord Nicholls with Lord Slynn concurring and in *Barrett*, it was Lord Slynn who gave a leading speech.

Stovin was applied by the Court of Appeal in the recent (pre-*Barrett*) decision of the Court of Appeal in *Hussain* v. *Lancaster City Council*.[73] This was an action in nuisance[74] and negligence brought by the owners of a shop and house

---

[68] F H Bohlen, "The Moral Duty to Aid Others as a Basis of Tort Liability", (1908) 56 *U Pa L Rev* 217; Weinrib, *supra* n.65.

[69] Not every failure to control the act of a third party will be an omission. The defendant may have created the opportunity for harm to occur through their carelessness: *Carmarthenshire County Council* v. *Lewis* [1955] AC 549.

[70] *Stovin* v. *Wise* [1996] 3 All ER 801 at 828, per Lord Hoffmann.

[71] [1999] 3 WLR 79.

[72] See text accompanying n.77 *et seq* in Chapter 4.

[73] [1999] 4 All ER 125.

[74] See text accompanying n.44 in Chapter 8.

on a notorious housing estate owned by the council. The plaintiffs alleged that they had been the targets of a sustained campaign of racial harassment and intimidation and that the defendant council was negligent in failing to exercise its powers (to seek eviction) under the Housing and Highway Acts. Hirst LJ, for the Court of Appeal, held that the plaintiffs did not bring themselves within the categories identified by Lord Hoffmann in *Stovin*. Even if they could, they would still have to show that it was fair, just and reasonable, to impose a duty of care and taking account of the policy factors outlined by Lord Browne-Wilkinson in *X (Minors)*, it would not be fair, just and reasonable to hold the council liable in negligence. The policy factors accepted by the Court of Appeal included the fact that dealing with racial harassment is a multi-agency task and that scarce resources might be diverted from the council's proper responsibility to defending court actions. Finally, Hirst LJ concluded by citing Lord Browne-Wilkinson in *X (Minors)*:

> "In my judgment, the courts should proceed with great care before holding liable in negligence those who have been charged by Parliament with the task of protecting society from the wrongdoings of others".[75]

It is unlikely that if deciding this case now, the Court of Appeal could come to the same conclusion. First, the Court of Appeal was effectively granting an immunity from suit to the council on the basis of *X*, and the Court of Appeal failed to give proper weight to the policy considerations that would speak in favour of a duty of care, as now requisite by virtue of *Osman*.[75a] Secondly, the House of Lords in *Barrett* has indicated the extreme caution that should attend decisions to strike-out. Finally, it should be noted that in *Z*, the Commission observed in its Report that: "[as] regards the multidisciplinary aspects of child protection work, this may provide a factual complexity to cases but cannot by itself provide a justification for excluding liability from a body found to have acted negligently".[76] It is also seems arguable that the Article 3 right not to suffer inhuman and degrading treatment is engaged. This right gives rise to a positive obligation on the state where there is "real and immediate risk of ill-treatment" (see *Z*) to take reasonable steps to protect the potential victim(s). The fact that a fundamental right is engaged is an important factor for the court to take into account in discharging its obligation in relation to whether a duty of care should be recognised in accordance with Article 6.

In other cases, the omissions argument has not been the pivotal concept through which liability has been denied explicitly: in *Hill*,[77] the claim has failed for want of proximity and policy considerations and in *Osman* v. *Ferguson*[78] the policy factors articulated in *Hill* were determinative.

---

[75]   *Supra* n.32 at 751.
[75a]   See Note on the Text for analysis of the impact of *Z* v. *United Kingdom*.
[76]   *Supra* n.31 at para. 114.
[77]   *Supra* n.37.
[78]   [1993] 4 All ER 344.

Where a claimant alleges that a public body has caused damage through a failure to exercise/failure to exercise with due care a statutory duty, the distinction between acts and omissions has not generally been employed. On one view, though, the impugned conduct was an omission, which is presumably why in *Osman* the plaintiffs argued that the police had assumed responsibility for their safety. In X *(Minors)*, the failure to take the children into care may be viewed as an omission. This analysis, while alluded to regarding the attribution of responsibility for another's wrongdoing was not generally adopted by the House of Lords, presumably in the light of the statutory duties under the relevant child welfare legislation. The potential denial of liability on the part of a public authority on the ground of omission has been attacked by Craig who has argued that it is inappropriate to apply the same principles of no liability for omissions to public and private actors:

"the position of a public body vested with discretionary power is not the same as that of a private individual who simply 'happens' upon some accident. The reasons for the reluctance to impose liability in cases of pure omission concerning private individuals, which are questionable in themselves, are not necessarily transferable to public bodies which are granted discretionary powers".[79]

He cites Arrowsmith who has observed that the main policy reason for denying affirmative duties on the part of private individuals is that "it would impose an unfair burden, and constitute excessive interference with private autonomy . . . This argument has no application where there is a public duty to consider whether and how to exercise a power".[80] While there is force in this argument, English courts have continued to apply the distinction between acts and omissions in a range of situations, not least the paradigmatic situation of rescue services.

A good example from recent English jurisprudence where omissions/ nonfeasance analysis did prevail is the Court of Appeal decision in *Capital and Counties plc v. Hampshire County Council*,[81] one of three consolidated appeals, which concerned the question of whether, and if so in what circumstances, a fire brigade owes a duty of care to the owner or occupier of premises which are damaged or destroyed by fire. In the *Capital and Counties* case, the fire officer in charge of the fire-fighting operation had broken the golden rule that sprinklers should not be turned off. The first instance judge had held that, but for the fire officer's action, a total loss of property would have been avoided. The finding of liability was confirmed by a unanimous Court of Appeal, which applied the reasoning of the House of Lords in *East Suffolk Rivers Catchment Board v. Kent*,[82] to the effect that "where a statutory authority embarks upon the execution of the power to do work, the only duty owed to any member of

---

[79] P Craig, *Administrative Law* (London, Sweet & Maxwell, 1999) at 868.
[80] S Arrowsmith, *Civil Liability and Public Authorities* (Winteringham, Earlsgate Press, 1992) at 179.
[81] [1997] QB 1004.
[82] [1941] AC 74.

the public is not thereby to add to the damages which that person would have suffered had the authority done nothing". Here the fire officer had quite clearly exacerbated the situation and in view of the fresh damage the fire brigade was liable. This case contrasted with the two appeals with which it was consolidated, in neither of which it was it possible to identify a positive act, or misfeasance, on the part of the fire service, and, therefore, there could be no liability.

It will be appreciated that the recognition of positive obligations by the Strasbourg machinery on the part of state authorities, as well as obligations to procure that private parties respect the human rights of others (to the extent that such are recognised by Strasbourg) may lead to tension between common law precepts and the obligation of the court to act compatibly with Convention rights under section 6 of the Act. Therefore, the next section will examine recent English authorities relating to liability for the acts of third parties and omissions from a Convention and Human Rights Act perspective in order to determine whether such a tension exists and how it might be resolved in the new constitutional climate.

There are two separate, but related questions, which arise: first, do the rules and principles developed by English courts comply with Convention standards? Secondly, is it appropriate for English courts to map the tort landscape so that Convention standards are accommodated by the common law, rather than using other remedies to achieve compliance? Now that the Human Rights Act has introduced a new remedy against public authorities it may be argued that there is no necessity to develop common law principles as well.[83] Clearly though, this argument cannot prevail in relation to private parties, whose behaviour, if it is not regulated appropriately, can lead to violation of the Convention by the state. The Human Rights Act does not create a scheme of remedies directly enforceable against private actors and the common law, therefore, is likely to be the preferred option as a means of securing redress where it can be shown that Strasbourg has recognised a positive obligation upon the state to act to control private behaviour. It would, therefore, be not only logical, but also necessary, in the light of the courts' obligation under section 6(1) of the Human Rights Act, to develop the common law so that it does not offend Convention principles.

OMISSIONS/LIABILITY FOR THE ACTS OF THIRD PARTIES IN NEGLIGENCE:
COMPATIBILITY WITH THE CONVENTION

Osman v. United Kingdom has established a test for determining when a positive obligation on state authorities will arise to take preventive operational measures to protect an individual whose life is at risk from the criminal acts of another. The test is whether the authorities "knew or ought to have known at

---

[83] See text accompanying n.116 in Chapter 2. See Note on the Text for an expanded discussion in the light of *Z v. United Kingdom*.

the time of the existence of a real and immediate risk to the life of an identified individual or individuals from the criminal acts of a third party and that they failed to take measures within the scope of their powers which, judged reasonably, might have been expected to avoid that risk".[84] It should be noted that the Court expressly rejected the UK government's argument that a failure to act should only engage liability where the failure to perceive a risk or take preventive measures amounted to "gross negligence or wilful disregard of the duty to protect life".[85] The "real risk" formula was applied by the Commission in *Z v. United Kingdom*, where the Commission examined the petition brought by the *Bedfordshire* children. The Commission stated that:

> "the protection of children who by reason of their age and vulnerability are not capable of protecting themselves requires not merely that the criminal law provides protection against Article 3 treatment but that, additionally, this provision will in appropriate circumstances imply a positive obligation on the authorities to take preventive measures to protect a child who is at risk from another individual (*Osman* v. *United Kingdom*) . . . the positive obligation [is to] take those steps that could be reasonably expected of them to avoid a real and immediate risk of ill-treatment contrary to Article 3 of which they knew or ought to have had knowledge".[86]

Essentially, the Court, in adopting a test of anticipation of the likelihood of an event happening, is employing a "high degree of" forseeability test (real and immediate risk of which they knew or ought to know) to determine when a positive obligation to protect the vulnerable party will arise. A number of cases in English law concerning omissions/liability for the acts of third parties have applied a similar threshold test, whether to discovery of duty or establishment of causation. The use of forseeability has been criticised as hopelessly vague,[87] but it is a test that accords with common-sense notions of justice: the reason that cases like *X (Minors)* (and possibly *Osman*) cause outrage is because the danger to the vulnerable was so obvious and there were reasonable preventive measures available to those charged with the statutory responsibility of protection. The language is reminiscent of the House of Lords' decision in *Dorset Yacht Co. v. Home Office*,[88] probably the most well known example of one party being held legally responsible for the wrongdoing of another. The preliminary issue which came before the House was whether on the facts, namely bringing the Borstal trainees to Brownsea Island, the Home Office owed any duty of care to the respondents. On the question of whether a duty of care was owed Lord Reid said that the risk of the boys escaping and interfering with the yachts was "glaringly obvious" and concluded therefore that a duty of care was owed. In *Osman v. United Kingdom* terms there was a real and immediate risk of the damage occurring.

---

[84] *Supra* n.4 at para. 116.
[85] *Ibid.*
[86] *Supra* n.31 at para. 93.
[87] M Lunney and K Oliphant, *Tort Law Text and Materials* (Oxford, Oxford University Press, 2000) at 390.
[88] [1970] AC 1004.

If we utilise the notion of the ability to control a third party's behaviour and therefore prevent them causing damage, we can see immediately the difference between *Hill* and *Osman* v. *Ferguson*. *Hill* was reasoned in terms of proximity as between the police force and the plaintiff; in Convention terms there was no knowledge of risk to an identified individual. However, there was also no suggestion that the police then had the means of knowledge that Peter Sutcliffe, who was subsequently convicted, was the perpetrator of the most appalling homicidal acts.

It is clear then that the effect of Article 2 is that state authorities may be engaged in positive obligations to protect the lives of others (*Osman*) and likewise to prevent the vulnerable suffering from inhuman or degrading treatment (*Z*) under Article 3. We have seen that the Human Rights Act sets out a framework of remedies (section 8) which are available where a victim can show that a public authority has acted unlawfully by acting incompatibly with Convention rights (section 6(1)). The court is also under an obligation to act compatibly with the Convention by virtues of section 6(3). It is likely that claimants will argue that the court in its role as public authority should develop the tort of negligence so that it is compatible with Convention rights and the following discussion will address this issue.

NEGLIGENCE: COMPATIBILITY WITH CONVENTION STANDARDS ON
POSITIVE OBLIGATIONS

The current approach of English law to public authority liability in negligence differs, depending upon whether the underlying legislation contains duties or powers, although these potential bases for action are not always distinguished.[89] Following the House of Lords' decision in *Barrett*, it would seem that the public law hurdle laid down by Lord Browne-Wilkinson in *X (Minors)* v. *Bedfordshire County Council*, requiring a claimant to establish *Wednesbury* unreasonableness in relation to discretionary decisions, has been removed in any case where it is alleged that a local authority has acted negligently. In cases concerning non-exercise of statutory powers it seems that the test still remains. The effect of *Barrett* seems to be that the public law threshold to liability is only relevant where, in the words of Lord Hutton, the court is of the opinion that any

---

[89] See, for example, R A Buckley, "Negligence in the Public Sphere: Is Clarity Possible?", (2000) 51 *Northern Ireland Legal Quarterly* 25, who described *X* v. *Bedfordshire* as a case where local authorities failed to exercise statutory *powers* (in fact the relevant legislation laid down duties, albeit duties involving the exercise of discretion in decision-making). Cf *Sheppard* v. *Glossop Corporation* [1921] 3 KB 132 and *Stovin* v. *Wise* [1996] AC 923 and R Kidner, *Casebook on Torts* (London, Blackstone Press, 1996), who includes *X (Minors)* v. *Bedfordshire* under the heading of "Exercise of Statutory Powers". In *Anns* v. *Merton London Borough Council* [1978] AC 728, Lord Wilberforce did say that it was irrelevant to the existence of a duty of care whether a statute lays down a power or a duty. He was of course seeking to erect a duty where the relevant statute gave only a power to inspect buildings. His approach has not been followed.

decision on the existence of negligence would involve the courts in "considering matters of policy raising issues which they are ill-equipped and ill-suited to assess and on which parliament could not have intended that the courts would substitute their views for the views of ministers or officials".[90] In such cases the courts would hold that the action for negligence was non-justiciable. Likewise for Lord Slynn the key issue was justiciability.[91]

The application of a requirement for a claimant to satisfy the *Wednesbury* test as a pre-condition to liability would effectively exclude all but the most irrational/unreasonable decisions from scrutiny, thus securing immunity to all but the most grossly negligent[92] decisions. This standard would appear to be incompatible with the Strasbourg Court's views as set out in *Osman v. United Kingdom*, where the government's argument that only gross negligence should lead to a violation of Article 2 was expressly rejected. The effect of *Barrett* is that only non-justiciable policy issues are removed from the court's scrutiny in a negligence action, thus reducing the likelihood of potential for incompatibility with the Convention. It will be recalled that in *Osman v. United Kingdom*, the Court held that, having regard to the operational choices that must be made in terms of priorities and resources, the obligation should not be interpreted to impose an impossible or disproportionate burden on the authorities.[93] Both Lord Slynn and Lord Hutton (Lord Steyn and Lord Nolan concurring) agreed that, absent non-justiciable policy issues, the *Caparo* criteria should determine the existence of a duty of care.

It is becoming increasingly difficult to predict outcomes where a claimant alleges that she has suffered damage through an omission/failure to have conferred upon her a benefit by a third party. The Court of Appeal decision in *Capital and Counties* exemplifies the traditional English pre-*Anns* approach: there can be no liability in the absence of fresh damage being caused by the defendants. All that had happened in three of the appeals was that the defendant had failed to confer a benefit upon the plaintiffs. Applying *Alexandrou v. Oxford*,[94] Stuart-Smith LJ concluded:

> "In our judgment the fire brigade are not under a common law duty to answer the call for help and are not under a duty to take care to do so. If, therefore, they fail to turn up, or fail to turn up in time, because they have carelessly misunderstood the message, got lost on the way or run into a tree, they are not liable".[95]

Stuart-Smith considered that, "the peculiarity of fire brigades, together with other rescue services" is that they do not usually create the danger that causes

---

[90] *Supra.* n.71 at 105 per Lord Hutton.

[91] For an excellent discussion of these issues, see P Craig and D Fairgrieve, "*Barrett*, Negligence and Discretionary Powers", [1999] *PL* 626.

[92] Cane has described the standard of care applied to public authorities through the application of *Wednesbury* principles as "extraordinary unreasonableness", P Cane, *The Anatomy of Tort Law* (Hart Publishing, Oxford, 1997) at 41.

[93] *Supra* n.4 at para. 116.

[94] [1993] 4 All ER 328.

[95] [1997] 2 All ER 865 at 878.

injury to person or property, and a claimant could not recover in the absence of danger created by the rescue services themselves.[96] The action failed because the fire brigade did not enter into a sufficiently proximate relationship with the owner/occupier of premises in order to come under a duty of care.

A number of points should be made about this decision. First, the case was decided in a pre-*Osman* v. *United Kingdom* climate and without any consideration of the Convention; secondly, all the appeals concerned damage to property (would the Court of Appeal have decided so readily in favour of the fire service had children been forced to jump to their deaths from a burning building because the service failed to arrive in a timely fashion) and not injury to the person and, finally, each of the appeals related to insured damage.

The implications of the Court of Appeal's decision in *Capital and Counties* must now be reviewed in the light of the Court of Appeal in *Kent* v. *Griffiths*.[97] The issue before the court was whether the ambulance service can owe a duty of care to a member of the public for whose benefit a "999" call is made. The claimant was an asthmatic who suffered a respiratory arrest and consequent brain damage when an ambulance took forty minutes to arrive. It was found that the ambulance could and should have taken fourteen minutes less to reach the claimant's house. It was also highly probable that the respiratory arrest would have been avoided had the ambulance proceeded with due care. Interestingly, in its original defence, the London Ambulance Service had admitted that it was under a duty to respond, but following the *Capital and Counties* decision, leave to amend was sought. As Lord Woolf MR, giving judgment for the Court of Appeal observed, unless *Alexandrou* and *Capital & Counties* could be distinguished, the appeal by the London Ambulance Service would have to be allowed. Lord Woolf acknowledged the potential difficulty *Osman* v. *United Kingdom* posed for the implementation of the new Civil Procedure Rules, but went on to observe that there is a much more positive consequence of *Osman*, namely:

> "It does draw attention to the fact that in this area of the law there is a danger that statements will be applied more widely and more rigidly than was in fact intended. The statements are intended to assist in the difficult task of determining whether a duty of care exists. They are tools not rules".[98]

Unfortunately, Lord Woolf did not identify the Convention as a possible tool through which the respective interests of the parties could be mediated. He concluded that while *Alexandrou* and *Capital & Counties* were similar, he had no reservations in agreeing with the first instance judge who had found against the ambulance service. He began by saying that even where a statutory power authorises a body to behave in a particular manner, there may be liability if there is a common law duty of care. Following Lord Hoffmann's approach in

---

[96] [1997] 2 All ER 865 at 878.
[97] [2000] 2 All ER 474.
[98] *Ibid.* at 484.

Stovin, this was a case where it would have been irrational not to have provided an ambulance. He distinguished *Alexandrou* and *Capital & Counties* on the basis that like medical and nursing services, the provision of an ambulance service is part of the provision of a health service included in section 3 of the National Health Service Act 1977. He also said that the public policy arguments are much weaker in the case of the ambulance service than in the case of the fire or police services. As far as Lord Woolf was concerned, the difference in part seemed to be a question of numbers, a new variant of the floodgates argument:

> "The police and fire services' primary obligation is to the public at large. In protecting a particular victim of crime, the police are performing their more general role of maintaining public order and reducing crime. In the case of fire the fire service will normally be concerned not only to protect a particular property where a fire breaks out but also to prevent fire spreading. In the case of both services, there is therefore a concern to protect the public generally . . . But . . . the ambulance service is part of the health service . . . providing services of the category provided by hospitals . . . Cases could arise where an ambulance is required to attend a scene of an accident in which a number of people need transporting to hospital. That could be said to be a different situation, but, as the numbers involved would be limited, I would not necessarily regard this as leading to a different result".[99]

One only has to imagine a multiple vehicle pile-up on the M6 at which all emergency services attend to envisage the potential arbitrariness these apparently conflicting rules might produce. In order to get the injured to hospital, the fire service must cut people from wreckage: they can be as efficient/as inefficient as they wish: no accountability in tort according to *Capital & Counties*. Although *Capital & Counties* did concern property damage, Stuart-Smith LJ did not attempt to restrict his observation that there is no duty on the fire service to respond to a call. The ambulance crews on the other hand must act with reasonable care in order to transport the injured to hospital.

The real difference between *Capital & Counties* (and *Alexandrou*) and *Kent v. Griffiths*, but not the one expressly alluded to by Lord Woolf, is the nature of the injury. In the earlier cases, insured damage to buildings which can be replaced,[100] in *Kent* the threat to the life of someone who cannot be replaced. Admittedly, life insurance may be available, but that will not replace the person. How, though, can that distinction be accommodated by the principles of tort law? One way of doing that is by taking account of the Convention in the development of substantive principles, as indeed now required by section 6(3) of the Human Rights Act. The rights to life and not to suffer inhuman and degrading treatment are accorded the highest protection by the Convention and *Osman* and *Kilic* demonstrate that states have positive obligations to put

---

[99] Ibid. at 486.
[100] Curiously, in *Stovin*, Lord Hoffmann in his discussion under the heading "Particular and General Reliance", did state that: "It is not obvious that there should be a right to compensation from a negligent fire authority which will ordinarily insure by right of subrogation to an insurance company", [1996] 3 All ER 801.

in place operational measures in certain circumstances, subject to the balancing of priorities and resources. *Osman* and *Kilic* both concerned danger from criminality, but other cases such as *LCB* v. *United Kingdom*,[101] outside the field of criminality confirm the wider application of positive obligations. The Convention was drafted in recognition of the fact that our humanity and our physical integrity have particular worth. The time has come for that to be recognised explicitly by the principles of negligence. As *Z* and *Osman* v. *United Kingdom* have made clear, in considering whether a duty of care is owed, the court should have regard to the fact that fundamental rights are engaged. In both cases, the Strasbourg organs held that the claimants were entitled to have the police and local authority, respectively, account for their actions in adversarial proceedings.[102] As Buckley has observed, courts appear more ready to impose liability where a claimant has suffered personal injury as opposed to pure economic loss or damage to property.[103]

In *Kent*, Lord Woolf did qualify his view potentially to exclude cases where what is being attacked is the allocation of resources. It was important in this case that there was no question of an ambulance not being available nor of a conflict in priorities. The fact that courts should be sensitive to difficult questions of priority and resource allocation was acknowledged by the Court in *Osman* when it elaborated upon the necessity for a state in certain circumstances to take operational measures to protect the life of an individual:

> "For the Court, and bearing in mind the difficulties involved in policing modern societies, the unpredictability of human conduct and the operational choices which must be made in terms of priorities and resources, such an obligation must be interpreted in a way which does not impose an impossible or disproportionate burden on the authorities".[104]

Lord Woolf did not express any explicit view in *Kent* as to the correctness of *OLL Ltd* v. *Secretary of State for Transport*,[105] but this decision must be open to attack in the wake of *Kent* and *Osman*. In *OLL*, May J struck out a claim against the coastguard by a tortfeasor for contribution on the basis that no distinction could be drawn between the fire brigade responding to a fire where lives were at risk and the coastguard responding to an emergency at sea. Clearly drawing on traditional nonfeasance rhetoric, May J stated that, "[directly] inflicted physical injury is the first building block of the law of negligence". It will be recalled that in *Capital and Counties*, the only source of liability could be "fresh damage". May J took the view that *Capital and Counties* was binding upon him so that the same principle applied. In *Kent*, Lord Woolf did take issue with the application of the *East Suffolk* principle and *Horsley* v. *Maclaren*[106]

---

[101] (1998) 27 EHRR 212.
[102] *Osman, supra* n.4 at para. 153 and *Z, supra* n.31 at para. 115.
[103] Buckley, *supra* n.89 at 39.
[104] *Supra* n.4 at para. 116.
[105] [1997] 3 All ER 897.
[106] [1971] 2 Lloyd's Rep 410.

outside the context of volunteer rescuers. He said that while cases like *Horsley* establish that the common law does not require members of the public to be "Good Samaritans", he had difficulty in applying the principle in the case of the ambulance service. This is because the ambulance service is under a public law duty to act: "it is wholly inappropriate to regard the [London Ambulance Service] as volunteers".[107] While Lord Woolf was at pains to distinguish *Capital and Counties*, this statement is a direct attack upon the appropriateness of the principles applied by Stuart-Smith LJ in relation to a public service rescuer.

DUTY TO RESCUE BY NON-STATE ACTORS: IMPLEMENTATION OF A EUROPEAN STANDARD?

It is not clear from Convention jurisprudence whether the Article 8(1) right to respect for private life demands that states should require individuals to undertake efforts to protect the vulnerable from injury or death, quite apart from situations where a defendant has created a source of danger. The cases which have required action in the private sphere have been those where a third party has been responsible for a source of danger, or where the third party has otherwise actively interfered with Article 8 rights. However, in view of the fact that it is common to impose some form of obligation to rescue (see the discussion below regarding France and Germany) it is arguable that the interest in protecting the physical and moral integrity of the individual requires that such a duty exist. One of the guiding principles in the Strasbourg case law is the search for a European standard.

If such an obligation were found to exist, the sanction imposed by the state could be civil or criminal. It would not follow from the recognition of the obligation that it should necessarily take the form of civil liability in tort. It is for the state to choose the means used in its domestic system in order to comply with the Convention or to redress the situation that has given rise to the violation of the Convention.

However, it is clear from *X and Y* v. *The Netherlands*, that the state does not enjoy totally unrestricted freedom of action in relation to the means by which a right is protected. Both the Court and the Commission took the view that in principle the means by which compliance with Article 8 is wrought in the sphere of relations between individuals themselves falls within the state's margin of appreciation.[108] Thus, it is primarily for the state to determine the way in which rights taking effect at horizontal level are protected. It will be recalled that in *X and Y*, the sixteen-year-old mentally disabled girl could have brought a civil action for damages against her assailant, as well as an injunction to restrain a repetition of the offence: her complaint was that a gap in the law meant there

---

[107] *Supra* n.97 at 479.
[108] *Supra* n.5 at para. 24.

could be no criminal prosecution of the attacker. The court was in no doubt that criminal law provisions were essential:

> "This is a case where fundamental values and essential aspects of private life are at stake. Effective deterrence is indispensable in this area and it can be achieved only by criminal-law provisions; indeed, *it is by such provisions that the matter is normally regulated*".[109] (emphasis added)

The Court was thus explicit that the *usual* way such matters are dealt with by a legal system will influence its assessment of the method of implementation. While civil law systems are in agreement as regards recognising the principle of an obligation to rescue there is no uniform approach to its implementation. Such obligations are frequently regulated by the criminal law and a failure to act will not always attract civil liability. In Germany, for example, the general view is that article 323c of the Criminal Code, which imposes a limited duty to rescue, is not a protective norm falling within article 823 II BGB,[110] so that civil liability for failure to rescue is not attracted.[111] Civil liability will arise where, analogously with English law, a duty to act can be discovered and this will be the case where the defendant through his activity creates a source of danger to others.[112] France, by contrast, has an expanded liability for failure to rescue. The duty to rescue is enshrined in article 223-6 of the New Penal Code and civil liability in tort is governed by articles 1382–6 of the Code Civil. The Cour de Cassation has held that an omission to act can only give rise to civil liability where the defendant has an affirmative duty to act.[113] However, such an obligation can be derived from the criminal law and in 1996 the Criminal Chamber of the French Cour de Cassation held a minor and his mother liable for the non-pecuniary loss suffered by the family of a deceased fellow joyrider. The defendant had pulled his friend from the wreckage, but fled without summoning assistance, in breach of the Penal Code. Thus the "civil action for damages was based solely upon the criminal offence of failure to assist a person in need".[114]

It is submitted that, in view of the range of responses on the part of states and the lack of a European consensus on the issue, it is unlikely that any duty to rescue on the part of a private actor found by the Strasbourg Court would take the

---

[109] *Supra* n.5 at para. 27.

[110] Article 823 II provides that: "The same obligation [to compensate for wilful or negligent injury to life, body, health, freedom, property or other right of another contrary to law] attaches to a person who infringes a statutory provision intended for the protection of others. If according to the purview of the statute infringement is possible even without fault, the duty to make compensation arises only if some fault can be imputed to the wrongdoer": B S Markesinis, *The German Law of Obligations, Volume II The Law of Tort: A Comparative Introduction* (Oxford, Clarendon Press, 1997).

[111] B S Markesinis, "Negligence, Nuisance and Affirmative Duties of Action", (1989) 105 *LQR* 104 at 114.

[112] See generally, Markesinis, *ibid.* at 117.

[113] Cass. Civ., 24 Dec 1924, D. 1925, 120 (case of *Compagnie des Messageries Maritimes*), quoted by M Vranken, "Duty to Rescue in Civil Law and Common Law: *Les Extrêmes Se Touchent?*", (2000) 47 *ICLQ* 934 at 939.

[114] Vranken, *ibid.* at 940.

form of mandatory civil liability. In *Stubbings* v. *United Kingdom*, the applicants petitioned Strasbourg after the House of Lords held that damages for deliberately inflicted personal injury fell within section 2 of the Limitation Act 1980 which meant that the applicants' civil claims for damages for childhood sexual abuse were time-barred. The Court held that Article 8 gave rise to a positive obligation to protect children from sexual abuse by providing effective deterrence and that the criminal penalties available provided this. It was held that Article 8 does not "necessarily require that States fulfil their positive obligation to secure respect for private life by the provision of unlimited civil remedies in circumstances where criminal law sanctions are in operation".[115] Thus, in the context of rescue, arguably, effective respect for private life could be achieved through the imposition of criminal sanctions. However, there is something distinctly unattractive about a legal system which denies redress where it can be shown that physical injury or death could have been avoided through the provision of assistance which would have involved no risk to the rescuer.

PROTECTION FOR THE RESCUER AND THE RIGHT TO RESPECT FOR PRIVATE LIFE

Hitherto, the discussion has focused upon whether as a matter of Convention jurisprudence an affirmative duty to assist others in danger can be divined. Another aspect of rescue is the extent to which legal protection is afforded to the person who is brave enough to set out to rescue others. What if they are injured in the process? Should they have a right of action against any negligent third party who created the source of danger? If domestic law does not compensate the altruistic intervener, it is obvious that an argument can be made that a state has failed to secure the right to respect for private life. Strasbourg has repeatedly stressed that a person's physical and emotional integrity are the core values encompassed by the Article 8 interest of private life and a law that is unfavourable to rescuers insofar as it discourages one citizen to come to the aid of another arguably embodies a lack of respect for private life.

English law has adopted the reasoning of Cardozo J in *Wagner* v. *International Rly Co*, that "danger invites rescue. The cry of distress is the summons to relief. The wrong that imperils life is a wrong to the imperilled victim; it is also a wrong to his rescuer".[116] Thus, in *Baker* v. *T. E. Hopkins*,[117] the plaintiff's husband had died during an attempt to rescue two men trapped in a well due to the negligence of the defendant and the Court of Appeal allowed the plaintiff's Fatal Accidents Act claim. *Chadwick* v. *British Transport Commission*,[118] has frequently been cited as an example of a judicial policy favouring rescuers. In

---

[115] (1997) 23 EHRR 213.
[116] (1921) 232 NY 176 at 180–1.
[117] [1959] 1 WLR 966.
[118] [1967] 1 WLR 912.

White v. *Chief Constable of Yorkshire*,[119] Lord Steyn acknowledged that "the law has long recognised the moral imperative of encouraging citizens to rescue persons in peril". It is disappointing, therefore, that a majority of the House of Lords in *White*, including Lord Steyn, has reinterpreted the decision in *Chadwick* to the effect that a rescuer who does not suffer physical injury will recover damages for psychiatric injury only where he was either in danger of physical injury to himself or reasonably believed himself to be so. If a rescuer cannot demonstrate this he is a secondary victim and must satisfy the criteria laid down in *Alcock* in order to succeed. It is appreciated that the House of Lords was strongly influenced by the fact that the claims of the bereaved relatives in the Hillsborough tragedy were denied and as Lord Steyn put it, the Court of Appeal decision had introduced an imbalance "which might perplex the man on the Underground".[120] The problem is that one imbalance has been substituted for another. In *Chadwick*, Waller J did refer to an element of personal danger in what Mr Chadwick was doing (a fact seized upon by Lord Steyn as demonstrating that the rescuer had passed the threshold of being in personal danger), but he took the view that Mr Chadwick's catastrophic neurosis was caused by the horror of the experience. He found as a fact that his shock was not caused by fear for his own safety. Lord Goff, who dissented in *White*, elaborated on the potential arbitrariness of the "fear for one's own safety" threshold, introduced by *White*:

> "Suppose that there was a terrible train crash and there were two Chadwick brothers living nearby, both of them small and agile window cleaners distinguished by their courage and humanity. Mr A. Chadwick worked on the front half of the train, and Mr B. Chadwick on the rear half. It so happened that, although there was some physical danger present in the front half of the train, there was none in the rear. Both worked for 12 hours . . . [both] suffered P.T.S.D. . . . Mr A. would recover but Mr B. would not . . . the same conclusion must follow even if Mr A. was unaware of the physical danger present in his half of the train . . .".[121]

The effect of *White* is that the scope of protection afforded to rescuers by the tort of negligence has been reduced and it seems arguable that this could amount to a violation of Article 8 for someone in Chadwick's position who is unable to demonstrate a fear for his own safety. While it is perhaps unlikely that anyone faced with the need to embark on a rescue attempt will have in mind the state of civil compensation law, the effect of the law is to discourage and undermine such activity: as such it is arguably a manifestation of a failure to respect private life. Such an inference can also be supported by a recent Report adopted by the Commission in *Cyprus* v. *Turkey*[122] where a reduction

[119] [1998] 3 WLR 1509.
[120] *Ibid.* at 1542.
[121] *Ibid.* at 1535.
[122] Application no 25781/94, Report adopted 4 June 1999. The complaint upheld related to the removal of secondary school education in northern Cyprus in the Greek language.

in the level of a right previously enjoyed was taken into account in finding that a violation of Article 2 of Protocol 1 had occurred.

CONCLUSION

The Strasbourg case law over the last five years reveals a distinct strengthening of the positive obligations on the state under Articles 2 and 3. The jurisprudence in relation to positive obligations affecting the behaviour of private individuals is confined to Article 8 and the margin of appreciation that has been allowed to states is significant. For this reason the indirect horizontal effect of the Act that was discussed in Chapter 2 may be less significant than anticipated. Margin doctrine has not been applied under Articles 2 and 3, although the Court has acknowledged that resource issues are implicated and should be taken into account in determining what measures should reasonably be employed to secure the right.

The challenge for English courts is to shape legal rules appropriately so that suitable mechanisms for redress exist at domestic level. Where the action/inaction of public authorities engages Convention rights, proceedings will lie under the Human Rights Act, while in relation to private individuals the duty of the court alone under section 6 of the Act is relevant. Where proceedings are brought under section 7 of the Act, a claimant has to demonstrate that a public authority has acted in a away that is incompatible with a Convention right. The Strasbourg jurisprudence reveals when a duty to act arises and the measures that are required to discharge that duty. If a public authority fails to act compatibly with the Convention rights, it will have acted unlawfully and a remedy may be sought under section 8 of the Act.

As we have seen in Chapter 4, the response of English courts to *Osman* v. *United Kingdom* has been potentially to open up tort liability by allowing claims to go to trial that would have been struck out previously. These developments have taken place in the light of the obligation perceived to arise from Article 6 and the *Osman* ruling, without, however, focusing on the substantive obligations created by the various Articles of the Convention, other than Article 6 itself. Now that the Court of Human Rights has rejected *Osman* in *Z* v. *United Kingdom*,[123] the focus of the courts and claimants is likely to shift to other Convention articles as the courts grapple with their own obligation under section 6 of the Act to develop the common law so that it is compatible with Convention rights.[124] Many outstanding claims relate to acts that are not caught by the Human Rights Act because section 7 of the Act applies only to claims brought against public authorities in respect of acts taking place after the commencement of the section (section 22(4)): appropriate development of the common law is therefore required if petitions to Strasbourg are to be avoided.

---

[123] Judgment dated 10 May 2001: see Note on the Text.
[124] See text accompanying n.32 *et seq* in Chapter 2.

6

Defamation and Freedom of Expression

INTRODUCTION

A NUMBER OF "justificatory"[1] theories have been advanced in support of the notion that freedom of speech is deserving of constitutional protection. First, this freedom is essential if there is to be dissemination of political information which fosters political debate, such that the polity is enabled to exercise the franchise in accordance with the democratic ideals of an open society. Secondly, freedom of expression enables the full development of the human person and should be a fundamental aspect of individual autonomy, enabling the full development of the human personality. Finally, there is the argument propounded by John Stuart Mill,[2] that freedom of speech will lead to the discovery of truth and hence enhance scientific and social progress.

Each of these theories finds support in the Strasbourg jurisprudence but it is clear that the highest degree of protection has been allotted to political speech. As the European Court of Human Rights has reiterated on many occasions, freedom of expression is at the very core of a democratic society: without freedom of expression there can be no free flow of political information which is so essential if the polity is to be informed on matters of political debate and free to form political opinion in a meaningful way. Not only that, freedom of expression augments self-fulfilment and enables the development of the human person. The Court in *Handyside* v. *United Kingdom* encapsulated both these ideals:

> "The Court's supervisory functions oblige it to pay the utmost attention to the principles characterising a 'democratic society'. Freedom of expression constitutes one of the essential foundations of such a society, one of the basic conditions for its progress and for the development of every man".[3]

Examples can be found also in Strasbourg jurisprudence to support the Mill thesis in that they expound the necessity for protection from state interference where a speaker is contributing to a debate on matters affecting the public

---

[1] G Marshall, "Press Freedom and Free Speech Theory" [1992] *PL* 40. See also E Barendt, *Freedom of Speech* (Oxford, Clarendon Press, 1985).

[2] J S Mill, *On Liberty and Other Essays* (Oxford, Oxford University Press, 1991).

[3] Series A no 24 at para. 49.

interest.[4] Ultimately, where there is uncertainty over scientific matters, public debate may lead to discovery of truth.

The right to freedom of expression enshrined in Article 10 shares the structure of the other personal freedoms articles contained in Articles 8 to 11. Each of these articles sets out the substantive right in the first paragraph and then lists the grounds upon which states may restrict the right in the second paragraph. Included within the scope of restrictions which may be permitted, assuming that they satisfy the other qualifying requirements of Article 10(2), are restrictions in the interests of "the protection of the reputation or rights of others, for preventing the disclosure of information received in confidence". Much of the jurisprudence which has developed under Article 10 concerns the compatibility of state defamation laws with the right to freedom of expression. It is fair to say that the Court has become increasingly vigilant to guard the free speech interest, particularly in the realm of political speech, but also where speech relates to matters considered to be in the public interest generally as issues for debate or concern. In contrast, where an applicant has complained that artistic expression has been curtailed on the grounds of obscenity or blasphemy, a greater margin of appreciation has been allowed to states in assessing the necessity for restrictions upon the right.[5]

It is incontrovertible that the Human Rights Act requires English courts to ensure that defamation law is compatible with the Convention, whether the parties are public or private.[6] *Reynolds* v. *Times Newspapers* was decided before the Act came into force, but it was common ground between the parties that the House of Lords should proceed upon the basis that the Act would very soon be in force.[7] According to Lord Nicholls (Lords Hope and Cooke concurring) this meant that the common law should be developed consistently with Article 10 and relevant decisions of the European Court of Human Rights should be taken into account in accordance with section 2 of the Act.

Any action for defamation represents an attempt to restrict freedom of expression in order to protect the reputation of another, which is a legitimate aim under Article 10(2), and permissible provided that two conditions are satisfied. First, the restriction must be "prescribed by law" and, secondly, the restriction must be "necessary in a democratic society". In order to satisfy the first requirement it must be shown that the law is adequately accessible:

---

[4] *Hertel* v. *Switzerland* (1998) EHRR 534.

[5] See for example: *Otto-Preminger-Institut* v. *Austria* Series A no 295-A (1994) where the seizure of a film depicting "God as a senile, impotent idiot, Christ as a cretin and Mary as a wanton lady" (Innsbrück Regional Court) was justified on the grounds that it was necessary to uphold the right to freedom of religion of others, notwithstanding that the applicant was a private cinema club, no entry was permitted to those under seventeen and advertising material for the film carried a warning of unsuitability for those of religious persuasion and *Wingrove* v. *United Kingdom* (1996) 24 EHRR 1 which concerned the refusal to grant a classification certificate for a video on the ground that it infringed the criminal law of blasphemy, pursued the legitimate aim of protecting the rights of others and was consonant with the aim of the protections afforded by Article 9 to religious freedom.

[6] *Reynolds* v. *Times Newspapers* [1999] 3 WLR 1010.

[7] Per Lord Steyn, *ibid.* at 1030.

"the citizen must be able to have an indication that is adequate in the circumstances of the legal rules applicable to a given case . . . a norm cannot be regarded as a 'law' unless it is formulated with sufficient precision to enable the citizen to regulate his conduct".[8]

In order to demonstrate that a restriction is necessary in a democratic society, it must correspond to a pressing social need and must be proportionate to the legitimate aim pursued.[9] The starting point for any assessment of a restriction on freedom of expression is that the right occupies a special place in the personal freedom hierarchy of Articles 8 to 11. The most frequently quoted dictum in relation to Article 10 is probably that of the Court in *Handyside v. United Kingdom*, where the Court stated that:

"Freedom of expression constitutes one of the essential foundations of [a democratic society], one of the basic conditions for its progress and for the development of every man. Subject to paragraph 2 of Article 10, it is applicable not only to 'information' or 'ideas' that are favourably received or regarded as inoffensive or as a matter of indifference, but also to those that offend, shock or disturb the State or any sector of the population. Such are the demands of that pluralism, tolerance and broadmindedness without which there is no 'democratic society'. This means, amongst other things, that every 'formality', 'condition', 'restriction' or 'penalty' imposed in this sphere must be proportionate to the legitimate aim pursued".[10]

The special role that is accorded to freedom of speech is recognised by section 12 of the Human Rights Act 1998, which requires courts to have particular regard to the importance of the Convention right to freedom of expression where the court is considering whether to grant any relief which might affect the exercise of the Convention right (section 12(1) and (4)).

The areas of English law that are likely to be subject to the most intensive scrutiny in the light of Article 10 are those concerning the defences available to a defamation action, particularly, in the context of "political" speech, and also privacy issues which may require a balance to be struck between the Article 8 right to private life and freedom of speech under Article 10. Privacy is discussed in Chapter 7. It seems likely that media defendants will continue to argue for greater protection to be accorded to political comment, particularly in the light of section 12. On the other hand, those defences, when viewed from the claimant's perspective, may be perceived as a restriction on the right of access to a court and consequently a violation of Article 6.[11] The jurisprudence in relation

---

[8] *Sunday Times* v. *United Kingdom* Series A no. 30 at para. 266. In this case the Court decided that the common law rules on contempt of court were sufficiently clear for the applicants to foresee the consequences of their actions. There were, however, three dissents on this point (Judges Zekia, O'Donoghue and Evrigenis) and the possibility cannot be excluded that some of the more arcane rules of the common law might fail the accessibility test.

[9] *Olsson* v. *Sweden* Series A 130 no 130.

[10] Series A no 24 (1976) at para. 49.

[11] See, for example, *Fayed* v. *United Kingdom* Series A vol. 294-B (1994), where the applicant argued unsuccessfully that English rules on qualified privilege amounted to a violation of Article 6: the complaint related to the report prepared by the Department of Trade and Industry into the applicants' take-over of the House of Fraser. The report alleged that the applicants were dishonest, but no civil claim could proceed because the report was a privileged. See text accompanying n.46 in Chapter 4.

to Article 6 was discussed in detail in Chapter 4 and the following discussion will therefore examine those features of the defences available in English defamation law, which may be vulnerable to attack on the grounds of incompatibility with the Convention. However, it is necessary first to evaluate the standards which have been laid down by the Strasbourg organs in relation to Article 10.

ARTICLE 10 JURISPRUDENCE

After initial hesitation,[12] Strasbourg has carved out a special rolé for "political comment" and comment on matters of public interest so that a strict scrutiny approach is applied to any interference with such speech. Although the Court and Commission have not gone so far as to require that states should introduce a *Sullivan*[13] type defence to political defamations, it is clear that the Strasbourg view of freedom of expression is that political speech serves a special role in the pursuit of a democratic society. It is entirely consonant with the spirit of the Convention, as described in the Preamble, that this should be so: it is only through "an effective political democracy" that Convention freedoms, the foundation of justice and peace in the world, will be best maintained.

The case that set the tone for Strasbourg jurisprudence is *Lingens* v. *Austria*.[14] Immediately after the Austrian general elections in 1975, Lingens had published two articles in the Vienna magazine, *Profil*, which were critical of the behaviour of Bruno Kreisky, the retiring Chancellor and President of the Austrian Socialist Party. In a television interview Kreisky had described the Jewish Documentation Centre (run by Simon Wiesenthal) as a political mafia and its activities as employing "mafia methods". These comments were prompted by Wiesenthal's accusation that Friedrich Peter (President of the Austrian Liberal Party) had served in the first SS Infantry Brigade during the Second World War. Against this background, Lingens wrote an article criticising Kreisky's attitude to Peter and said that had Kreisky's comments about Wiesenthal "been made by someone else this would probably have been described as the basest opportunism". The second article in which he described Kreisky's behaviour as "immoral, undignified" was a development of the first.

Kreisky brought two private prosecutions under article 111 of the Austrian Criminal Code against Lingens, who was found guilty of defamation. He was fined, but in view of his good faith no damages award was made. After his appeals failed, Lingens complained to Strasbourg that his conviction for

---

[12] *Lingens* v. *Austria*, Application no. 8303/79 (1981) 26 D & R 171.

[13] In *Sullivan* v. *New York Times* (1964) 376 US 254, the US Supreme Court decided that no action for defamation would lie in respect of political speech, unless the plaintiff could prove "actual malice" on the part of the disseminator: for a comparative account of this area of defamation law see the scholarly work of I Loveland, *Political Libels* (Oxford, Hart Publishing, 2000).

[14] Series A no 103 (1986).

defamation through the press in accordance with article 111.2 of the Criminal Code was a violation of Article 10. According to article 111.3, proof of truth is a defence to the action.

There was no dispute between the parties that the conviction was "prescribed by law" and that it was designed to protect "the reputation or rights of others", thus fulfilling two of the conditions laid down in Article 10(2). Argument centred on the question of whether the conviction "was necessary in a democratic society". The Court quoted from its judgment in *Handyside*, and continued:

> "These principles are of particular importance as far as the press is concerned . . . it is incumbent on it to impart information and ideas on political issues just as on those in other areas of public interest. Not only does the press have the task of imparting such information and ideas: the public also has a right to receive them . . . freedom of political debate is at the very core of the concept of a democratic society which prevails throughout the Convention . . . Article 10(2) enables the reputation of . . . all individuals to be protected, and this protection extends to politicians too, even when they are not acting in their private capacity; but in such cases the requirements of such protection have to be weighed in relation to the interests of open discussion of political issues".[15]

In an important passage, that was conclusive for the applicant, the Court held that:

> "a careful distinction needs to be made between facts and value-judgements. The existence of facts can be demonstrated whereas the truth of value-judgments is not susceptible of proof . . . As regards value-judgements [the requirement to prove truth in article 111.3 Austrian Criminal Code] is impossible of fulfilment and it infringes freedom of opinion itself, which is a fundamental part of the right secured by Article 10 of the Convention".[16]

In addition, the Court alluded to the fact that although the penalty in terms of the fine and confiscation of the articles had not in fact prevented the applicant from expressing himself, it would be likely to have a chilling effect on political debate by deterring journalists from contributing to public discussion of issues affecting the life of the community.[17]

This distinction between facts and value-judgements is crucial and one that pervades the jurisprudence. However, the indications as to how statements are to be classified as falling within either category are few and the discussion is opaque. It is possible to discern a general trend toward classifying a statement as a value judgement if it constitutes a statement of opinion. The Strasbourg view of value judgements is that they are not susceptible of proof and a defence of justification in relation to such statements cannot therefore be regarded as necessary in a democratic society.

---

[15] *Ibid.* paras 41 and 42.
[16] *Ibid.* para. 46.
[17] *Ibid.* para. 44.

In *De Haes and Gijsels* v. *Belgium*, the applicants, an editor and a journalist, had published five articles in which they had accused three judges and the Advocate-General in the Antwerp Court of Appeal of bias, after they awarded custody to a father who was suspected of having committed child abuse. The applicants based their allegation of bias on the fact that the judges were part of the same social circle as the child's father and shared the same right-wing political views. The journalists were convicted of the crime of defamation under articles 275–276 of the Belgian Penal Code, according to which it is a crime to insult members of the judiciary. The Strasbourg Court found that Article 10 had been violated. It was held that the views regarding bias amounted to opinion, which was not susceptible of proof, but held that such an opinion may be excessive in the absence of *any* factual basis. Proof of bias based on the ideological leanings of the judges could not be established, but there were facts in the articles regarding the father's behaviour to his children that were capable of justifying the criticism of the decisions taken by the judges, and with the aid of the Advocate-General. It may reasonably be inferred from *De Haes and Gijsels* that the Court will not require proof of underlying facts to support an opinion: a lack of factual basis may lead to the view that an opinion is excessive, but will not *per se* justify a restriction on such expression.

The decision in *De Haes and Gijsels* is a departure from *Barfod* v. *Denmark*,[18] where the Court upheld the criminal conviction of a journalist for libel because he had insulted two judges, by accusing them of bias. There appeared to be reasonable grounds for making the comment since the article related to a tax case and the judges were employed by one of the parties to the proceedings. However, the Court held that "[the composition of the court] may give rise to a difference of opinion as to whether the court was properly composed, it was certainly not proof of actual bias and the applicant cannot reasonably have been unaware of that".[19]

The Court has emphasised on a number of occasions that the context against which defamatory words are spoken is important, even though that context may not be fully articulated by the applicant. Thus in *Lingens*, the Court stated that:

> "In exercising it supervisory jurisdiction, the Court cannot confine itself to considering the impugned decisions in isolation; it must look at them in the light of the case as a whole, including the articles held against the applicant and the context in which they were written".[20]

It should be noted that in the earlier case of *Prager and Oberschlick* v. *Austria*,[21] the Court held that the manner in which a statement is classified, either as a statement of fact or a value judgement, comes within the ambit of a state's margin of appreciation. This approach is open to criticism on the basis

---

[18] Series A no 149 (1989).
[19] *Ibid.* at para. 33.
[20] *Lingens* v. *Austria*, *supra* n.14 at para. 40.
[21] (1995) 21 EHRR 1.

that the state could arbitrarily remove the supervisory jurisdiction of Strasbourg through applying a legal technicality. There is no further support for this margin in the jurisprudence and it could be argued therefore that this ruling does not form part of the *jurisprudence constante*. It is also a dictum that does not sit comfortably with the general approach to restrictions on freedom of expression: they must always be narrowly interpreted and the necessity for any restrictions convincingly justified.[22]

De Haes and Gijsels has been described as confirming the "extension of Article 10's public-private defamation divide that was introduced in *Thorgeirson* v. *Iceland*,[23] from matters affecting just politicians to all information raising a legitimate matter of public interest".[24] In *Thorgeirson*, the applicant had been convicted of defamation after he published two articles in a daily newspaper in which he made allegations of brutality against the police force. The Court refused to accept the government's argument that the wide limits of acceptable criticism in political discussion did not apply to other matters of public interest: there was no warrant in the case law for distinguishing between the two. The Court took the view that it was unreasonable, if not impossible, for the applicant to be required to establish the truth of his statements, in view of the fact that he was reporting what others had said about police brutality. The motive of the applicant was to encourage a public investigation into the activities of the police force and having regard to that fact the Court did not find the language excessive.

It should be noted that the margin of appreciation allowed to the state in deciding whether there is a pressing social need to restrict expression is generally greater in the fields of commercial and artistic speech. However, in *Hertel* v. *Switzerland*,[25] the margin in the commercial sphere was reduced where the applicant had been banned under unfair competition legislation from publishing the results of his scientific research which showed that food prepared in microwave ovens was a danger to health. The Court found that Article 10 had been violated and that the state's margin of appreciation is reduced when the freedom to take part in a debate affecting the public interest, for example, public health, is at stake.

In *Bladet Tromso* v. *Stensaas*,[26] the Norwegian courts had found that statements of fact published by the applicants were defamatory and not proved to be true. The statements were taken from a report into seal hunting by an inspector. The newspaper had not verified the information by independent research. The Court said that account must be taken of the overall background and public controversy surrounding seal hunting when the statements were made. The

---

[22] *Sunday Times* v. *United Kingdom (No 2)* Series A no 217 (1992).
[23] 14 EHRR 843 (1992).
[24] Loveland, *supra* n.13 at 154.
[25] (1998) 28 EHRR 534.
[26] (1999) 29 EHRR 125.

reporting was fair and it was balanced, since different views were presented. The chilling effect of defamation laws was highlighted:

> "The most careful scrutiny on the part of the Court is called for when, as in the present case, the measures taken or sanctions imposed by the national authority are capable of discouraging the press in debates over matters of legitimate public concern".[27]

The Court held that whether the newspaper could be dispensed from the ordinary obligation of verifying the information depended on two factors: the "nature and degree of the defamation . . . and the extent to which the newspaper could reasonably regard the [report] as reliable".[28] As to the first, a number of the allegations were not serious, those that were could be understood as being exaggerated. More importantly, none of those accused of committing "reprehensible acts" were named (the ship was named). With regard to the second factor, the report had been drawn up by an inspector appointed by the Ministry of Fisheries and the press should normally be entitled to rely on the contents without undertaking independent research.[29] In English law, unless the newspaper could establish that the publication attracted the defence of qualified privilege, the facts set out in the newspaper report would have to be justified. The necessity to establish qualified privilege has a chilling effect on publication and this is one of the considerations that has led other Commonwealth courts to adopt a generic defence of qualified privilege.[30]

The *Bladet Tromso* case is yet a further enlargement of press freedom under the Convention. Here, admittedly the issue of seal hunting was a matter of considerable public interest, but the defamed were private individuals and the statements were statements of fact.

Another element the Court uses to evaluate the necessity for restrictions on freedom of expression is the good faith of the speaker, which is tested by reference to two issues: what was the motive of the speaker in making a defamatory statement and did the speaker exercise due care in disseminating the information. In *Bladet Tromso*, the aim of publication was to stimulate debate and it was reasonable for the newspaper to rely on the inspector's report. In *Lingens*,[31] the Court noted that the good faith of the applicant was undisputed by the Austrian courts, his motive was to voice political criticism of politicians on political questions and politicians were expected to show greater tolerance of defamation than other individuals.[32] Similarly, in *Thorgeirson*, the Court was not convinced that the aim of the articles was to besmirch the reputation of the police force; rather, the journalist's aim was to urge the Minister of Justice to establish an official investigation into the allegations. On the other hand, the

---

[27] (1999) 29 EHRR 125, at para. 64.
[28] *Ibid.* at para. 66.
[29] *Ibid.* at para. 68.
[30] See discussion *infra.*
[31] *Supra* n.14 at para. 46.
[32] *Ibid.* at para. 21

journalist applicant in *Prager and Oberschlick*, who was convicted of defaming a judge in a periodical was unable to invoke his:

> "good faith or compliance with the ethics of journalism. The research that he had undertaken [did] not appear adequate to substantiate such serious allegations . . . the applicant had not attended a single criminal trial before Judge J. Furthermore, he had not given the judge any opportunity to comment on the accusations levelled against him".[33]

Thus, motive and due diligence are taken into account in order to test the necessity of restricting the Article 10 right.

COMPATIBILITY OF THE COMMON LAW ACTION FOR DEFAMATION WITH ARTICLE 10

The structure of Article 10 contemplates that the right to freedom of expression may be restricted for the protection of the reputation of others.[34] It can be inferred from the cases that have gone to Strasbourg that English defamation laws will generally surmount the first two hurdles laid down under Article 10(2), namely that such restrictions are prescribed by law[35] and pursue a legitimate aim. The third requirement, that any restriction should be necessary in a democratic society, is the one against which English law requires to be evaluated. The following discussion will examine aspects of the defences available in English law that appear most susceptible to attack for non-compliance with Article 10 standards.

It is trite to observe that not every defamatory statement will ground a cause of action in English law. There is in place a range of defences which may be invoked and which can be seen to be supportive of a free speech principle. Thus, in *McDonald's Corp. v. Steel*,[36] Neill LJ commented that:

> "It is to be remembered that the defences of justification and fair comment form part of the framework by which free speech is protected. It is therefore important that no unnecessary barriers to the use of these defences are erected".

As in the case of other Member States of the Council of Europe, the defence of justification is generally available under English law, save with regard to certain types of criminal libel. The treatment of defamation as a matter of criminal law is not incompatible with the Convention; indeed, many states routinely prosecute. However, it might be argued that a failure to allow a defendant to justify a statement is incompatible with the Convention:[37] the decision in *Barfod*

---

[33] *Supra* n.21 at para. 37.

[34] Note that unlike Article 17 of the International Covenant on Civil and Political Rights, the Convention does not enumerate amongst the human rights protected the right to reputation.

[35] See discussion accompanying n.9, *supra*.

[36] [1995] 3 All ER 615 at 621.

[37] According to Libel Act 1843, s. 6, it is a defence to an action for criminal libel if the defendant can prove that publication was for the public benefit: see P Milmo and W V H Rogers (eds), *Gatley on Libel and Slander*, 9th edn (London, Sweet & Maxwell 1998) at 22.6.

upheld a conviction for insulting the judiciary and the relevant domestic law did not permit the defence of truth where words used were "unduly insulting". However, while *De Haes and Gijsels* did not overrule *Barfod*, its correctness must be open to doubt.

In addition to justification, a defendant may, where appropriate plead fair comment on a matter of public interest or that the defamatory words were spoken on a privileged occasion. The question which arises is whether these defences are sufficiently accommodating of freedom of expression that they satisfy the Article 10 standard.

The defence of fair comment has been described as a "bulwark of free speech".[38] However, in order for a defamatory statement to qualify for this defence:

> "it must be recognisable by the ordinary, reasonable reader as comment and the key to this is whether it is supported by facts, stated or indicated, upon which, as comment, it may be based".[39]

If a statement is found to be a statement of fact, rather than comment, then subject to the rules on privilege, only a plea of justification will exonerate the defendant. If the statement is a comment, the speaker must prove the truth of the underlying facts on which the comment is based. A speaker is not required to set out all the facts he is commenting on. As Gatley states, this would be a completely impracticable rule: "if the law required even serious newspapers to be like doctoral theses the right of discussion of public affairs would be destroyed".[40] What is important is that there should be a "sufficient substratum of fact stated or, at least where the subject matter is well-known or easily ascertainable, indicated in the article complained of".[41] Section 6 of the Defamation Act 1952 affords some relief to a defendant by providing that the defence will not fail if not every fact is proved provided that "the expression of opinion is fair comment having regard to such of the facts alleged or referred to in the words complained of as are proved".

The previous section on Strasbourg jurisprudence has emphasised the difference in treatment by the Court between facts and value judgements. It may[42] be acceptable to require proof of the truth of statements of fact, but the truth of value judgements is not susceptible of proof. It has been suggested by Young that, "a strong argument can be made that English law would be incompatible with Article 10 if value judgements are classified as statements of fact".[43] This

---

[38] Faulks Committee (Cmnd. 5909, 1975) at para. 151, quoted by Milmo and Rogers, *ibid.* at 12.1.

[39] *Gatley, supra* n.37 at 12.7.

[40] *Ibid.* at 12.12.

[41] *Ibid.*

[42] Subject to *Bladet Tromso, supra* n.26.

[43] A Young, "Fact, Opinion and the Human Rights Act 1998: Does English Law Need to Modify its Definition of 'Statements of Opinion' to Ensure Compliance with Article 10 of the European Convention on Human Rights?", (2000) 20 *OJLS* 89 at 97.

statement must be read in the light of *Prager and Oberschlick*, where it was held that classification was within the state's margin of appreciation, but as the previous discussion has indicated this view would seem to be out of step with Strasbourg jurisprudence.

In order to plead the defence of fair comment, a statement of opinion must be based on true facts. Whether a statement is one of fact or opinion will depend upon whether it is "evaluative or descriptive".[44] In order for it to be evaluative and therefore a statement of opinion it must identify or refer to relevant facts.

Taking account of these principles and comparing them with the scope of protection given to freedom of expression by Strasbourg, one is driven to the conclusion that English law falls short of the Convention goals. Strasbourg has emphasised how important it is to take account of "context", although that is not clearly defined, and has not imposed such an exacting standard regarding the necessity to establish the truth of underlying facts. A case like *Telnikoff* v. *Matusevitch*,[45] illustrates the problems defendants may face where they plead fair comment. It should be recalled, in particular, that according to Convention jurisprudence any restrictions on freedom of expression must always be "narrowly interpreted and the necessity for any restrictions must be convincingly established".[46]

In *Telnikoff*, the plaintiff a Russian émigré and an employee of the BBC's Russian service, had written an article, published by the *Daily Telegraph* newspaper, criticising the BBC's Russian service for employing too many people from the ethnic minorities of the Soviet Union and not enough from among those who "associate themselves ethnically, spiritually or religiously with the Russian people". The defendant, also a Russian émigré, wrote a letter which was published in the same newspaper in which he indicated that the article was anti-semitic and he said that Mr Telnikoff was advocating that the management of the Russian service should "switch from a professional test to a blood test" and that "his racialist recipe required that ethnically alien" employees should be dismissed from the Russian service. The plaintiff took exception to the letter and instituted libel proceedings. The defendant argued that these were statements of opinion, commenting on the plaintiff's article.

The House of Lords considered that the letter should be examined on its own in determining whether the statements were fact or comment, with the result that the statements described above must be regarded as fact, and with regard to which the defendant had not pleaded any defence. This seems a remarkably tough approach, given that the defendant had been provoked into writing a letter in response to the polemical tone of the plaintiff's article, and it was apparent from the letter that the defendant was responding to the opinions the plaintiff had expressed.

---

[44] Young, *ibid.* at 98.
[45] [1992] AC 343.
[46] *Sunday Times* v. *United Kingdom* Series A no 217 *supra* n.22.

Lord Ackner, a lone dissenting voice, was the only member of the House of Lords to acknowledge the human rights dimension to the case, beginning his speech with a reference to the fundamental freedom of speech. He referred to a number of dicta which emphasise the importance of fair comment in order to facilitate free discussion on matters of public interest and he cited Lord Denning in *Slim* v. *Daily Telegraph*,[47] who said that:

> "the right to fair comment is one of the essential ingredients which go to make up our freedom of speech. We must ever maintain this right intact. It must not be whittled down by legal refinements".

Lord Ackner concluded that the essential question is clearly what is the "context" in which the letter was to be construed and he shared the view of Woolf LJ that if the court was not entitled to look at the material on which it was alleged that the words complained of were commenting that would be unduly restrictive of the defence. Lord Ackner did not refer to the Convention in his speech; indeed it is surprising that no Convention argument was made, but his reasoning is in tune with Convention jurisprudence and if the decision on the same facts were to be examined today against the new legal landscape the respondent's arguments seem irrefutable. The Convention jurisprudence stresses the importance of context, that not only political issues, but also other matters of public debate deserve the greatest protection and that if a person puts himself in the limelight he may expect to be the subject of discussion, which may at times be exaggerated.

The defence of privilege may be available for defamatory statements of fact. Privilege may be absolute, for example statements made during parliamentary or judicial proceedings, or it may be qualified. Qualified privilege will apply to "an occasion where the person who makes a communication has an interest or a duty, legal, social, or moral, to make it to the person to whom it is made, and the person to whom it is made has a corresponding interest or duty to receive it".[48] Qualified privilege is defeasible on proof of malice.[49]

Despite the advent of the Human Rights Act, the House of Lords, when given the opportunity recently in *Reynolds* v. *Times Newspapers*,[50] has refused to categorise "political information" as benefiting from qualified privilege. This conservatism is to be contrasted with the creativity of the High Court of Australia and the New Zealand Court of Appeal which have both recognised political expression as deserving of qualified privilege, although in each system the scope of political expression and the effect of such expression are treated differently. In *Reynolds*, Lord Nicholls (Lord Hobhouse and Lord Cooke concurring) confidently asserted that "the common law approach accords with the present state

---

[47] [1968] 1 All ER 497 at 503.

[48] *Adam* v. *Ward* [1917] AC 309 at 334 per Lord Atkinson.

[49] Cf the application of a good faith test by Strasbourg in evaluating whether a restriction on freedom of expression is necessary in a democratic society, *supra* n.31.

[50] [1999] 3 WLR 1010.

of human rights jurisprudence",[51] a view perhaps open to question as the following discussion will demonstrate. The stance taken by the House of Lords has recently, and emphatically, been rebuffed by the New Zealand Court of Appeal in *Lange* v. *Atkinson*,[52] even after the Privy Council had considered that the New Zealand court would find it advantageous to consider both the English Court of Appeal and House of Lords decisions in *Reynolds*. Not for the first time we see that a major cleavage in policy between the higher Commonwealth courts has been revealed. While local conditions clearly demanded a New Zealand answer[53] to the *Murphy* v. *Brentwood* question, freedom of expression is surely a different issue in that it serves to promote the democratic quality of a society, wherever that society may be. This is an example of jurisprudence where the English courts have much to learn from their Commonwealth counterparts.

In *Reynolds*, the former Taoiseach of Ireland alleged that he had been defamed by the headline and a number of paragraphs in an article in the *Sunday Times* newspaper which was published three days after his resignation at a time of political crisis. The title was "Goodbye Gombeen Man. Why a Fib Too far Proved Fatal for the Political Career of Ireland's Peacemaker and Mr. Fixit" and the article alleged that the plaintiff had knowingly misled the Dail by suppressing information. The plaintiff had no complaint regarding the coverage of the story by the Irish edition of the *Sunday Times*.

The defendant argued that the time had come for English law to recognise political speech as a generic category of expression deserving of qualified privilege, specifically that English law should adopt the scope of such speech indicated by the formulation laid down by Brennan J in *Lange* v. *Australian Broadcasting Corporation*,[54] namely, the dissemination of information, opinions and arguments concerning government and political matters affecting the people of the United Kingdom.[55] However, defendant's counsel, Lord Anthony Lester QC, argued that, unlike Australia, English law should not subject the speaker to a requirement to prove reasonableness, proof of malice being a sufficient brake on the effect of the defence.[56]

This argument was rejected by the House of Lords in a speech by Lord Nicholls which seems completely out of step with what would be desirable in the interests of the "common convenience and welfare of society"[57] (the traditional justification for the recognition of qualified privilege) as this might presently be understood. Although His Lordship stated that his starting point was freedom of expression and he noted that "freedom to disseminate and

---

[51] *Ibid.* at 1026.

[52] [2000] NZLR 257.

[53] See *Invercargill City Council* v. *Hamlin* [1996] 1 All ER 756.

[54] (1997) 71 ALJR 818.

[55] *Reynolds, supra* n.6 at 1022.

[56] As Loveland notes, *supra* n.13 at 165 n.39, though, Lord Lester acknowledged that "most juries would regard gross negligence on a newspaper's part as *prima facie* evidence of malice".

[57] *Toogood* v. *Spyring* (1834) 1 CM & R 181 at 193 per Parke B.

receive information on political matters is essential to the proper functioning of the system of parliamentary democracy cherished in this country", he proceeded on the basis that he was addressing two interests of equal importance. He rather swiftly moved from freedom of speech to stating that:

> "Protection of reputation is conducive to the public good. It is in the public interest that the reputation of public figures should not be debased falsely. In the political field, in order to make an informed choice, the electorate needs to be able to identify the good as well as the bad. Consistently with these considerations, human rights conventions recognise that freedom of expression is not an absolute right. Its exercise may be subject to such restrictions as are prescribed by law and are necessary in a democratic society for the protection of the reputation of others".

According to Strasbourg, the starting point for analysis is the importance attached to freedom of expression. Freedom of expression, particularly political expression, is deserving of the highest degree of protection: the interests in speech and reputation are not accorded equal weight. Any restriction on freedom of expression must be *convincingly justified*. Lord Nicholls went on to hold that the availability of the defence should be determined on a case by case basis, taking account of all the circumstances in order to decide whether publication was privileged because of the value to the public. The matters to be taken into account in making this assessment would include:

> "2. The nature of the information, and the extent to which the subject matter is a matter of public concern 3. The source of the information. Some informants have no direct knowledge of the events. Some have their own axes to grind, or are being paid for their stories.4. The steps taken to verify the information. 6. The urgency of the matter. News is often a perishable commodity. 7. Whether comment was sought from the plaintiff".

It is arguable, but by no means certain, that if the facts that arose in *Bladet Tromso* came before an English court, the newspaper report would constitute a privileged occasion. Given that the newspaper was relying on a report and did not verify/take any steps to verify the information, an English court might say the defence did not apply. On the other hand, as the criteria in *Reynolds* indicate, the fact that a story is of public interest and that news is a perishable commodity would argue in favour of applying the defence.

As indicated, the House of Lords' approach has been rejected by the New Zealand Court of Appeal in *Lange* v. *Atkinson*,[58] where the court confirmed its previous decision that the defence of qualified privilege would be available in respect of a statement published generally and in respect of the actions and qualities of those currently or formerly in Parliament and those with immediate aspirations to such election, so far as those actions and qualities directly affected their capacity (including their personal ability and willingness) to meet their public responsibilities. Thus, the scope of privileged speech is narrower than in

---

[58] [2000] 1 NZLR 257.

the Australian *Lange* test, but there is no requirement to prove reasonableness.[59] The New Zealand court expressed disquiet with the *Reynolds* decision for two very important reasons.

First, the principles laid down in *Reynolds* exacerbate the undoubted chilling effect of English defamation law. The New Zealand court referred to the important empirical work conducted in this area by Barendt, Lustgarten, Norrie and Stephenson resulting in *Libel and Media: The Chilling Effect* where the authors concluded that:

> " 'the chilling effect genuinely does exist and significantly restricts what the public is able to read and hear' and that 'uncertainty in both the principles of defamation law and their practical application induce great caution on the part of the media. Virtually every interviewee, in all branches of the media, emphasised the lottery aspect attached to this area of the law' ".

Secondly, for the New Zealand Court of Appeal, Lord Nicholls' list of factors to be taken into account in determining whether the public had an interest in receiving information added to the uncertainty in this area, because of the blurring of the distinction between the occasion and its abuse. Lord Nicholls was of the view that it makes no practical difference when these questions are asked, but the New Zealand court was not so sanguine, since it would reduce the role of the jury in freedom of speech cases.

Perhaps the most telling comment in *Reynolds* is Lord Nicholls observation that: "the sad fact is that the overall handling of these matters by the national press, with its own commercial interests to serve, does not always command general confidence".[60] It could equally be said that the fact that Jonathan Aitken believed he could bring a successful libel action against the *Guardian* newspaper demonstrates just how difficult it may be for a newspaper to defend a truthful story disseminated in the public interest. Perhaps the real problem with English law and freedom of speech has lain in the failure to introduce a privacy law. The newspaper headlines which provoke the most frequent (and justifiable) outrage are those relating to the private life of individuals where there is arguably no public interest to pursue in publication. The "incorporation" of the Convention means that English courts can no longer sit on the fence when faced with arguments that the right to privacy should be recognised explicitly. The worst excesses of the press will thereby be checked and the courts will feel able to uphold the constitutional right to free speech which is so important for a free flow of political information. Loveland has rightly identified the approach of the English courts as reflecting a particular and peculiarly common law cast of mind which fails to appreciate the constitutional dimension to defamation law: He says that:

[59] For a detailed analysis, see generally Loveland, *supra* n.13.
[60] *Supra* n.50 at 1024.

"while the [European Court of Human Rights] and the courts in the USA, Australia and New Zealand now categorise political libels as a facet of constitutional law, the English Court of Appeal continues to approach them as a part of the law of torts".[61]

In *Lange* v. *Atkinson* (heard by the Judicial Committee identically composed as *Reynolds*), Lord Nicholls giving judgment stated that a feature of the law of England, Australia and New Zealand is the "recognition that striking a balance between freedom of expression and protection of reputation calls for a value judgement which depends upon local political and social conditions".[62] As we have seen, this is not a correct representation of the law in England following the Human Rights Act. The courts are required to ensure compatibility with the Convention and to take account of Strasbourg jurisprudence. Although in some respects the transposition of principles from Strasbourg into English law is a matter of uncertainty, one thing is clear. In the field of political speech, so essential to the functioning of a democratic society, any margin of appreciation allowed to states will be very limited. Although the margin of appreciation doctrine is applied to evaluate state behaviour for compliance with the Convention,[63] the extensive body of case law under Article 10 illustrating its application must affect the judgement of the English courts as to where to draw the line between legitimate comment and reporting, and actionable defamation.

---

[61] Loveland, *supra* n.13 at 166.
[62] LEXIS transcript Privy Council, 28 October 1999.
[63] See text accompanying n.152 in Chapter 3.

7

Privacy

T HE TERMS "PRIVACY" and "private life" are used in a wealth of different contexts to indicate interests deserving of protection by the state from interference either by private third parties or by the state itself.[1] The range of interests protected by Article 8 of the Convention was outlined in Chapter 3, where it was observed that matters affecting one's sexual orientation, gender identity, physical and psychological integrity and the disclosure of personal information are all encompassed under the umbrella of "private life". In the USA, privacy rights and interests are usually considered to refer to matters of individual autonomy, such as sexuality[2] and reproductive freedom,[3] which are protected as matters of constitutional law and the ability to restrict the dissemination of personal information[4] which is achieved through tort law.

This chapter will examine that aspect of private life or privacy that relates to the non-consensual disclosure of personal information, in other words, the ability to seek a remedy where the defendant has made/proposes to make an unauthorised disclosure of private facts. The paradigm case for the purposes of this discussion would arise where the defendant has acquired private personal information regarding a claimant and proposes to publish that information in the media (broadcasting or press). The fact that information may be gleaned from the public record should not necessarily prevent the information from being "private" for these purposes. Private information is information relating to the intimate sphere of a person's life; the author would argue that the flow of such information to those with no legitimate interest in it may be restricted in order to enhance the free development of the human personality. A distinction should be drawn between "secret" information, traditionally the province of actions for breach of confidence and explicitly/implicitly designated as secret by the confider of information, and "private" information which by virtue of the subject matter has the capacity to embarrass or inhibit a person in the free development of their personality and relationships with others.

Until the Human Rights Act, in the absence of a tort action directed specifically to protect privacy, a victim of press intrusion was forced to try to

---

[1] See E Barendt, "Privacy as a Constitutional Right and Value", in P Birks (ed), *Privacy and Loyalty* (Oxford, Clarendon Press, 1997).

[2] *Bowers* v. *Hardwick* 85 US 140 (1986).

[3] *Griswold* v. *Connecticut*, 381 US 479 (1965).

[4] *Melvin* v. *Reid* 112 Cal App 285 (1931).

"pigeonhole"[5] her claim into the established criteria of a range of legal and equitable remedies in order to achieve redress. It might be that a plaintiff would be successful in finding the appropriate peg on which to hang a claim,[6] but it is undeniable that English law has often protected privacy "in a patchy, capricious and uncertain way".[7] *Kaye* v. *Robertson*[8] is probably the most frequently cited example of the legal gymnastics required in order to try to restrain publication of private facts. Gorden Kaye, a well-known actor was recovering in hospital following brain surgery. He was in a private room, with a notice on the door restricting access by visitors. Journalists gained access to the room, conducted an "interview", took photographs and left. Fifteen minutes later Mr Kaye had no recollection of their visit. In an action to restrain publication, the plaintiff could not argue that his right to privacy had been invaded, there being no recognised cause of action or right.[9] Instead, an injunction was sought on the basis of four causes of action: trespass, passing off, libel and malicious falsehood. While the Court of Appeal considered that it was certainly arguable that the plaintiff would establish a libel by innuendo[10] at full trial, and that a jury would "probably" find that Mr Kaye had been libelled, such a conclusion was not "inevitable". Thus, the injunction on the ground of libel was refused. Limited relief was granted on the basis of malicious falsehood: the newspaper was restrained from publishing anything which could be understood as conveying the impression that the plaintiff had consented to the interview or being photographed. This case is a classic example of the limitations to the protection of human rights in a system which has developed as a system of "remedies", rather than rights. It is of interest to note that in this field, a significant divergence between the common law systems in the USA and England emerged nearly a century ago.

So incensed was Samuel Warren by newspaper speculation about the impending nuptials of his daughter that, in 1890, in conjunction with his law partner Louis Brandeis, he was driven to write what is arguably one of the most famous academic articles ever published, "The Right to Privacy". Despite the temporal

---

[5] To adopt the metaphor employed by Markesinis: B Markesinis, "Our Patchy Law of Privacy—Time to do Something About It", (1990) 53 *MLR* 802.

[6] For examples, see D Seipp, "English Judicial Recognition of a Right to Privacy", (1983) 3 OJLS 325.

[7] Markesinis, *supra* n5.

[8] [1991] FSR 62.

[9] See Megarry J in *Malone* v. *Metropolitan Police Commissioner* [1979] 1 Ch 344 at 372 where he held that there is no general right to privacy in English law and stated that: "No new right in the law, fully-fledged with all the appropriate safeguards, can spring from the head of a judge deciding a particular case: only Parliament can create such a right". In *Malone*, it will be recalled that the court held that Article 8 was not a right in English law, see text accompanying n.15 inChapter 1.

[10] By analogy with *Tolley* v. *Fry* [1931] AC 333. The implication that would be raised by publication of the Kaye story would presumably be that he had consented to give a first "exclusive" interview to the *Sunday Sport* and to be photographed by their photographer. In view of the fact that this is a newspaper described by Potter J as having a "lurid and sensational style", the plaintiff argued that the implication in the article "would have the effect of lowering Mr. Kaye in the esteem of right-thinking people generally" (per Glidewell LJ).

distance, the article has contemporary resonance for anyone who is critical of the prurient activities of the press:

> "Of the desirability—indeed of the necessity—of some such protection, there can, it is believed be no doubt. The press is overstepping in every direction the obvious bounds of propriety and decency. Gossip is no longer the resource of the idle and vicious, but has become a trade, which is pursued with industry as well as effrontery".[11]

Warren and Brandeis charted the development of the common law from its early preoccupation with physical interference with life and tangible property to the recognition of man's spiritual nature, his feelings and his intellect. Over the centuries the common law had gradually extended the range of interests deserving of protection from land and cattle to a recognition of the legal value of "sensations". Thus, gradually the interest in reputation was protected through actions for slander and libel. The development of copyright laws and the protection of trade secrets and trade marks were but aspects of the legal protection of intellectual and emotional life. Warren and Brandeis argued that the unifying general principle emanating from the common law was the "right to be let alone". Their call for law reform, initially unheeded, was gradually taken up by the states, which accorded privacy protection to individuals, either through common law development or statute.

Similarly, in England over the last twenty years there has been a groundswell of both judicial and academic opinion arguing that a right to privacy should be recognised by English law. In *Kaye*, Bingham LJ expressed trenchant criticism of the state of English law: "If ever a person has a right to be let alone by strangers with no public interest to pursue, it must surely be when he lies in hospital recovering from brain surgery and in no more than partial command of his faculties".

Since 1 January 1991 the activities of the press have been regulated by the Press Complaints Commission (PCC) a non-statutory self-regulatory body which has no powers to fine offenders nor to seek injunctions. Its powers are limited to investigation of complaints and the issuing of adjudications. The PCC will request editors to publish findings, but it has no right to require publication and it cannot investigate anticipated breaches of the Code, unless there is an allegation of harassment. In practice editors regularly publish the findings of the PCC. However, in the light of continuing circulation wars among the tabloid press, and prurient standards of journalism, which can lead to the callous exploitation of those in whom there is no legitimate public interest,[12] it is clear that the PCC is inadequate to the task.

---

[11] (1890) 4 *Harv L Rev* 193.

[12] To take just one example, in April 2001, the *News of the World* exposed a woman who, unbeknown to her three children, earned her living by prostitution. Her mistake had been to appear on a television gameshow where she was recognised by a member of the public. The effects on her family were devastating.

In his Review of Press Self-Regulation in 1993, Sir David Calcutt concluded that:

> "The Press Complaints Commission is not, in my view, an effective regulator of the press. It has not been set up in a way, and is not operating a code of practice, which enables it to hold the balance fairly between the press and the individual . . . As constituted, it is in essence a body set up by the industry and operating a code of practice devised by the industry and which is over favourable to the industry".[13]

Since that time there have been changes to the Code of Practice, but legitimate concerns remain that, overall, the existence of the PCC is not sufficient to ensure that appropriate standards of journalism are applied.

There are signs that English law has been moving very tentatively towards the de facto protection of a right to privacy through the incremental development of the action for breach of confidence and the recent decision of the Court of Appeal in *Douglas* v. *Hello Ltd*[14] seems to confirm that, as a result of the Human Rights Act, there is now an obligation on English courts to protect the right to privacy in English law. The more perplexing question relates to the appropriate cause of action to be employed and how precisely the right should be circumscribed, taking account of the interface between any right to privacy and the right to freedom of expression under Article 10 of the Convention. These developments, and the question of whether privacy would more appropriately be protected through the equitable remedy for breach of confidence or the recognition of a dedicated privacy tort, are described below.

The following discussion will be conducted under three main headings: first, the analysis will attempt to determine the scope of privacy as recognised by Strasbourg in order to determine what aims English law should seek to achieve in this field; secondly, an account of English law will be provided with a view to ascertaining whether Convention objectives are being met; and, finally, and linked to the above, the discussion will conclude with a consideration of whether the action for breach of confidence is an appropriate cause of action by which to protect privacy.

PRIVACY JURISPRUDENCE UNDER THE CONVENTION

As we have seen, the Convention does not cast duties directly upon third parties; it is states that agree to be bound to secure to everyone within the jurisdiction the rights and freedoms set out (Article 1). In view of the fact that the present discussion focuses on the rights of private actors *inter se*, it is necessary to examine the Strasbourg jurisprudence regarding any positive obligation on states to control the behaviour of non-state actors, the jurisprudence regarding "positive obligations". The Court has held that there may be positive obligations upon the

---

[13] Cm 2135, 1993 at xi.
[14] Court of Appeal judgment dated 21 December 2000, http:www.courtservice.gov.uk/

state in relation to Article 8. Positive obligations are fully discussed in Chapter 5, and it will be recalled that they take two forms: first, they may be such that the state itself must take positive steps to fulfil the Article 8 obligation, for example, by the enactment of legislation regarding illegitimacy,[15] or the provision of access to a decree of judicial separation;[16] or, secondly, the state may be required to procure that private parties behave in a way that that is respectful of the right to private life.[17] Thus, the Court in *X and Y* v. *The Netherlands* held that:

> "[positive obligations] may involve the adoption of measures designed to secure respect for private life even in the sphere of the relations of individuals between themselves".[18]

Although a positive obligation is discovered through the interpretation of Article 8(1), the Court has held that the limitations set out under Article 8(2) may be relevant, since the permitted aims in Article 8(2) are relevant in shaping the content of the right. In *Rees* v. *United Kingdom*,[19] the Court stated that:

> "In determining whether or not a positive obligation exists, regard must be had to the fair balance that has to be struck between the general interest of the community and the interests of the individual, the search for which balance is inherent in the whole of the Convention. In striking this balance the aims mentioned in the second paragraph of Article 8 may be of certain relevance, although this provision refers in terms only to 'interferences' with the right protected by the first paragraph—in other words is concerned with the negative obligations flowing therefrom".

One of the grounds upon which interference with the rights in Article 8(1) is permitted is where such interference is necessary, "for the protection of the rights and freedoms of others". Clearly, in most cases of privacy intrusion, as understood in the context of present discussion, the argument will be that the right to freedom of expression under Article 10 of the Convention, as another right, should prevail.

It is clear also that, in relation to positive obligations, states:

> "enjoy a wide margin of appreciation in determining the steps to be taken to ensure compliance with the Convention with due regard to the needs and resources of the community and of individuals".[20]

There have been very few occasions upon which the Strasbourg organs have considered alleged violations of Article 8, arising from the dissemination of personal information by members of the media. This is probably not surprising, in view of the fact that the United Kingdom is unusual among parties to the Convention in failing to accord a general right to privacy. Since citizens in other

[15] *Marckx* v. *Belgium* Series A no 31 (1979).
[16] *Airey* v. *Ireland* Series A no 32 (1979).
[17] *X and Y* v. *The Netherlands* Series A no 91 (1985), *Plattform "Ärtzte für das Leben"* v. *Austria* Series A no 139 (1988).
[18] *X and Y, supra* at para. 23.
[19] Series A no 106 (1986).
[20] *Johnston* v. *Ireland* Series A no 112 (1986) at para. 55.

Contracting States can avail themselves of protection at domestic level there is no need to look for recourse to Strasbourg. Those applications that have been made have failed at the admissibility stage for a variety of reasons, including the fact that the state has been acting/failed to act within its margin of appreciation. However, recent jurisprudence would suggest that a failure to protect an individual from the unauthorised disclosure of truthful personal information by the media will amount to a violation of Article 8.

The initial weakness of Strasbourg and its reluctance to supervise Convention compliance in this field effectively is illustrated by *Winer* v. *United Kingdom.*[21] Here, the applicant complained that publication of a book containing intimate details of his married life constituted a violation of his right to respect for private life. In relation to parts of the book, which were accepted by the publishers as being defamatory, the applicant had settled a claim out of court. His application to Strasbourg related to the parts of the book that contained true facts. The Commission took into account the Article 10 right to freedom of expression of both the author and publisher in establishing the extent of positive obligations under Article 8 of the Convention and alluded to the wide margin of appreciation allowed to states in fulfilling positive obligations: "the way in which a High Contracting Party may meet such obligations is largely within its discretion".[22] The Commission concluded that the applicant's right to privacy was not wholly unprotected, as was shown by his defamation action and settlement, and his own liberty to publish. The Commission also took the view that, in the light of the uncertainty surrounding the scope of action for breach of confidence, there was no necessity to bring such an action in the English courts: he had therefore exhausted domestic remedies. This decision fails to distinguish appropriately between the rights to reputation[23] and privacy,[24] respectively, and signifies an undue deference to the state in determining whether a state has met its positive obligations.

More recently, in *Spencer* v. *United Kingdom,*[25] the Commission considered the applications of the Earl and Countess Spencer in relation to newspaper reports of the latter's stay at a private clinic for the treatment of bulimia and alcoholism. The petitions alleged that the United Kingdom had violated Articles 8 and 13 (the right to an effective remedy) in failing to provide appropriate redress where private information and photographs had been published and re-published. The applications were declared inadmissible because, in failing to

---

[21] (1986) 48 D & R 154.

[22] *Ibid.* at 170.

[23] By implication, the Convention acknowledges that the interests of reputation and private life are different: Article 8 protects "private life", while the list of permitted aims for limitation of the right to freedom of expression set out under Article 10(2) includes "the protection of the reputation or rights of others". Cf Article 17 of the International Covenant on Civil and Political Rights which protects privacy and reputation.

[24] See G Gilbert and J Wright, "The Means of Protecting Human Rights in the United Kingdom", (1997) 1 *International Journal of Human Rights* 23 at 49.

[25] (1998) 25 EHRR CD 172.

invoke an action for breach of confidence in the English courts, the Commission found that the applicants had failed to exhaust domestic remedies as required by then Article 26 (now Article 35) of the Convention. However, of significance for the present discussion, the Commission declared that:

> "On the facts as presented by the parties, the Commission would not exclude that the absence of an actionable remedy in relation to the publications of which the applicants complain could show a lack of respect for their private lives. It has regard in this respect to the duties and responsibilities that are carried with the right of freedom of expression guaranteed by Article 10 . . . and to the Contracting States' obligation to provide a measure of protection to the right of privacy of an individual affected by others' exercise of their freedom of expression".

This dictum supports the notion that informational privacy should be protected by Article 8. It is also consonant with the evolutive interpretative technique applied by Strasbourg that this right should be recognised, given that there is a European consensus on this matter.[26]

It should be noted that following formal complaints by the Spencers, the PCC ruled that the press had breached the Code of Practice and did not accept that a photograph taken of an indisputably ill person walking in private secluded grounds could be anything other than a breach of the Code. In view of its finding on Article 8, the Commission also rejected the Article 13 complaint as manifestly ill-founded. However, the corollary of the Commission's reasoning regarding the availability of a breach of confidence (in view of the fact that the PCC had ruled on the matter) must be that the possibility of complaint to, and adjudication by the PCC, is not sufficient to secure the right under Article 8 and nor is it an effective remedy for the purposes of Article 13. If the possibility of recourse to the PCC was sufficient to discharge the Article 13 obligation, presumably the Commission would have indicated as much.

The views of the Commission in *Spencer* allude to the conundrum which any complaint regarding privacy as understood in the present context raises, namely, how to balance any Article 8 privacy right against the right to freedom of expression under Article 10. In particular, at what point does the Article 8 right yield to the Article 10 interest in freedom of expression? There is little in the Convention jurisprudence to guide us here, and the difficulty is exacerbated by the opaque nature of the margin of appreciation doctrine as applied to positive obligations. What does emerge, though, from the Convention jurisprudence is the importance that must be attributed to freedom of expression if a society is to embody a healthy democracy, which is after all recognised as the very cornerstone of the protection of human rights (Preamble to the Convention). As we have seen there is a large measure of discretion allowed to states in fulfilling those positive obligations: the existence of this discretion, however, cannot be taken to negate the existence of the obligation. In *Winer*, greater weight

---

[26] See G Phillipson and H Fenwick, "Breach of Confidence as a Privacy Remedy", (2000) 63 *MLR* 660 at 666.

attached to the interest in freedom of expression; in *Spencer*, the interest in privacy was acknowledged, but on the facts no substantive evaluation for compliance was carried out because of the failure to exhaust domestic remedies. The implication in *Spencer* is that had the breach of confidence action been tried and had failed to yield a remedy, then there would have been a violation of Article 8. The applicants' complaint related to a private matter (health) and a private occasion (treatment at a clinic).

The author is not aware of any case under the Convention where a violation of Article 8 arising from the publication of private facts has been found, but a number of cases under Article 10 indicate that sanctions applied regarding the publication of private facts will be appropriate.

It was implied in *Lingens* v. *Austria*,[27] that a political figure may have recourse to Article 8 in relation to private matters. *Lingens*, is primarily a defamation case and was described in detail in Chapter 6, but observations were made by the Court regarding privacy. In *Lingens*, the applicant journalist complained that his criminal conviction for defamation of a politician violated his Article 10 right. Lingens had criticised public statements made by then Chancellor Kreisky regarding Simon Wiesenthal, the Nazi hunter, and also Kreisky's attitude to former Nazis and National Socialism. The Court held that there was no need to read Article 10 in the light of Article 8 because the statements made by Kreisky were public and the applicant's criticisms related to Kreisky the politician. The implication is that private statements would have raised an issue under Article 8, the public character of Kreisky notwithstanding, so that a public figure will be able to seek the protection of Articles 8, the ultimate balance between Article 8 and 10 depending upon context.

In *N* v. *Portugal*,[28] an application was made by the publisher of photographs under Article 10. He had been convicted of defamation and invasion of privacy for publishing intimate photographs of a businessman. The application was rejected as manifestly ill-founded and a sentence of 15 months' imprisonment, as well as the payment of a fine and damages, was considered by the Commission to be proportionate and necessary to protect the rights of others.

The facts in *Spencer* clearly raised a private life issue. The photograph was taken with the aid of a telephoto lens of activity on private property and the text of the newspaper articles related to the applicant's health, a private matter. One of the difficulties that will arise in relation to assessment of intrusion by the media is whether what a person does in public may be included in the notion of private life, so that, for example, a photograph of a person sunbathing topless on the beach might be the subject of protection. Should a person who is photographed eating in a restaurant be able to keep that occasion private and prevent the publication of photographs recording the occasion? When Princess Caroline

[27] Series A no 103 (1986).
[28] Application no 20683/92 (1995), discussed by S H Naismith, "Photographs, Privacy and Freedom of Expression", [1996] *EHRLR* 150.

of Monaco and her boyfriend were photographed by the French press at a garden restaurant, the German Supreme Court has held that this was a private occasion, because:

> "she had retreated to a place of seclusion where [she wished] to be left alone, as [could] be ascertained by objective criteria, and in a specific situation, where [she], relying on the fact of seclusion acts in a way that [she would not have done in public]. An unjustified intrusion into this area occurs where pictures of that person are published if taken secretly or by stealth".[29]

However, Strasbourg authorities that are directly on point are scarce. In *Friedl* v. *Austria*,[30] the Commission decided that there had been no interference with Article 8 rights where the applicant was photographed during a demonstration in a public place. The Commission laid stress on the fact that since the authorities had not entered the applicant's home there was no intrusion into the "inner circle" of the applicant's private life and the photographs related to a public incident. It was also noted that the photographs were taken with a view to investigating road traffic offences. In *Friedl*, a friendly settlement was reached between the Austrian government and the applicant after the case had been referred to the court.

Harris, O'Boyle and Warbrick have observed that where intrusion is "slight and forseeable . . . the judgment in *Costello* v. *Roberts* would suggest that there is no infringement of private life".[31] In *Costello-Roberts*,[32] the applicant complained that the state's responsibility was engaged under Article 8 where corporal punishment was administered at a private school. On the facts, the adverse effects for the applicant's physical and moral integrity were not sufficient to engage Article 8.

Article 8 as a personality right

A number of decisions under Article 8, but outside the sphere of informational privacy, have alluded to the rationale behind the right to respect for private life and they may assist in determining where boundaries should be drawn in cases of conflict between Article 8 and Article 10. In *Friedl*, the Commission, drawing on previous jurisprudence,[33] stated that:

> " 'private life' is not limited to an 'inner circle' in which the individual may live his own personal life as he chooses and to exclude therefrom entirely the outside world not encompassed within this circle. Respect for private life must also comprise to a certain

---

[29] BGH 19 December 1995, BGHZ 131, quoted by Lord Bingham, "The Way We Live Now: Human Rights in the New Millennium", [1998] *WJCLI* 1.

[30] Series A no 305-B (1994).

[31] D J Harris, M O'Boyle and C Warbrick, *Law of the European Convention on Human Rights* (London, Butterworths, 1995) at 309.

[32] *Costello-Roberts* v. *United Kingdom* Series A no 247-B (1993).

[33] *Niemitz* v. *Germany* Series A no 251-B (1993).

degree the right to establish and develop relationships with other human beings and the outside world".[34]

In *Botta* v. *Italy*,[35] the Court stated that "the guarantee afforded by Article 8 of the Convention is primarily intended to ensure the development, without outside interference, of the personality of each individual in his relations with other human beings". There are strong echoes here of the general right to the free development of the personality, recognised by article 2 of the Basic Law of Germany, and the subject of extensive teleological interpretation by the German Constitutional Court.[36] Although neither the Basic Law of 1949, nor the German Civil Code, contain a general right to privacy, such a right has been recognised, first as an aspect of the general right to the free development of personality enshrined in article 2 of the Basic Law and, secondly, as "another right" within article 823 I BGB. The personality right includes the right to one's picture and word and the right to decide what personal information may be communicated to others. In the famous *Lebach* decision, the petitioner was a convicted criminal who was about to be released on parole and discovered that a television documentary was being prepared that would name him and show his likeness during the programme. He succeeded in obtaining an injunction to prevent the film-makers from naming or otherwise identifying him. On facts such as these, where there was no public interest in the reporting of current crime, the greater societal interest lay in the rehabilitation of the offender. The Constitutional Court stated that:

> "The importance of the right to personality, which is a cornerstone of the Constitution, requires not only that account must be taken of the sacrosanct innermost personal sphere . . . but also a strict regard for the principle of proportionality. The invasion of the personal sphere is limited to the need to satisfy adequately the interest to receive information, and the disadvantages suffered by the culprit must be proportional to the seriousness of the offence or its importance otherwise for the public".[37]

If the purpose of Article 8 is to underpin the free development of the personality, there is a strong argument for including within the concept of privacy, information that is discoverable from the public record, such disclosure to be prevented where there is no legitimate public interest to be served by publication. Such a case would arise, for example, where the media threatened to expose details regarding a person's criminal record. In contrast with German law, the Rehabilitation of Offenders Act 1974 offers so little protection,[38] that

---

[34] *Supra* n.30 at para. 44.
[35] (1998) 26 EHRR 241 at para. 32, citing *Niemitz* v. *Germany*, *supra* n.33.
[36] See B S Markesinis, *The German Law of Torts*, 3rd edn (Oxford, Clarendon Press, 1994) at 31.
[37] BverfGE 35, 202 extracted in Markesinis, *ibid.* at 390, 396.
[38] A number of sentences are excluded from rehabilitation, including terms of imprisonment of more than thirty months (section 5(1)(b)), and the defence of justification remains available even after a sentence has become spent, provided that the publication is not proved to have been made with malice (section 8(5)).

any possibility of rehabilitation of an offender may be seriously jeopardised by unwelcome publicity. That is not to say that in all cases publication should be prevented: there may be a greater public interest to be served from the disclosure of true facts regarding convicted criminals;[39] each case must be examined on its own facts.

Historically, these are the types of case where the ex-offender's privacy might be indirectly protected through the invocation of the wardship or inherent jurisdiction of the court: an injunction may issue to protect details regarding a child from being disclosed by the media and indirectly the parent's privacy is protected also.[40] While there may be strong social and moral arguments that can be weighed in favour of supporting the ex-offender, the scope of the state's margin of appreciation in relation to positive obligations is so great that Strasbourg would be likely to defer to the state's judgment as to where the boundary between public and private should be drawn. On the other hand, the search for a fair balance between the interests of the community and the interests of the individual is inherent in the Convention jurisprudence as a whole, and in some cases it is highly arguable that the interest in rehabilitation of the offender should outweigh the public's right to know.

The focus of discussion in this chapter is on the rights that a person may have to restrain the publication of true facts by the media. Where a public body, such as the police, discloses private information, that disclosure is likely to be classified as an interference with the Article 8(1) right (rather than a failure to fulfil a positive obligation), which must then be justified under Article 8(2). So, for example, a decision to disclose the whereabouts and identity of paedophiles, as happened in *R v. Chief Constable of North Wales, ex parte Thorpe*,[41] would have to be justified by showing that it pursued a legitimate aim and was necessary in a democratic society: the action must pursue a pressing social need and be proportionate to the aim pursued. While the limitations set out in Article 8(2) are relevant strictly speaking to "interferences by a public authority", it will be recalled that the Strasbourg Court has held that they may be relevant in determining the scope of positive obligations arising under Article 8(1).[42] In practice, however, Strasbourg has not applied the Article 8(2) criteria in its consideration of positive obligations.[43]

As far as remedies are concerned, the most effective remedy to protect private life, is clearly the injunction. The issue of injunctions against the press was considered in *The Observer and The Guardian* v. *United Kingdom*, where it was

---

[39] See *R v. Chief Constable of North Wales, ex parte Thorpe*, *The Times* 23 March 1998, CA.

[40] *Re X* [1984] 1 WLR 1422.

[41] *Supra* n.39. See R Mullender, "Privacy, Paedophilia and the European Convention on Human Rights: a Deontological Appoach", [1998] PL 384.

[42] *Rees* v. *United Kingdom* Series A no 106 (1986) at para. 37; *Gaskin* v. *United Kingdom* Series A no 160 (1989) at para. 42.

[43] See the concurring opinion of Judge Wildhaber in *Stjerna* v. *Finland* Series A no 229B (1994), text accompanying n.19 in Chapter 5.

held that Article 10 does not prohibit prior restraints, but in view of the chilling effect on free speech, they call for "the most careful scrutiny on the part of the court".[44]

The impact of the Act

It has been argued[45] that the effect of section 6(1) and (3) of the Human Rights Act is that the English courts are now required to develop the principles of the common law to ensure that they are compatible with Convention rights, even where any alleged violation of such a right has occurred as a result of the acts of a non-state actor. The Act in other words has indirect horizontal effect. This principle is crucial in determining the appropriate response of the English courts to arguments that the time has now come to recognise an explicit right to privacy, since any complaint is likely to lie against a non-public body ie the privately-owned press. Obviously, where a public sector broadcaster, such as the BBC, acts incompatibly with Article 8, a complaint will lie directly against that body under the Act.

The House of Lords in *Reynolds*[46] proceeded upon the basis that their obligation under section 6(1) as a judicial body is to render the principles of English defamation law compatible with the Convention. The actions for slander and libel for the protection of reputation are of respectable antiquity, so there was no question in *Reynolds* of the court being forced to consider the recognition of a new cause of action. Privacy is a different issue, because the English courts have refused to recognise explicitly such a right. In *Kaye*, the Court of Appeal was appalled by the "monstrous invasion" of the plaintiff's privacy, but Glidewell and Leggatt LJJ were compelled to observe that the introduction of an appropriate law was a matter for Parliament. It is to be hoped that the Human Rights Act will put an end to judicial handwringing and take us into a new era, one in which privacy is properly protected.

The courts have been moving incrementally towards the recognition of a de facto privacy right in the guise of breach of confidence. The issues of privacy and the effect of the Act were considered recently by the Court of Appeal in *Douglas* v. *Hello Ltd*,[47] and very shortly thereafter by the High Court in *Thompson and Venables* v. *News Group Newspapers Ltd*.[48]

In *Douglas*, the action was brought by the claimants after the "star-studded" wedding celebrations of Michael Douglas and Catherine Zeta-Jones in New

---

[44] Series A no 216 (1991) at para. 60.
[45] See text accompanying n.25 in Chapter 2.
[46] *Reynolds* v. *Times Newspapers Ltd* [1999] 3 WLR 1010.
[47] *Supra* n.14.
[48] Judgment dated 8 January 2001: http://www.courtservice.gov.uk/

York. The action arose from the circulation war between two celebrity-watching magazines. *OK!* magazine paid a large sum to Douglas and Zeta-Jones for exclusive rights for a nine month period to publish photographs taken by a photographer hired by the couple and to publish an article about the wedding. The claimants had agreed to use their best efforts to ensure that:

> "no other media (including but not limited to photographers, television crews or journalists) shall be permitted access to the Wedding, and that no guests or anyone else present at the Wedding (including staff at the venues) shall be allowed to take photographs".

Despite tight security, *Hello!* magazine obtained copies of the photographs and injunctive relief was sought by the claimants, including Northern & Shell plc, the proprietors of *OK!* magazine, in order to restrain publication by *Hello!*. An injunction had been granted over the telephone by Buckley J late in the evening, and then continued by Hunt J on the basis that the images were confidential and that the defendants were in breach of confidence and probably breach of contract and malicious falsehood as well. The injunction was discharged because the balance of convenience[49] as between the two magazines favoured *Hello!*, since it would be difficult to compute *Hello!*'s losses if publication were wrongfully prevented. On the other hand, if *OK!* were to win at trial it would be able to pursue the equitable remedy of an account of profits or damages (per Brooke LJ, Sedley LJ concurring) and any damage to the claimants could be adequately dealt with in monetary terms (Keene LJ). Sedley LJ considered also that while the first two claimants would be likely to establish a breach of their privacy at trial, they had sold "by far the greater part of that privacy [which] falls to be protected, if at all, in the hands of the third claimant. This can be done without the need of an injunction".[50]

As to the effect of including the court within the definition of public authority in section 6 of the Human Rights Act, only Sedley LJ discussed in any detail the consequences in relation to recognition of a privacy right. Brooke LJ considered that the claimants would be likely to establish that publication should not be allowed on confidentiality grounds: such a finding would be based on the equitable action for breach of confidence and would not involve recognising a new cause of action. Brooke LJ accepted counsel's argument that the law is "adequately configured to respect the Convention", by virtue of the action for breach of confidence. However, the scope of the action for breach of confidence is by no means as certain as Brooke LJ implied and it might be established at full trial that the photographs had not been obtained in breach of confidence because there were no circumstances "importing an obligation of confidence" on the part of the photographer.[51] How would the courts deal with a situation where there was no appropriate cause of action? According to

[49] *American Cyanamid Company* v. *Ethicon* [1975] AC 396.
[50] *Supra* n.14 at para. 144.
[51] The action for breach of confidence is discussed *infra*.

Sedley LJ, section 6 of the Act would step in to enable the court to recognise a new right:

> "If [counsel] is right in his primary submission then the law is today adequately configured to respect the Convention. If it is not—for example if the step from confidentiality to privacy is not simply a modern restatement of the scope of a known protection but a legal innovation—then I would accept his submission (for which there is widespread support among commentators on the Act: see in particular M. Hunt, 'The "Horizontal Effect" of the Human Rights Act' [1998] PL 423) that this is precisely the kind of incremental change for which the Act is designed: one which without undermining the measure of certainty which is necessary to all law gives substance and effect to s. 6".[52]

Keene LJ was more cautious and referring to the court's role as a public authority stated that:

> "[section 6(1)] arguably includes their activity in interpreting and developing the common law, even where no public authority is a party to the litigation. Whether this extends to creating a new cause of action between private persons and bodies is more controversial, since to do so would appear to circumvent the restrictions on proceedings contained in section 7(1) of the Act and on remedies in section 8(1)".

However, he considered it unnecessary to decide this issue because in these proceedings reliance was placed on an established cause of action, namely the action for breach of confidence.

In relation to the need to recognise a privacy right, all members of the Court of Appeal proceeded on the basis that English law should now, in the light of Article 8, protect privacy. Sedley LJ, alone, was explicit on this point when he spoke in terms of the claimants having a "legal right to respect for their privacy". Brooke LJ analysed the Convention jurisprudence on positive obligations and implied that following cases such as *Spencer*, English law should protect privacy, although he expressed no conclusion regarding the appropriate cause of action. He was open to the view that such protection might be otherwise than through the law of confidence:

> "Whether they do so in future by an extension of the existing frontiers of the law of confidence, or by recognising the existence of new relationships which give rise to enforceable legal rights (as happened in relation to the law of negligence ever since the 3–2 decision of the House of Lords in *Donoghue* v. *Stevenson*) is not for this court, on this occasion to predict".[53]

Keene LJ, having identified what he saw as a potential difficulty under section 7 of the Act in recognising a new cause of action (he said that to do so would circumvent the scheme of remedies established by the Act) said that it was unnecessary to do so anyway, since the action for breach of confidence must now be informed by Convention jurisprudence under Article 8.

---

[52] *Supra* n.14 at para. 129.
[53] *Ibid.*, at para. 88.

While Keene LJ could envisage no difficulty in utilising breach of confidence as a remedy to afford redress for breaches of privacy claims, there are un-resolved issues in this field which would lead one to argue that it would be preferable for the courts to shape a new remedy to address privacy claims, not the least of which is whether damages may be claimed for the distress attendant upon this form of wrong.

In *Thompson and Venables*,[54] Dame Butler-Sloss appeared rather more scep-tical of the extent to which English law should protect privacy. The claimants were the notorious killers of James Bulger and the proceedings were precip-itated by the fact that they have reached the age of majority and it is anticipated that the Parole Board will shortly be making a decision regarding their release. During the period of the offenders' detention in secure units, the Bulger story has rarely been far from newspaper headlines, and Venables and Thompson have been the subject of extensive coverage alluding to the possibility of vigil-ante attacks on their release. In these proceedings, Venables and Thompson sought an indefinite continuation of injunctions to restrain the press from dis-closing their identities (they will be given new identities on their release) or whereabouts.

Butler-Sloss had no doubt that by virtue of section 6(3) of the Act, the court should act compatibly with Convention rights, but only in adjudicating on existing common law causes of action. On the evidence that, if the public could identify their whereabouts, there would be a real and serious risk to the claimants under Articles 2 (right to life) and 3 (not to be tortured or suffer in-human and degrading treatment) Butler-Sloss granted the injunctions on the basis of the law of confidence. In *Douglas*, Sedley LJ alluded to the uncertainty that surrounds the scope of the action for breach of confidence (the action is dis-cussed in the next section), but Butler-Sloss had no doubt that the duty of con-fidence arises independently of a transaction or relationship between the parties. Butler-Sloss made clear that she granted the injunction in view of the "excep-tional circumstances" of the case: "it will only be necessary to grant injunctions to restrain the media where it can be convincingly demonstrated within the exceptions [set out in Article 10(2)] that it is strictly necessary".[55] According to Butler-Sloss, the effect of section 12[56] of the Human Rights Act is that English law has given enhanced protection to freedom of the press, and consequently the right to publish, and had the application been based upon the likelihood of Article 8 being breached, she was uncertain that an injunction would be appro-priate. Despite the fact that there would be a serious breach of Article 8 when Venables and Thompson were discovered and an adverse impact on their

---

[54] *Supra* n.48.

[55] *Ibid.* at "Conclusions on jurisdiction" para. 11.

[56] Section 12(1) states: section 12 "applies if a court is considering whether to grant any relief which, if granted, might affect the exercise of the Convention right to freedom of expression". According to subs (4): "The court must have particular regard to the importance of the Convention right to freedom of expression".

prospects for rehabilitation, she was not convinced that such matters would meet the "importance of the preservation of the freedom of expression in Article 10(1)".[57]

For proponents of the effective protection of privacy, these observations are alarming. Where privacy is threatened, the only effective remedy is the injunction. Many examples demonstrate that the fabric of a person's life can be destroyed for the sake of titillation by an avaricious press eager for copy to satisfy the prurient interest of the public.[58] The decision in *Thompson and Venables* emasculates Article 8, because it is a decision in which Article 8 is effectively rendered otiose. It is in fact a decision that is not really *based* upon privacy at all, rather the obligation to protect the claimants that derives from the positive obligation upon the state under Articles 2 and 3 of the Convention.

The action for breach of confidence to exert a privacy right?

In *Douglas*, counsel for the claimants argued that English law is adequately configured to respect the Convention through the action for breach of confidence and he argued that the publication of the photographs would be a breach of confidence, although he acknowledged that the case had "more to do with privacy than confidentiality".[59] However, Sedley and Brooke LJJ had doubts that the ingredients for the breach of confidence action were made out; hence, the need to establish that English law should now protect privacy per se. Keene LJ, on the other hand, considered that the breach of confidence action would afford a remedy on the facts, and, moreover, that a case like *Kaye* would be decided differently in the light of recent developments in the law of confidence and the obligation of the courts to take account of the right to respect for private life under Article 8. In *Kaye*, there was no attempt to seek a remedy on the ground of breach of confidence, presumably because the view was taken that the necessary indicia were not made out. In *Winer*, the Commission had expressed the view that the failure to bring an action for breach of confidence did not constitute a failure to exhaust domestic remedies in view of the uncertainty as to the scope and extent of that remedy. In *Spencer*, on the other hand, "the eloquence of the advocate for the United Kingdom government persuaded the Commission that English law provided [Victoria Spencer] with a potentially satisfactory remedy in an action for breach of confidence".[60] What, then, is the current state of the law regarding the action for breach of confidence?[61] Is this action an appropriate vehicle through which to protect the right to privacy?

---

[57] *Supra* n.48 at para. 12.

[58] *Melvin* v. *Reid, supra* n.4; *Briscoe* v. *Readers' Digest Association Inc.* 4 Cal 3rd 529; (1971) R v. *Central Independent Television PLC* [1994] Fam 192.

[59] *Supra* n.14 at para. 164.

[60] *Douglas*, supra n.14 at para. 86.

[61] The following discussion draws extensively on J Wright, "How Private is my Private Life?", in L Betten (ed), *The Human Rights Act 1998: What it Means* (The Hague, Martinus Nijhoff, 1999).

The *locus classicus* for identification of the criteria on which the action is founded is the summary of Megarry J in *Coco v. A. N. Clark Engineers Ltd*,[62] to the effect that:

> "three elements are normally required if, apart from contract, a case of breach of confidence is to succeed. First, the information itself, in the words of Lord Greene M.R. in the *Saltman*[63] case on 215 must have the 'necessary quality of confidence about it'. Secondly, that information must have been imparted in circumstances importing an obligation of confidence. Thirdly, there must be an unauthorised use of that information to the detriment of the party communicating it".

A duty of confidence will arise even where information is given to the recipient without an express undertaking that it will remain confidential.[64] What is more difficult to determine is precisely when information is imparted in "circumstances importing an obligation of confidence"; in particular, whether there is scope for arguing that it is not necessary for a relationship of confidence (whether contractual or otherwise) to exist between confider and confidant. There is now considerable support for the argument that an obligation of confidence will arise where there is no relationship as such between the parties and that the duty of confidence is predicated on the principle of unconscionability.[65] Thus, in *Stephens v. Avery*,[66] Browne-Wilkinson VC stated that the "basis of equitable intervention is that it is unconscionable for a person who has received information on the basis that it is confidential subsequently to reveal that information . . . [The] relationship between the parties is not the determining factor. It is the acceptance of the information on the basis that it will be kept secret that affects the conscience of the recipient of the information". Lord Goff went even further in *Spycatcher (No 2)* when he stated that a duty of confidence would arise "independently" of a relationship or transaction between the parties, to include situations:

> "where an obviously confidential document is wafted by an electric fan out of a window in a crowded street, or where an obviously confidential document, such as a private diary, is dropped in a public place and is then picked up by a passer-by".[67]

If this view is correct, an obligation of confidence may arise where the parties have never met and where it should be apparent from the text that the information is confidential: in this way, the action for breach of confidence may become a vehicle to protect "privacy". Laws J was prepared to extend the

---

[62] [1969] RPC 41.

[63] [1948] 65 RPC 203.

[64] "If the circumstances are such that any reasonable man standing in the shoes of the recipient of the information would have realised upon reasonable grounds that the information was being given to him in confidence, then this should suffice to impose upon him the equitable obligation of confidence," per Megarry J in *Coco v. A. N. Clark (Engineers) Ltd, supra* n.62.

[65] See R Wacks, *Privacy and Press Freedom* (London, Blackstone Press, 1995) at 53.

[66] [1988] 1 Ch 449.

[67] [1990] 1 AC 109 at 281.

principle further in *Hellewell* v. *Chief Constable of Derbyshire*, where he stated, *obiter*, that:

> "If someone with a telephoto lens were to take from a distance and with no authority a picture of another engaged in some private act, his subsequent disclosure of the photograph would, in my judgment, as surely amount to a breach of confidence as if he had found or stolen a letter or diary in which the act was recounted and proceeded to publish it. In such a case, the law would protect what might reasonably be called a right of privacy, although the name accorded to that cause of action would be breach of confidence".[68]

Further, in *Creation Records Ltd and others* v. *News Group Newspapers Ltd*, Lloyd J granted an interim injunction to restrain *The Sun* newspaper from further publishing a photograph, already in the public domain, but in a different format, where the photograph had been taken on an occasion of confidentiality. *The Sun*'s photographer had managed to take a photograph at a photo shoot set up by a pop group. Extensive security precautions had been taken by the group, but despite this, the photographer who was registered as a hotel guest managed to photograph the objects which were to form the artwork for an album sleeve. The obligation of confidence arose from the factual context, which was an occasion of confidentiality, in the words of Lloyd J:

> "any reasonable man in the shoes of [the photographer] would have realised on reasonable grounds he was obtaining the information, that is to say the view of the scene, in confidence, at least to the extent that he was obliged by that confidentiality not to photograph the scene".[68a]

From this survey of the authorities it is apparent that in many cases where an applicant seeks to protect what is in truth a privacy right the action for breach of confidence may provide a cause of action. But uncertainty as to precisely when an obligation of confidence will arise remains. Whether a "relationship" is required has not been considered at the highest level. Lord Goff's comments in *Spycatcher* were clearly *obiter* since Peter Wright, the former member of MI5, who had published his memoirs in Australia, was bound by an obligation of confidence both as a matter of contract and under the Official Secrets Act 1911. In *Spencer* v. *United Kingdom*, where it will be recalled the Commission held that the applicants had not exhausted domestic remedies, a telling feature, as far as the Commission was concerned, was that the personal details reported by the press had been gleaned directly from former friends of the applicant, so that on the facts there was a relationship of confidence from which the equitable obligation would derive.

In *Douglas*, both Sedley LJ and Brooke LJ explored the law relating to privacy and the United Kingdom's obligations under the Convention and the Human Rights Act precisely because the trial judge might find "that the photographer was

---

[68] [1995] 1 WLR 804, discussed by D Eady, "Opinion: A Statutory Right to Privacy", (1996) 3 *EHRLR* 243.

[68a] *The Times*, 29 April 1997.

an intruder with whom no relationship of trust or confidence had been established".[69] In Sedley LJ's view, if the covert photographer of the wedding celebrations were a guest or employee then the action for breach of confidence would suffice, because the information would have fulfilled Megarry J's second criterion that the information was "imparted in circumstances importing an obligation of confidence". In *Thompson and Venables*, Butler-Sloss held that the duty of confidence may arise independently of a transaction or relationship; in this case, it arose from the fact that the information required a special quality of protection, because if it were published it would lead to possibly fatal consequences. Thus, it is the information itself and the consequences attaching to disclosure that give rise to the duty.

SUITABILITY OF BREACH OF CONFIDENCE TO PROTECT PRIVACY

There is uncertainty regarding the range of remedies available in breach of confidence. The author is not aware of any case where damages have been awarded for the distress attendant on the disclosure of private information in breach of confidence. In *Spycatcher (No 2)*, Lord Goff considered that damages are available through a "beneficent interpretation of the Chancery Amendment Act 1858 (Lord Cairns' Act)".[70] In *Malone*, Megarry J had expressed doubt regarding the availability of damages since under the Act they can be awarded in substitution for an injunction: where the court had no jurisdiction to award an injunction, because for example the information was in the public domain, no damages could be awarded.[71] However, in *Spycatcher (No 2)*, Lord Goff clarified the position by pointing out that when confidential information ceases to exist, because of publication, the obligation of confidence ceases to exist and what remains is the remedy or remedies, which include an account of profits and damages.

Wacks has argued that the action for breach of confidence is:

> "inadequate to deal with the archetypal 'privacy' claim because the action is largely concerned with: (a) disclosure or use rather than publicity, (b) the source rather than the nature of the information, and (c) the preservation of confidence rather than the possible harm to the plaintiff caused by its breach".[72]

Thus, while, in principle, a privacy action would lie to restrain disclosure of information acquired through independent investigation by the media, for example, an action for breach of confidence is unlikely to lie, if the focus of the action is on the source, rather than the nature of the information. Wacks was writing in 1995, and while there have been cases recently, including *Thompson*

---

[69] See Brooke LJ, *supra* n.14 at para. 59 and Sedley LJ, *supra* n.14 at para. 112.
[70] *Supra* n.67 at 286.
[71] *Supra* n.9 at 360.
[72] Wacks, *supra* n.65 at 56.

and Venables, that suggest the quality of the information itself is determinative, doubts remain.

Wacks has suggested, and this is supported by the cases, that the theoretical underpinning of the confidence action is the control of/retribution for "unconscionable" conduct. In *Stephens* v. *Avery*, the Vice-Chancellor said that the foundation of the obligation of confidence is that it would be unconscionable for a particular person to disclose information, where it was revealed in confidence. The focus of the action in other words is the source, not the nature of the information. In relation to the need for prior relationship, this "may be explained as the threshold of the circumstantial evidence that the plaintiff must establish in order to show that the recipient's conscience has been pricked by the confidential nature of the information".[73]

Others have argued that the requirement of a relationship of confidence exists because the rationale for the action is "maintaining the integrity of relationships of confidence".[74] Writing in 1990, Wilson was critical of the decision in *Stephens* v. *Avery*, although he acknowledged that it had received the seal of approval by Lord Goff in *Spycatcher (No 2)*. In particular, Browne-Wilkinson VC had failed to explore the argument that personal (or commercial) confidences should be imparted in a particular type of relationship in order for them to receive legal protection. In Wilson's view, a large number of authorities demonstrated that the obligation of confidentiality has a "social rather than a simply ethical basis".[75] Wilson's view has been overtaken by the body of precedent described above, but uncertainties remain and it is the author's view that it would be preferable to shape a true privacy right and appropriate remedy in preference to the adaptation of a cause of action ill-suited to the purpose.

The inherent limitation of the confidence action is evidenced also in cases where the actions impugned involve the publication of information already in the public domain. Section 12 of the Human Rights Act erects a hurdle for the claimant who seeks an injunction on the basis of breach of confidence, but this remedy may be of little use in privacy claims in any event, because very often information is in the public domain and is obtained through independent investigation. As Wacks has pointed out, the chief complaint in a breach of confidence action is that there has been *disclosure* of information, rather than *publicity*, and once information is in the public domain, it will no longer be protected from further dissemination.[76] Thus, if the action for breach of confidence is the vehicle adopted by English courts as the means of fulfilling Article 8 obligations, it would seem that the fears of the press lobby that gave rise to section 12 of the Human Rights Act will have been misplaced.

---

[73] Wacks, *supra* n.65 at 64.
[74] G Virgo, *The Principles of the Law of Restitution* (Oxford, Clarendon Press, 1999) at 545.
[75] W Wilson, "Privacy, Confidence and Press Freedom", (1990) 53 *MLR* 43 at 51.
[76] Spycatcher (No 2), *supra* n.67, applied in *Attorney-General* v. *Blake* [1998] 2 WLR 805.

8

Environmental Protection, the Convention and Private Nuisance

INTRODUCTION

THERE IS NOW a substantial body of jurisprudence under the Convention, regarding the extent to which a state must take positive steps to secure the protection of individuals from agents that may either impact on the quality of life, or present danger to health, without actual injury having occurred. This dual aspect to environmental obligations raises particular concerns for English tort law, which has refused to contemplate a freestanding award of damages in tort for mental distress or loss of amenity, short of diagnosable psychiatric injury.[1] In *Hunter* v. *London Canary Wharf Ltd*,[2] Lord Hoffmann suggested such damages ought to be recoverable in the case of intentional harm because the policy factors that are relevant to limit recovery in negligence do not apply. On that basis he said *Khorasandjian* v. *Bush*,[3] was not wrongly decided, but it was a case of intentional harassment, not nuisance.

Gilliker has argued that, "mental distress should be recognised as a distinct head of damages", as part of a general compensation claim and states that "there is no evidence to support a right to claim such damages in their own right".[4] This is certainly the case in relation to English law prior to the Human Rights Act, but the Act invites us to reconsider that orthodoxy in the process of determining how Convention obligations should be met. It has been forcefully argued that the role of the courts in the development of the common law is engaged by section 6 of the Act and it is appropriate, therefore, that a number of established tenets of English law should be revisited.[5] On one hand, the range of harms recognised by the Convention is much wider than those recognised by the tort of negligence,[6] and, on the other, the jurisprudence in relation to the right to respect for private and family life and the home, under Article 8, does

---

[1] See generally H McGregor, *Mcgregor on Damages*, 16th edn (London, Sweet & Maxwell, 1997). The term mental distress is used loosely by the English courts: in this chapter it is used to encompass feelings of distress, discomfort and loss of amenity.

[2] [1997] 2 All ER 426.

[3] [1993] 3 All ER 669 and see now the Protection from Harassment Act 1997.

[4] P Gilliker, "A 'New' Head of Damages: Damages for Mental Distress in the English Law of Torts", (2000) 20 Legal Studies 19.

[5] See text accompanying n.25 in Chapter 2.

[6] See text accompanying n.79 in Chapter 2.

not require any form of qualifying property interest for a person to be a victim of a violation where the quality of life is impaired, short of danger to health. The question arises, therefore, as to whether English law currently meets Convention standards and, if not, what developments would be appropriate in order to meet those obligations.

It is perhaps helpful to consider the type of factual situation that arose in *Hunter*: a person's life may be made a misery over an extensive period of time because their home is infiltrated by clouds of dust from building works, but they do not suffer physical injury. The harm is essentially a temporary loss of amenity. There can be no claim in negligence in the absence of physical or recognisable psychiatric injury; there can be no claim in private nuisance in the absence of a right to exclusive possession of the land affected. It has also been argued most forcefully that damages for personal injury should be excluded from nuisance altogether,[7] and that claims for physical damage should also be excluded from the action in private nuisance.[8] This situation is the paradigmatic consequence of English law's conceptualisation of rights and responsibilities as forms of action. One is put in mind, not for the first time, of Maitlands's oft-quoted aphorism, "[t]forms of action we have buried, but they rule us from their graves".[9] Markesinis has aptly summed up the protection of privacy in English law prior to the Human Rights Act as both patchy and a system which required the plaintiff to "pigeonhole" their claim into a range of torts, ill-suited to the purpose. The same can be said regarding the protection of the right to respect for private life and the home. As in the case of privacy, perhaps the time has come for English law to stop thinking in formulary terms and to think instead in terms of protected interests, to move, in other words, from torts to rights.

The framework of this chapter is arranged in three parts: first, Convention obligations regarding the environment, and in particular the impact of the environment on the right to respect for private and family life and the home, are identified; secondly, the tort of private nuisance as a mechanism for securing Convention rights is examined and its limitations identified. It will be argued that the dissenting speech of Lord Cooke of Thorndon in *Hunter* v. *Canary Wharf Ltd* is more reflective of human rights obligations and contemporary concerns than the majority opinions in that case; and, finally, the discussion reverts to the theme identified in Chapter 2, namely the differential treatment of defendants by the Human Rights Act, which distinguishes between public and private actors. Where a public authority acts incompatibly with Convention rights, there is a remedy under the Act, and to that extent it might be argued that an action in private nuisance regarding the same set of facts would be otiose. Clearly, that argument cannot apply in the case of private defendants against whom no action under the Act will lie. However, as far as private defendants are concerned, the

---

[7] F H Newark, "The Boundaries of Nuisance", (1949) 65 LQR 480.

[8] C Gearty, "The Place of Private Nuisance in a Modern Law of Tort", (1989) 48 *CLJ* 214.

[9] F W Maitland, *The Forms of Action at Common Law* (A H Chaytor and WJ Whittaker (eds), (Cambridge, Cambridge University Press, 1987).

extent of the state's obligation may be obscured by the margin of appreciation doctrine and by the permitted variety of remedies. It goes without saying that these factors do not lend support to the predictive quality of litigation.

CONVENTION STANDARDS

Convention jurisprudence demonstrates a concern to protect life itself, so that a failure on the part of the state to take operational measures to protect the existence of life may give rise to a violation of Article 2,[10] and a concern also to protect the quality of life (where impugned conduct need not be health threatening to give rise to a violation) and a failure to act in this regard may give rise to a violation of Article 8 as a failure to respect the right to private and family life and the home.[11] There has yet to be a finding of a violation of Article 2 in relation to damage to the environment.

Article 2

In *Guerra* v. *Italy*,[12] the applicants brought complaints under Articles 2 and 8: they argued that Article 2 had been violated as a result of the failure to take appropriate steps to reduce pollution and the risk of accident from a privately-owned factory producing fertilisers and caprolactam (a number of workers at the factory had died of cancer) and classified as "high risk" by Presidential Decree;[13] and that the right to respect for family life under Article 8 was violated by the failure to provide information about risks and what to do in the event of an accident. A number of accidents had occurred, the most serious in 1976, when 150 people were taken to hospital with acute arsenic poisoning. With regard to the Article 8 right, the European Court of Human Rights held that the state could not be said to have "interfered" with the private or family life of the applicants, because they were complaining, not of an act by the state, but of a failure to act; the state had failed in its positive obligation to secure effective protection of the right to respect for private and family life under Article 8 because there had been a failure to provide information to enable the local population to assess the risks they and their families might run if they continued to live in Manfredonia. The Court considered it unnecessary to consider Article 2, as a violation of Article 8 had been found. This decision is a weak decision when compared with the earlier case of *Lopez Ostra* v. *Spain*,[14] where the Court

---

[10] *Kilic* v. *Turkey* App no 22492/93, judgment dated 28 March 2000.

[11] *Lopez Ostra* v. *Spain* Series A no 303-C (1995).

[12] (1998) 26 EHRR 357.

[13] Presidential Decree No 175 transposed into Italian law by Council Directive 82/501/EEC (the "Seveso" Directive).

[14] Series A no 303-C (1995).

found that the actual operation of a factory was a violation of Article 8. The finding in *Guerra* was limited to the failure to provide information, so that, effectively, the responsibility for addressing the issue of pollution was shifted onto the shoulders of the local population.

In *LCB v. United Kingdom*,[15] the applicant was diagnosed with leukaemia at the age of four. She alleged that her condition was caused by her father's presence at Christmas Island during nuclear tests in 1957 and 1958 and that the government should have informed her parents of the nature and impact of her father's participation in the programme and the consequence of risk to her health. She argued that she would then have received "earlier monitoring, diagnosis and treatment" and the "fatal course of the disease could have been avoided".[16] The Commission's approach is reminiscent of *Barnett* v. *Chelsea & Kensington Hospital Management Committee*,[17] because it decided that there could be no violation of Article 2, unless it could be demonstrated that the fatal nature of the illness could have been altered by earlier diagnosis and consequent treatment. The Commission accepted that the provision of information might have helped to alleviate anxiety about the applicant's condition, but any such anxiety did not reach the minimum level of severity required for a violation of Article 3.[18] The Court imposed what can reasonably be described as a negligence standard and held that the quality of information available to the state at the relevant time (the period from 14 January 1966 when the right of individual petition was accepted to October 1970 when the leukaemia diagnosis was made) would mean that the authorities "could reasonably have been confident that [the applicant's father] had not been dangerously irradiated".[19] The evidence from which this conclusion could be inferred included in particular contemporaneous records that showed radiation did not reach dangerous levels where the servicemen were stationed. However, the evidence on this point was not conclusive so the Court went on to consider whether, if there had been information that the applicant's father had been exposed to radiation, the government could then have been expected to provide advice to her parents and monitor her health. The test for liability was whether "if it had appeared likely at that time that any such exposure . . . might have engendered a real risk to health".[20] The Court held that a causal link between paternal exposure to radiation and leukaemia in children had not been established[21] and so there was no duty to take action. The Court differed from the Commission in that, if there had been reason to believe that her father's presence at the tests could lead to her suffering a life-threatening condition, then it was arguable that the state should have made this known to the applicant, even if possession of that information might not have assisted the

---

[15] (1997) 27 EHRR 212.
[16] *Ibid.* at para. 58.
[17] [1969] 1 QB 428.
[18] See text accompanying n.18 in Chapter 3.
[19] *Supra* n.15 at para. 37. Cf *Roe* v. *Ministry of Health* [1954] 2 QB 66.
[20] *LCB* v. *United Kingdom, supra* n.15 at para. 38.
[21] Relying in part on *Reay and Hope* v. *British Nuclear Fuels PLC* [1994] 5 Med LR 1.

applicant.[22] However, it was not necessary to decide the point. Having made a finding under Article 2, it was not necessary to consider the complaint under Article 8.

Even where information establishing a causal connection between a risk and harm is established, the *Osman* v. *United Kingdom* line of jurisprudence under Article 2 will be relevant so that an evaluation of state behaviour will include consideration of resources and the balancing of priorities. The positive obligation is not to be interpreted to impose a disproportionate liability upon the state.[23]

Article 8

In *Powell and Rayner* v. *United Kingdom*,[24] the applicants complained that the noise levels generated by aircraft operating out of Heathrow Airport interfered adversely with their Article 8 rights to respect for private life and the home. The Commission stated that noise nuisance can affect the physical well-being of a person and may affect the enjoyment of the amenity of the home adversely. However, the Commission found that the interference with Article 8 rights was justified since the operation of the airport was in the interest of the economic well-being of the country and the principle of proportionality had been observed: the authorities had taken measures to control the level of noise by reducing flight levels and dividing the area into two sectors in response to local objections.

The balance between individual and community was struck differently in *Lopez Ostra* v. *Spain*, where the applicant complained of violations of Articles 3 (inhuman and degrading treatment) and 8, as a result of the operation of a waste treatment plant situated a few metres from her home. The plant had emitted smells, noise and fumes over a number of years and had been permitted to operate without the necessary licence. Her appeal to the Spanish Constitutional Court had been declared inadmissible because, *inter alia*, the applicant's life and physical integrity had not been endangered and the presence of fumes, smells and noise did not amount to a breach of the right to inviolability of the home.[25] The Strasbourg Court held that:

> "severe environmental pollution may affect individuals' well-being and prevent them from enjoying their homes in such a way as to affect their private and family life adversely, without, however, seriously endangering their health. Whether the question is analysed in terms of a positive duty on the State to take reasonable and appropriate measures to secure the applicant's rights under paragraph 1 of Article 8, as the applicant wishes in her case, or in terms of an 'interference by a public authority' to

[22] Cf the action for medical negligence at common law, see text accompanying n.21 in Chapter 3.
[23] See text accompanying n.38 in Chapter 5.
[24] Series A no 172 (1990).
[25] *Lopez Ostra, supra* n.14 at para. 15.

be justified in accordance with paragraph 2, the applicable principles are broadly similar. In both contexts regard must be had to the fair balance that has to be struck between the competing interests of the individual and of the community as a whole, and in any case the State enjoys a certain margin of appreciation. Furthermore, even in relation to the positive obligations flowing from the first paragraph of Article 8, in striking the required balance the aims mentioned in the second paragraph may be of a certain relevance".[26]

The Court held that, despite the margin of appreciation, the state had not struck a fair balance between the interest of the town's economic well-being and the applicant's rights under Article 8. The claim under Article 3 was rejected on the ground that although living conditions were "very difficult", they did not reach the level of severity required by Article 3.[27]

More recently, in *Khatun* v. *United Kingdom*,[28] the group of residents who lost their appeal before the House of Lords in *Hunter*[29] petitioned Strasbourg. The proceedings in *Hunter* were based, *inter alia*, on the nuisance caused by excessive dust created by the construction of the Limehouse Link Road which was built to provide access from the Docklands area to central London. The residents alleged that their Article 8 rights to respect for their private and family lives had been violated and that they had suffered discrimination, contrary to Article 14, on the grounds of poverty, "in that the amount of compensation they may receive for dust nuisance depends on the difference in value between the property as affected by dust and the property when not affected". Since the properties concerned were at the lower end of the scale in terms of amenity and cost, the presence of dust had little effect on the value of property, although causing significant personal discomfort. They also complained that their Article 13 rights (to an effective remedy) were violated because the decision of the House of Lords in *Hunter* meant that they had no effective remedy to seek compensation for the Article 8 violation.

The Commission began by observing that the notion of "home" is an autonomous concept and is determined by factual circumstances, such as the existence of sufficient and continuous links,[30] and no distinction is to be drawn between those applicants with a proprietary interest in land and those who do not have such an interest. Even where occupation of property is illegal, this will not necessarily prevent that occupation from falling within Article 8.[31] Therefore, the Commission considered that Article 8(1) applied to all the applicants and, although none of the applicants alleged that they had

---

[26] *Lopez Ostra, supra* n.14 at para. 51.
[27] See text accompanying n.35 in Chapter 3.
[28] (1998) 26 EHRR 212.
[29] *Supra* n.2.
[30] See *Gillow* v. *United Kingdom* Series A no 109 (1986) and *Mentes* v. *Turkey* (1998) 26 EHRR 595.
[31] *Buckley* v. *United Kingdom* (1997) 23 EHRR 597. Cf *Pemberton* v. *South London Borough Council* [2000] 3 All ER 924: a tolerated trespasser who has the right to exclusive possession has sufficient interest to sustain an action in private nuisance.

suffered ill-health as a result of dust contamination, "the fact that they could not open windows or dry laundry outside for a period of three years severely impaired their right to enjoy their homes and private or family lives". Therefore, there was an interference with Article 8(1) rights which required to be justified under Article 8(2), by demonstrating that the interference corresponded to a pressing social need and was proportionate to the aim pursued. The Commission held that the construction of the road pursued the legitimate aim of the well-being of the country. On the question of whether the interference was necessary in a democratic society, the Commission held that the construction of the road was essential to the development of the area and fulfilled an important public interest, against which the applicants' position must be weighed. The Commission found that although the dust was unpleasant, there were no health problems associated with it. On the facts, therefore, a fair balance between the interests of the community and the individuals had been struck. The Commission drew attention to the fact that no proceedings were instituted while the works were in progress and that the applicants were probably affected to different degrees at different times over the three-year period.

The Article 14 claim was declared manifestly ill-founded, because there were no other persons in "relevantly" similar situations who had been treated more favourably than the applicants.[32]

THE ACTION FOR PRIVATE NUISANCE

A common feature of *Guerra*, *Lopez Ostra* and *Powell and Rayner* is that they concerned allegations that the defendant states had failed to fulfil their positive obligations to secure the effective enjoyment of Article 8 rights through appropriate regulation of non-state actors. In analogous cases under English law, no claim will lie directly against a public body under section 7 of the Human Rights Act for a failure to act compatibly with the Convention under section 6(1) of the Act. Instead, a claimant will have to rely on common law principles and argue that the court is obliged, by virtue of the obligation imposed on it under section 6(1) and (3), to develop the common law so that its principles are compatible with the Convention.

Two distinct principles emerge from the Strasbourg jurisprudence which are problematic for English law. First, there is no requirement of a property interest in order for an individual to assert his right to respect for private and family life and the home. Thus, the English law of private nuisance as currently configured will not afford a remedy for an Article 8 violation. Secondly, according to Strasbourg jurisprudence a claim can arise for loss of amenity,[33]

---

[32] See text accompanying n.111 in Chapter 3.
[33] *Lopez Ostra, supra* n.14.

or for inconvenience and unpleasantness,[34] so that, likewise, an action in negligence cannot be a remedy for an Article 8 violation.

In *Hunter*, the House of Lords, by a four to one majority (Lord Cooke of Thorndon dissenting), confirmed that private nuisance is a property tort, the essence of which is that the enjoyment of property rights are infringed as a result of injury to property. Lord Hoffmann observed that:

> "Once it is understood that nuisances 'productive of sensible personal discomfort' do not constitute a separate tort of causing discomfort to people but are merely part of a single tort of causing injury to land, the rule that the plaintiff must have an interest in the land falls into place as logical and, indeed, inevitable (see *St Helen's Smelting Co* v. *Tipping* (1865) HL Cas 642 at 650, 11 ER 1483 at 1486)".[35]

Clearly, it cannot be said that the land has suffered "sensible" injury: rather "its utility has been diminished by the existence of the nuisance".[36] In view of this rationale, it is not surprising that Lord Hoffmann disapproved Stephenson and Scarman LJJ's "tentative" suggestion regarding the calculation of damages in *Bone* v. *Seal*.[37] It is not appropriate to fix damages by analogy with loss of amenity in personal injury actions. Instead, the correct approach is to assess diminution in capital value, and where this cannot be shown (as in *Bone* v. *Seal*), there should be an award to reflect diminution in the amenity value[38] of the property during the period of the nuisance. As Lord Lloyd pointed out there is no suggestion in *Bone* v. *Seal* that the sum awarded by way of damages should vary according to the number of occupants: damages are assessed "*per stirpes* and not *per capita*".[39] Thus, the majority of the House overruled *Khorasandjian* v. *Bush*[40] on the issue of standing to claim in private nuisance and signalled a refusal to effect a desirable degree of modernisation in the law.

By contrast Lord Cooke's speech demonstrated a desire to cast off the historical technicalities of the nuisance action, in order to render the law reflective of contemporary values, in particular the standards of international human rights law. He began by pointing out that while the majority opinions achieved a "symmetry" in the law of nuisance, this was not necessarily to strengthen the "utility" or the "justice" of the common law. As he said, "the choice is in the end a policy one between competing principles".[41] He pointed out that legal analysis does not assist in identifying what the policy of the law should be. As the author has argued, the development of international human rights standards should inform the policy that is reflected in the legal principles applied by the courts.

---

[34] *Khatun, supra* n.28.

[35] *Hunter, supra* n.2 at 452.

[36] *Hunter*, supra n.2 at 451, per Lord Hoffmann.

[37] [1975] 1 All ER 787.

[38] Lord Hoffmann drew the analogy of amenity damages in contract: *Ruxley Electronics and Construction Ltd* v. *Forsyth* [1995] 3 All ER 268.

[39] *Hunter, supra* n.2 at 444.

[40] [1993] 3 WLR 476.

[41] *Hunter, supra* n.2 at 456.

Lord Cooke identified the nub of the claim as interference with the amenity of the home, an interest protected by a range of international instruments, including Article 16 of the United Nations Convention on the Rights of the Child, as well as Article 12 of the Universal Declaration of Human Rights and Article 8 of the Convention. He cited, *inter alia*, *Lopez Ostra* and the comments of Harris, O'Boyle and Warbrick to the effect that the Convention right in Article 8 goes beyond possession or property rights[42] and held that a test of "residence" would be an acceptable basis of standing in cases such as *Hunter*. He also surveyed academic opinion, the preponderance of which rejected confining the tort to those with proprietary interests and stated that:

> "The reason why I prefer the alternative advocated with unwonted vigour of expression by the doyen [Fleming in *The Law of Torts*, 8th edn (1992)] of living tort writers is that it gives better effect to widespread conceptions concerning the home and family".[43]

In contrast, in two recent decisions of the Court of Appeal, no mention was made of the Convention: *Hussain* v. *Lancaster City Council*[44] and *Lippiatt* v. *South Gloucestershire Council*.[45] In *Hussain*, the plaintiffs were owners of a shop and residential premises on the notorious Ryelands Estate, owned by the defendant council in Lancaster. For a number of years the plaintiffs were victims of a vicious campaign of racial harassment that included property damage, verbal threats and abuse and attempts to burn the plaintiffs out of the premises. A number of the perpetrators had been prosecuted for breach of the peace or criminal damage, but only fines or bind-over orders were made and the criminal courts could not require their removal from the estate. The plaintiffs therefore instituted proceedings in negligence and nuisance against the defendant council. It should be noted that this decision predates *Osman* v. *United Kingdom*.[46]

The Court of Appeal's decision in *Hussain* was discussed in Chapter 5,[47] and a brief summary will suffice. The gist of the negligence action was that the defendants had improperly failed to institute possession proceedings or other effective action against the perpetrators. The defendant had statutory power to seek possession under Schedule 2, ground 2 to the Housing Act 1985 and section 84 of the 1985 Act, which provides that a court may order possession in respect of a secure tenancy if it considers it reasonable to do so and "the tenant or a person residing in the dwelling-house has been guilty of conduct which is a nuisance or annoyance to neighbours". The Court of Appeal applied the House of Lords' decision in *Stovin* v. *Wise*,[48] and held that the plaintiffs did not come within the categories identified by Lord Hoffmann: the council had not acted irrationally

---

[42] Harris, O'Boyle and Warbrick, *Law of the European Convention on Human Rights* (London, Butterworths, 1995) at 319.

[43] *Hunter, supra* n.2 at 462.

[44] [1999] 4 All ER 125.

[45] [1999] 4 All ER 149.

[46] [1999] 1 FLR 193.

[47] See text accompanying n.73 in Chapter 5.

[48] [1996] 3 All ER 801.

in failing to exercise its powers under the Housing Act and the Act did not require the payment of compensation to those who suffered loss as a result of the failure to exercise a power. Moreover, it would not be "fair, just and reasonable" to impose a duty of care: dealing with racial harassment is a multi-agency responsibility and "it would cut across effective multi-agency working if one of the agencies involved is required by injunction to take specific steps";[49] if the claim was allowed to proceed, scarce public resources would be diverted to litigation. In the light of *Osman*, the reasoning is difficult to defend against a charge that the Article 6 right of access to a court has been violated: there was a clear failure to give adequate consideration to policy arguments that would militate in favour of a duty of care, not least that, contrary to Article 3, the applicants had suffered inhuman and degrading treatment in the form of severe racial harassment (there were attempts to burn the applicants out of their home). It is likely that if the same facts arose now, a remedy would lie against the local authority under section 7 of the Act.

The nuisance claim failed on two grounds: first, it was held that the acts complained of did interfere with the plaintiffs' enjoyment of their land, but these acts did not involve the use of the tenant's land and were therefore outside the scope of the tort; secondly, applying the rule in *Smith* v. *Scott*,[50] the council was not liable for the acts of its tenants because it had not authorised or adopted them. The first ground for the decision has been subject to criticism, appropriately, because:

> "nuisance is universally defined simply as unlawful interference with the plaintiff's enjoyment of his property, whether or not it derives from the defendant's use of his property. This accords with the elementary principle that it is the creator of the nuisance who is primarily liable for it, while the occupier of land from which it emanates might also be liable if he continued or adopted the nuisance (in other words if he was at fault)".[51]

Doubt has been cast upon the correctness of *Hussain* on this point in *Lippiatt*, where *Hussain* was distinguished. Here, the plaintiffs complained of the nuisance that arose from the occupation of council-owned land by a group of travellers. The plaintiffs farmed adjoining property and over a period of several years the travellers trespassed onto their land, dumping rubbish and excrement on it, obstructed access to a field, stole timber gates and fences, tied up animals and threatened and assaulted the plaintiffs and their families. The travellers were evicted after occupying the defendant's land for almost three years and the plaintiffs sought damages. In the light of *Hussain*, the council raised a preliminary objection, arguing that the claim had no prospect of success and should be struck out, because the impugned activities took place on the plaintiffs' land, rather than that of the defendant. At first instance these submissions were

---

[49] *Hussain, supra* n.44 at 145.
[50] [1972] 3 All ER 645.
[51] J O'Sullivan, "Nuisance, Local Authorities and Neighbours From Hell", [2000] CLJ 11 at 13.

accepted, but the plaintiffs appealed and a differently constituted Court of Appeal distinguished *Hussain* and allowed the appeal. Evans LJ (Mummery LJ and Sir Christopher Staughten concurring) referred to Lord Goff's statement of general principle in *Hunter*, to the effect that the action "will generally arise from something emanating from the defendant's land . . . noise, dirt, fumes . . . and such like",[52] and held that in the instant case what emanated from the defendant's land was the travellers themselves. According to Evans LJ, *Hussain* was different, because the disturbance was a public nuisance for which the perpetrators could be held liable and they lived in council property, "but their conduct was not in any sense linked to, nor did it emanate from, the homes where they lived".[53] It should be noted that two relevant authorities were not cited in *Hussain's* case: *AG v. Corke*[54] and *Thompson-Schwab v. Costaki*,[55] each of which support the argument that it is not necessary that the acts complained of occur on the defendant's land.

THE CONVENTION PERSPECTIVE

The English authorities referred to above are examples of attempts to use the tort of nuisance to seek redress for very different types of harm. On the one hand, *Hunter* was an attempt to use nuisance as a vehicle to vindicate the protection of a clean environment and the home and falls squarely within the jurisprudence that has developed under Article 8 of the Convention. Where a public authority is responsible for or adopts a nuisance, then it is highly likely that the offending behaviour will be caught by Article 8 as an infringement of the right to respect for private and family life, as well as the home, so that a claim will lie under the Human Rights Act, on the basis that the relevant authority has acted incompatibly with Article 8. Where the offending behaviour is that of a public authority, a claim can be made under the Act regardless of whether the claimant has any property interest, because the issue of standing is determined by the question of whether the claimant is the victim[56] of a violation of a Convention right. On facts such as *Hunter*, the public authority would then seek to justify any interference under Article 8(2) on the ground that urban regeneration is in the interest of the economic well-being of the country and it is difficult to envisage an English court reaching a different conclusion than that of the Commission on Human Rights in *Khatun*.[57] It will be recalled that similar economic arguments were upheld in *Powell and Rayner*. Essentially, the outcome of litigation will be assessed by balancing the community and individual interests, and applying the proportionality principle to any interference.

[52] *Supra* n.2 at 685–6.
[53] *Hussain, supra* n.44 at 157.
[54] [1933] Ch 89.
[55] [1956] 1 All ER 652.
[56] Human Rights Act 1998, s. 7(1).
[57] *Supra* n.28.

The difficulty for English courts will now be to establish how they, in the exercise of their obligation under section 6 of the Human Rights Act, will act compatibly with the Convention in responding to the demands of Article 8 jurisprudence. As far as actions against private actors are concerned, a claimant will argue that the court must implement a positive obligation to regulate the control of non-state actors so that Article 8 rights are secured. As we have seen in the context of these positive obligations: the notion of respect is not "clear cut", so that the state enjoys a particularly wide margin of appreciation; a balance should be struck between individual and community interests; and the aims set out in Article 8(2) may be relevant in determining where the balance should be struck. Nevertheless, these factors cannot be taken to negate the Article 8 obligation, of which English courts now have a duty to be cognisant. As Lord Cooke observed in his speech, his view was supported by the preponderance of academic opinion and what is more has now been given a very strong legal steer by the Human Rights Act. It is time for English law to move beyond the straitjacket of the forms of action, so that the boundaries of private nuisance are determined by the link with one's home.

Appendix

Schedule 1

THE ARTICLES

PART I
THE CONVENTION RIGHTS AND FREEDOMS

Article 2
Right to Life

1. Everyone's right to life shall be protected by law. No one shall be deprived of his life intentionally save in the execution of a sentence of a court following his conviction of a crime for which this penalty is provided by law.

2. Deprivation of life shall not be regarded as inflicted in contravention of this Article when it results from the use of force which is no more than absolutely necessary:

(a) in defence of any person from unlawful violence;
(b) in order to effect a lawful arrest or to prevent the escape of a person lawfully detained;
(c) in action lawfully taken for the purpose of quelling a riot or insurrection.

Article 3
Prohibition of Torture

No one shall be subjected to torture or to inhuman or degrading treatment or punishment.

Article 4
Prohibition of Slavery and Forced Labour

1. No one shall be held in slavery or servitude.
2. No one shall be required to perform forced or compulsory labour.
3. For the purpose of this Article the term "forced or compulsory labour" shall not include:
(a) any work required to be done in the ordinary course of detention imposed according to the provisions of Article 5 of this Convention or during conditional release from such detention;

(b) any service of a military character or, in case of conscientious objectors in countries where they are recognised, service exacted instead of compulsory military service;

(c) any service exacted in case of an emergency or calamity threatening the life or well-being of the community;

(d) any work or service which forms part of normal civic obligations.

Article 5
Right to Liberty and Security

1. Everyone has the right to liberty and security of person. No one shall be deprived of his liberty save in the following cases and in accordance with a procedure prescribed by law:

(a) the lawful detention of a person after conviction by a competent court;

(b) the lawful arrest or detention of a person for non-compliance with the lawful order of a court or in order to secure the fulfilment of any obligation prescribed by law;

(c) the lawful arrest or detention of a person effected for the purpose of bringing him before the competent legal authority on reasonable suspicion of having committed an offence or when it is reasonably considered necessary to prevent his committing an offence or fleeing after having done so;

(d) the detention of a minor by lawful order for the purpose of educational supervision or his lawful detention for the purpose of bringing him before the competent legal authority;

(e) the lawful detention of persons for the prevention of the spreading of infectious diseases, of persons of unsound mind, alcoholics or drug addicts or vagrants;

(f) the lawful arrest or detention of a person to prevent his effecting an unauthorised entry into the country or of a person against whom action is being taken with a view to deportation or extradition.

2. Everyone who is arrested shall be informed promptly, in a language which he understands, of the reasons for his arrest and of any charge against him.

3. Everyone arrested or detained in accordance with the provisions of paragraph 1(c) of this Article shall be brought promptly before a judge or other officer authorised by law to exercise judicial power and shall be entitled to trial within a reasonable time or to release pending trial. Release may be conditioned by guarantees to appear for trial.

4. Everyone who is deprived of his liberty by arrest or detention shall be entitled to take proceedings by which the lawfulness of his detention shall be decided speedily by a court and his release ordered if the detention is not lawful.

5. Everyone who has been the victim of arrest or detention in contravention of the provisions of this Article shall have an enforceable right to compensation.

Article 6
Right to a Fair Trial

1. In the determination of his civil rights and obligations or of any criminal charge against him, everyone is entitled to a fair and public hearing within a reasonable time by an independent and impartial tribunal established by law. Judgment shall be pronounced publicly but the press and public may be excluded from all or part of the trial in the interest of morals, public order or national security in a democratic society, where the interests of juveniles or the protection of the private life of the parties so require, or to the extent strictly necessary in the opinion of the court in special circumstances where publicity would prejudice the interests of justice.

2. Everyone charged with a criminal offence shall be presumed innocent until proved guilty according to law.

3. Everyone charged with a criminal offence has the following minimum rights:

   (a) to be informed promptly, in a language which he understands and in detail, of the nature and cause of the accusation against him;
   (b) to have adequate time and facilities for the preparation of his defence;
   (c) to defend himself in person or through legal assistance of his own choosing or, if he has not sufficient means to pay for legal assistance, to be given it free when the interests of justice so require;
   (d) to examine or have examined witnesses against him and to obtain the attendance and examination of witnesses on his behalf under the same conditions as witnesses against him;
   (e) to have the free assistance of an interpreter if he cannot understand or speak the language used in court.

Article 7
No Punishment Without Law

1. No one shall be held guilty of any criminal offence on account of any act or omission which did not constitute a criminal offence under national or international law at the time when it was committed. Nor shall a heavier penalty be imposed than the one that was applicable at the time the criminal offence was committed.

2. This Article shall not prejudice the trial and punishment of any person for any act or omission which, at the time when it was committed, was criminal according to the general principles of law recognised by civilised nations.

Article 8
Right to Respect For Private and Family Life

1. Everyone has the right to respect for his private and family life, his home and his correspondence.

2. There shall be no interference by a public authority with the exercise of this right except such as is in accordance with the law and is necessary in a democratic society in the interests of national security, public safety or the economic well-being of the country, for the prevention of disorder or crime, for the protection of health or morals, or for the protection of the rights and freedoms of others.

Article 9
Freedom of Thought, Conscience and Religion

1. Everyone has the right to freedom of thought, conscience and religion; this right includes freedom to change his religion or belief and freedom, either alone or in community with others and in public or private, to manifest his religion or belief, in worship, teaching, practice and observance.

2. Freedom to manifest one's religion or beliefs shall be subject only to such limitations as are prescribed by law and are necessary in a democratic society in the interests of public safety, for the protection of public order, health or morals, or for the protection of the rights and freedoms of others.

Article 10
Freedom of Expression

1. Everyone has the right to freedom of expression. This right shall include freedom to hold opinions and to receive and impart information and ideas without interference by public authority and regardless of frontiers. This Article shall not prevent States from requiring the licensing of broadcasting, television or cinema enterprises.

2. The exercise of these freedoms, since it carries with it duties and responsibilities, may be subject to such formalities, conditions, restrictions or penalties as are prescribed by law and are necessary in a democratic society, in the interests of national security, territorial integrity or public safety, for the prevention of disorder or crime, for the protection of health or morals, for the protection of the reputation or rights of others, for preventing the disclosure of information received in confidence, or for maintaining the authority and impartiality of the judiciary.

Article 11
Freedom of Assembly and Association

1. Everyone has the right to freedom of peaceful assembly and to freedom of association with others, including the right to form and to join trade unions for the protection of his interests.

2. No restrictions shall be placed on the exercise of these rights other than such as are prescribed by law and are necessary in a democratic society in the interests of national security or public safety, for the prevention of disorder or

crime, for the protection of health or morals or for the protection of the rights and freedoms of others. This Article shall not prevent the imposition of lawful restrictions on the exercise of these rights by members of the armed forces, of the police or of the administration of the State.

Article 12
Right to Marry

Men and women of marriageable age have the right to marry and to found a family, according to the national laws governing the exercise of this right.

Article 14
Prohibition of Discrimination

The enjoyment of the rights and freedoms set forth in this Convention shall be secured without discrimination on any ground such as sex, race, colour, language, religion, political or other opinion, national or social origin, association with a national minority, property, birth or other status.

Article 16
Restrictions on Political Activities of Aliens

Nothing in Articles 10, 11 and 14 shall be regarded as preventing the High Contracting Parties from imposing restrictions on the political activity of aliens.

Article 17
Prohibition of Abuse of Rights

Nothing in this Convention may be interpreted as implying for any State, group or person any right to engage in any activity or perform any act aimed at the destruction of any of the rights and freedoms set forth herein or at their limitation to a greater extent than is provided for in the Convention.

Article 18
Limitation on Use of Restrictions on Rights

The restrictions permitted under this Convention to the said rights and freedoms shall not be applied for any purpose other than those for which they have been prescribed.

Index